On Textual Understanding and Other Essays

Theory and History of Literature:
Edited by Wlad Godzich and Jochen Schulte-Sasse

On Textual Understanding
and Other Essays

Peter Szondi

Translation by Harvey Mendelsohn

Foreword by Michael Hays

Theory and History of Literature, Volume 15

University of Minnesota Press, Minneapolis

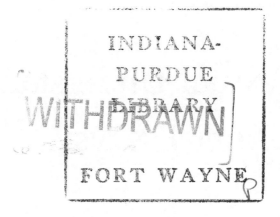
Published by the University of Minnesota Press
2037 University Avenue Southeast, Minneapolis MN 55414.
Published simultaneously in Canada
by Fitzhenry & Whiteside Limited, Markham.
Printed in the United States of America.

Library of Congress Cataloging-in-Publication Data
Szondi, Peter.
   On textual understanding and other essays.
   (Theory and history of literature ; v. 15)
   First essay is a translation of: Traktat über
philologische Erkenntnis
   Bibliography: p.
   Includes index.
   1. Literature—Addresses, essays, lectures.
I. Title. II. Series.
PN37.S96 1986   809   85-21022
ISBN 0-8166-1289-7
ISBN 0-8166-1288-9 (pbk.)

10-27-88

The University of Minnesota
is an equal-opportunity
educator and employer.

Contents

Foreword
Tracing a Critical Path:
Peter Szondi and the
Humanistic Tradition
Michael Hays

> The metamorphosis of criticism did not leave [its] theo-
> retical content untouched, for its truth evaporate [d].
>   T. W. Adorno and Max Horkheimer
>   *Dialectic of Enlightenment*

> What we savor in our laughter is the distance that come-
> dy establishes by reflecting on its own structure.
>   Peter Szondi
>   "Friedrich Schlegel and Romantic Irony"

I

Toward the close of his essay on "Friedrich Schlegel and Romantic Irony,"
Peter Szondi discusses Ludwig Tieck's brief comedy entitled *A Prologue.*
Szondi's attention is drawn to this particular play not because of its narrative content or because it is a model "prologue," but precisely because it
undermines such traditional notions of content and form. This prologue
does not serve as an introduction to a later and more complete text.
Neither does it provide a closed narrative of its own, despite the fact that
it is meant to stand as an independent dramatic work. As Szondi points
out, by refusing to prepare the way for another text, as its title implies, or
to complete the logical and linguistic progression its status as a play
demands, Tieck's *Prologue* opens the way for reflection on the formal
expectations that underlie the notions "prologue" and "drama."
    Traditional dramatic theory and practice suppose that "every speech
is binding, irrevocable and fraught with consequences. The drama is the
genre of 'presentness' in both senses of the word: the *present* and *presence.*
It is also the form most suited to convey immanence of meaning" (Szondi,
p. 70). In Tieck's "drama," however, text and character function differently.
Rather than generating a dialogic context, a setting in which the dramatis
personae could both "be" and be referents of a meaning inscribed within
their language and actions, neither place nor point of view nor character

is established. In another play, one of the central figures, an innkeeper, instead of "playing" innkeeper, speaks about himself as a role. He names the types of situation in which his role has or might appear and, thus, he not only announces that his existence is determined by the formal expectations of the drama itself, he also severs the connection between himself as signifier and any external signified. "Through its self-consciousness, the role becomes objective to itself, on the model of the divided ego of the early romantic writers, of which it is the aesthetic projection. This transposition of self-consciousness to the aesthetic realm is not without effect on the dramatic structure. In his role, the character is conscious not so much of his specific existence as it is revealed in the play, as he is of the very nature of his existence . . . ," (Szondi, p. 71).

What Szondi has discovered in Tieck's *Prologue* is not simply the difference between the textual reality of language and character, and the traditional notions embedded in "prologue" and "drama"; he has also located within this difference the point at which we can recognize these forms as the manifestation of a particular, historically bound, aesthetic consciousness—and within that consciousness, a locus of the critical act itself. Szondi's interest in Tieck is, therefore, not simply incidental to the rest of his work—an accident of critical *fortuna*. Neither is it by chance that it appears here in this foreword as the point of entry into Szondi's critical enterprise. His reflections on Tieck are a comment on and demonstration of his own method, one that seeks out the spaces of historical, formal, and linguistic difference in order to develop a critical understanding of the relationship between the text and its context, between the critic and the object of his or her investigation.[1]

A Prologue appears here in my text in two different relations, then. First, as read by Szondi, it is an indication of the possibility of locating a moment of difference within a textual tradition and thereby commenting on both the closure and the historicity of certain forms of dramatic, literary, and critical practice. Second, by exposing its own textuality (and, in Szondi's commentary, the textuality of criticism as well), Tieck's play calls into question the notion of introductions and places a barrier between my own text and the possibility of a "simple," "narrative" discussion of Peter Szondi and his work.[2]

In order to do justice to Szondi's critical theory and method, one must abandon the pretense of a linear discourse that can present the reader with a closed system of references or meanings couched within a framework that "names" and, thus, gives hierarchic value to Szondi's critical activity. Names will, of course, appear here, they are an inevitable aspect of the development of critical language as we know it, but they will be used, as was Tieck's play, to designate the momentary stance of a method (Szondi's) that insists upon positioning itself *in relation to* the texts and theories of others in order to understand them as terms in the interaction between literature and criticism, between poetics and history.[3]

To conclude from the above that Szondi was yet another "poststructuralist" deconstructor would be a mistake, however. Although he makes reference to Heidegger, Derrida, Foucault and others, Szondi provides us with a different kind of critical and historical awareness. Szondi would have described his practice as hermeneutic—the ongoing interest in Schleiermacher and the hermeneutic tradition demonstrated in the essays found in this volume makes his point of view quite obvious. But since Szondi's method is meant to provide a means of situating oneself in relation to one's own critical discourse, as well as in relation to the textual object and its socioaesthetic context, it is incumbent upon the reader to note when Szondi distances himself from or uses the hermeneutic method *against* the hermeneutic tradition itself. Indeed, much of Szondi's work bears on the discourse of this tradition as it evolved in the late nineteenth century and in the era of the Weimar Republic.

The reader's task is not simple, however. Szondi, like Schlegel, whom he invokes in the essay on romantic irony, subscribes in his texts to the "dignity of self-restraint." He chooses to eliminate as much as possible the subjective trace, the presence of an all-comprehending "competent reader," from his criticism. This decision results in a very precise, "objective" discourse, though one without any claim to "scientific" objectivity. What is exposed by this discourse also, of necessity, raises the question of what has been hidden by it: the links between Szondi as critical subject and the objects and terms of his investigation. It is these connections rather than a survey and evaluation of his essays that will occupy the rest of this foreword. Szondi's texts will be treated as fragments to be examined in an archaeological mapping that intends not to restore a completed site in the past, but, rather, to establish relationships in a process of disclosure. Szondi's method stands as the model for this activity, one in which the text becomes the source of questions about its context, about the intersection of language, text, and history.

II

When he discusses Walter Benjamin's reminiscences, printed in *Berliner Kindheit um Neunzehnhundert* (*A Berlin Childhood ca. 1900*), Szondi pauses over a comment Benjamin made at the time he was writing the book. Benjamin told T. W. Adorno "he did not wish to read a word more of Proust than what he needed to translate at the moment, because otherwise he risked straying into an addictive dependency."[4] This statement

raises the question of influence, but instead of submitting to the temptation of using this quote to establish a precedent for Benjamin's memoirs
and, thus, a mode of interpretation, Szondi chooses to use it as a "starting
point in the attempt to convey something of the distinctive nature of
Benjamin's work," not simply as a literary event but as the inscription of
a particular historical and aesthetic consciousness. Again, it is an appreci-
ation of difference that opens Szondi's project. He does not reject the
notion of "influence." On the contrary, he elicits numerous connections
between Benjamin's book and Proust's *A la recherche du temps perdu*. But,
he says, "little can be gained by this approach," since the search for lost
time in the two works arises out of fundamentally different motives.
Proust's narrator wishes to escape the present, while Benjamin's reminiscences are an effort to save it—to discover what the present *might have
been* by a re-cognition of the past. Benjamin's "lost time" is not the past
but a future (situated outside but also through Benjamin's book) that looks
back on the shattered dream of an ideal world to come.

In the light of this reading of Benjamin's text and the extraordinary and
moving essay in which it is found, we should not wonder about Szondi's
own interest in the past, his elucidation of two earlier moments in particular: the romantic epoch, when Schleiermacher's hermeneutics (to name
only one aspect of Szondi's investigations) both separated the self from
the other and also promised a path to their (temporary) reunion; and that
period at the end of the last century when European culture, which had
once more come to see itself as whole, generated a literature and art in
which this sense of presence began to vanish again.[5]

It was this process of literary-cultural fragmentation that became the
focus of Szondi's first book, *Theory of the Modern Drama* (1956). It
reappears in his work on Benjamin and in his final essays on Celan. We
might assume, therefore (taking as our guide Szondi's careful description
of Benjamin's nostalgia for a past that held the promise of wholeness—a
coherent sense of experience), that Szondi's criticism embodies the desire
to negate the painful realities, social, academic, and political, that are part
of his own experience as well as Benjamin's: the horrendous collapse of
European and especially "high" German culture and intellectual life during and just after the Weimar period.

Szondi's treatment of Benjamin's "City Portraits" lends support to
such a conclusion, since the whole of the essay can be read as a metaphor
for Szondi's own shattered, and therefore silenced, hope for a world in
which literature and criticism could serve a positive function, one in
which the difference between the critical ideal and political reality is
overcome. At a certain point in the essay Szondi elicits the reader's interest in this historical context by shifting his discussion from Benjamin's
written work to his biography:

The city portraits are products of the years between 1925 and 1930; *A Berlin Childhood* was written after 1930. Anyone familiar with Benjamin's biography and works will grasp the significance of these dates. From the period before 1925, we may mention an essay he wrote at the age of twenty-two on Hölderlin, a work that *would have marked a new epoch* in the study of that poet had it become known at the time. (The essay was first published in 1955.) Then came the great study on "Goethe's *Elective Affinities*" (1924) along with the major work on German baroque drama (1923-25), with which Benjamin vainly sought to qualify as a university lecturer at Frankfurt. It was only after Benjamin was obliged to give up the prospect of an academic career (his mind having been judged insufficiently academic) that he became a man of letters and a journalist.

The fact that Benjamin wrote no more city portraits can also be explained by the dates in question.

With the loss of one's homeland the notion of distance also disappears. If everything is foreign, then that tension between distance and nearness from which the city portraits drew their life cannot exist. The emigrants' travels are not the kind one looks back upon; his map has no focal point. . . .

These lines not only evoke an awareness of Walter Benjamin's personal fate—the academic elitism and the anti-Semitism that led to his dismissal from the university,[6] and the persecution that led to his suicide while fleeing the Nazi terror—they also circumscribe the period in twentieth-century German history from Wiemar to Hitler, one in which the map of human experience also lost its focal point.

Peter Szondi obviously stood in a very particular relation to the man and the events traced in the lines I have quoted. He too was Jewish, but unlike Benjamin, Szondi survived the Nazi era in the relative safety of Switzerland.[7] Furthermore, his desire to pursue an academic career was crowned with early success. Shortly after taking up his first teaching position at the Free University in Berlin, he was promoted to *Ordinarius* (full professor) and became head of the Institute for General and Comparative Literature. Although these accolades came early and Szondi's stature in the university community continued to grow, this does not mean that Szondi felt himself "at home" while noting in passing that Benjamin had been made homeless. On the contrary, the rupture in the continuity of German cultural and academic life traced by the events here associated with the name "Walter Benjamin" could be ignored by Szondi only at the expense of denying history, history as embodied in Benjamin's life *and* his own.

Szondi was not the only academic critic to face this problem. Indeed certain questions had to be faced by anyone in the university who was concerned about his own integrity or that of his profession. How *does* one place oneself in relation to an academic and critical tradition that produced the extraordinary intellectual achievements of the nineteenth and early twentieth German university and also played a role in the evolution of the German state toward Nazi dominance? How do the ideals of the university coincide with the reality of the death camps?

In response to these questions we may be reminded of the manner in which Georg Steiner dealt with this rupture in his book *Language and Silence* : since no words are adequate to deal with the horror of the Nazi era, only silence remains possible.[8] T. W. Adorno would say that, "after Auschwitz, . . . [it] became impossible to write poetry";[9] and, one might add, impossible to write criticism as well. For critical language, too, had, in the name of "higher values," collaborated in the destruction of human life and values. Once again the name "Walter Benjamin" traces this connection.

But Peter Szondi was obviously not satisfied with silence alone as a response. Such silence covers over history and prevents one from dealing with the past or the present; but at the same time there was, as Szondi began to write, no uncompromised language with which to address these subjects. Thus, a central but (for this and other reasons that will later become clear) *unspoken* question in the essays printed in this volume remains, how can one feel at home and produce critical interpretations in a language (not necessarily German) and an institutional structure (academic criticism) that could directly or indirectly support the rise of fascism?

This question may not seem very pressing for English-speaking readers whose good fortune it has been to be born on the "right" side of these political, historical, and geographical boundaries. If Szondi's position and his critical concerns are "only" those of a European (Jewish) academic and critic coming to grips with the gap between his present world and the cultural and intellectual "origins" that ought to represent his "home," then we can empathize with him, but we may not consider his problem to be our own.

But would we be correct in making such an assumption? Empathy itself is out of place here. Szondi vehemently rejected the term, and it is our critical and intellectual obligation to understand why. To do so it is not sufficient simply to note that "empathy" was a term adopted earlier by right-wing German critics. Szondi saw that it had become a historical necessity to *give up* the tainted pleasure of spontaneous emotional response for the rigor of rational inquiry in order to understand both literature and criticism. If we do so, and much of what follows is an effort in that direction, Szondi's essays and his terminological preferences become "documents" of modern intellectual history as well as statements of a particular critical position. Through these "documents," but not in them, one can learn how the language of empathy, which is supposed to indicate a natural and immediate understanding of a person or a work of art, is also the language that allowed a group of university professors and critics both to reject Walter Benjamin as "academically insufficient," and at the same time to espouse the ideal of academic freedom. It is the language that helped perpetuate the notion of a "natural bond" between what today might be referred to as "right thinking people," a union of people supposed to have common instincts, values, and heritage.[10] Such notions helped frame an academic discourse that fit comfortably with the antirationalism and the cultural idealism of National Socialism, and that remained silent as the concentration camps were filled.

Szondi speaks of none of this, however; he maintains the "dignity of silence" in his essays in order to give the reader an opportunity to discover for himself or herself the terrible polysemy of such words. Only in his last work, that on Paul Celan, did he come close to a direct, personal confrontation with this history, but even here his reticence remains.[11] The earlier essays are far more discreet in their evocation of the terrible history embedded in the language and ideals of our critical heritage. Still, this gap in his texts and the silence that fills it cries out against that earlier silence, and also cries out for our reading of it, for our discovery of the history of which Szondi was not yet able to speak since to name it would be to transform the event—would indeed be to erase the event by inscribing it in an unexamined language, the very language used earlier and by others to cover over this history.

Thus, it is through such silences, as well as through the moments of difference he elicits, that Szondi's texts can be entered most fruitfully. This "absence" points to the metaphoric and historically charged aspects of his tightly controlled, "objective" criticism. It refers to and opens up to our observation the closure and complicity of earlier critical modes and demands that we establish our own connections to literature, criticism, and history.

As Szondi says in "City Portraits," "the tension between name and reality ... is only experienced painfully, as the distance separating man from things." Szondi is speaking of poetry and metaphor here, but the statement serves as well to describe the multiple connotations of certain moments in Szondi's discussion of our literary-critical past, of romantic idealism and after; moments that, like Benjamin's metaphors, "tear reality asunder and abolish the identity that made naming possible in the first place." What remains is the observed entity itself, which, Szondi suggests, is, as such, "perhaps closer to man than if he possessed it by virtue of knowing its name."[12]

It is also when we confront the "meaning" of his silence and his search for difference that we can distinguish most clearly between Szondi and three immediate and powerful "influences" on his critical perspective, Walter Benjamin, Georg Lukács and T. W. Adorno. All three appear in Szondi's work. Adorno's application of the Hegelian notion of the form-content relation is especially important for Szondi, and fundamental to his book on the modern drama. It appears later too, when Szondi searches out and uncovers textual traces of the moment at which an author is no longer able to operate within the formal, "poetological" categories of his age and inscribes this rift in his work.[13] We see this process of discovery in Szondi's analysis of Tieck as well as in his discussions of Hölderlin's "other arrow" and Diderot's notions of *tableau* and *coup de théâtre*. But if Szondi is indebted to Adorno for certain conceptual tools—and I would include here the concept of a "negative dialectic"—Szondi's use of these tools has different ends than those we see in Adorno. This difference can be captured most succinctly in Szondi's response to Adorno's assertion that poetry was impossible after Auschwitz. In an essay on Paul Celan's "Engführung," Szondi cites Adorno's statement in order to go beyond it. "After Auschwitz, poetry is impossible—unless it arises out of Auschwitz."[14] Unlike Adorno, who refuses a confrontation with language and art *after* the fall, a refusal that maintains only the negative side of the dialectic, Szondi insists on examining not only the present, and the possibility of poetry and criticism in the present, but also the past—all that lies hidden behind the name "Auschwitz." He also openly criticizes what he calls the "eschatological impulse" in Adorno's writing, the impulse found most clearly in Adorno's assertion that "in the face of despair, the only way philosophy can still be justified is as an attempt to consider all things as they look from the standpoint of salvation."[15] To this other worldly and static position Szondi prefers the painful "tension between name and reality,"[16] the tension of difference and the possibility of a philosophy that may allow one to speak and understand in the present.

In order to maintain this tension Szondi must also move away from the sociological impulse as it is manifested in Georg Lukács's work. As we see in "*Tableau* and *Coup de théâtre*," Szondi's method is based on the assumption that the text itself generates the propositions, the formal and aesthetic terms from which an understanding of an author's language and his or her cultural and ideological position are derived. As in Lukács, there is a historical dialectic at work, but it is not established within the framework of an extratextual set of notions about the objective emergence of specific (class) conflicts in the literature of a given epoch. Szondi demonstrates that this is precisely what *did not* occur in early French middle-class drama. His reading of Diderot, therefore, functions as a deconstruction of sociological critiques based on extrinsic categories. It does not reject the social and historical, though; on the contrary, Szondi's method stimulates an awareness of the relationship between author, text, and society, an awareness that arises out of language itself.

Here, he is perhaps closer to Benjamin than to Adorno or Lukács, but as I indicated above, "hope in the past" is not sufficient for Szondi. His project moves through the labyrinth of language and memory (here memory evokes both social history and the critical tradition) in order to proceed out and away from the utopian desire for a future reconstituted from the past, into a present that is animated by a confrontation with language, past and present—by an inquiry into the availability of language as a means of expressing a *critical* relationship between subject and object, idea and event.[17] A fundamental question posed by all the essays printed here is, therefore, what *can* we understand and how, not on the level of epistemological abstraction but on the level of the literary event itself. It is no doubt for this reason that Szondi's "On Textual Understanding" was selected as the text with which to begin this volume. It opens a passage for the reader into literary history and criticism, a history and criticism that are also a philosophy of history.

Before proceeding to some rather more specific comments on these essays, I want to remind the reader that they are a selection and in no way correspond to a systematic presentation of the context and development of Peter Szondi's critical thought.[18] They do, however, indicate the scope of his interests and, more important, his methodological procedure and assumptions—and the results of his method. This is especially true of the first six essays, all of which focus on material related to German romanticism and idealism, terms which stand for the momentous social, aesthetic, and philosophical developments that transformed German culture between 1795 and 1830, and then once again between 1900 and 1930.

Of course, Szondi is not the only recent critic to have shown interest in the romantics. In fact, in the past few years there has been a revival of interest in German romanticism and a major revision in critical thinking about the romantic contribution to linguistics, philosophy, and literature.[19] Szondi no doubt has a significant place in the history of this revival since he was one of the major German critics of the early 1960s who began to look behind the stock assumptions that had come to define academic treatment of the period,[20] a treatment that even today appears in textbooks in the guise of a series of catch phrases (the German's say *Stichwörter*) invoked in relation to the term "romanticism."

To understand both the said and the unsaid in these first six essays, we must keep this academic-critical context in mind. When Szondi, in "On Textual Understanding," begins by citing Schleiermacher's insistence on confining understanding to "understanding a text," instead of "relating the concept of cognition to the ideas and structure of a work of art and to its historical setting," he is not rejecting the study of structure or context. He is, rather, reopening a vast network of philosophical and aesthetic problems that had been effectively eliminated from critical purview.[21] Already in 1962, in the first version of this essay Szondi had noted that "there exists no guide to the study of German literature that attempts to acquaint the student with the theoretical questions involved in understanding a text."[22] These questions, as Szondi makes clear, are not first concerned with a given set of notions about form, literary tradition, and meaning, but with the epistemological grounds for generating a possible relationship of understanding between the critical subject and the textual object. Such understanding, Szondi was certain, could only emerge if the critical inquiry posed questions about itself, its method, and assumptions. This process, the development of this "hermeneutical consciousness," is essential to criticism since without reflection there can be no "science" of criticism at all and, thus, no valid means of making generalizations about literature.[23] Szondi's reference to a "science" of criticism indicates a further link between his interest in the romantics, especially Schleiermacher and Schlegel, and his experience of critical practice in the German university of the postwar era. The term for literary study in Germany, *Literaturwissenschaft* (literary science) is, in many ways, connected with the positivist science and history that developed in the mid and late nineteenth century. In that sense, it can be equated with a "commonsense" view of literature which indicates that there is a concrete relationship between the reader's experience of the text and the statements the text makes about the empirical world. To put this idea in more contemporary terms, it was assumed that there was a direct relationship between the signifier in a text and a signified external to it.

Whatever arguments might be made today for such a position, in terms of Szondi's work, it must be kept in mind that the notion of such concrete connections and, therefore, of an objective literary science is precisely what produced the "guides" to which Szondi alludes in the remarks quoted above—manuals that made of German literary history a series of linearly ordered periods, often defined positively in terms of a combination of formal types and references to "natural" aspects of art based in the German national character. This is, of course, the most obviously dangerous element in the positivist orientation, its tendency to submit not just to "commonsense" judgments, but to the racist and chauvinist ideological biases that lie behind them.

In the academic realm, this positivism was the opponent of the idealist position that was in evidence in the founding of the modern German university in the early nineteenth century, an idealism that had reemerged in the work of Wilhelm Dilthey, Georg Simmel, Max Weber, and others at the beginning of our century.[24] These neo-Kantians proposed an alternative notion of *Wissenschaft* (science), one that was more subjective. It espoused the *Geist* (mind, spirit) and instinct as the keys to understanding rather than the quantitative method proposed by positivism. This new idealism unhesitatingly made metaphysical assumptions about the nature and existence of the external world, and about the relationship between objects and ideas.[25] Dilthey and the other neo-Kantians proposed a *discontinuous* world, one in which reflection upon experience was to be kept separate from any notion of empirical reality. To understand, according to Dilthey, was a process, a technique of analysis, whereby we come to grasp not the external world, but the "meanings" expressed in the structures (language, law, literature) elaborated by the intellect (*Geist*). Since the individual is isolated from these *intellectual* objectifications in his or her own subjectivity, to understand a poem, for example, required the ability to empathize with or reexperience the poem. Such action focused on the structure of the text, the manner in which it was objectified.[26]

This position is obviously akin to the critical theories developed later and elsewhere, to Russian formalism and the American New Criticism as well as to Szondi's own. But, as I mentioned above, and to return to the German situation at the beginning of the century, the idealist position that envisioned empathy as the bridge between subject and object also began to serve the needs of Fascist dogma. The elitist tendency in this position, its willingness to privilege the "competence" of the professor's intellect over that of his student or a nonacademic, helped maintain a rigid hierarchy of authority within the university. And the belief that one had to be able to empathize in order to understand the way in which a culture objectified its *Geist* was easily transformed into a part of the discourse that glorified the need to submit to the *Geist,* the higher moral order, objectified by the state—and to eliminate those who did not.

A nostalgic attachment to the abstract value of subjective spirit and the hierarchic tradition associated with the founding of the German university (and its intellectual achievements) was readily transformed into the equally abstract and nostalgic myth of a "pure" German culture. Thus, even the neo-Kantian potential for a *critical,* not "commonsense," reason could be hypostatized in the ideals of German fascism. Ideal critical categories, like canonical literary categories, provided no means of reflecting on their historical implications. Walter Benjamin was obviously not the only German intellectual to experience the sordid upshot of this process.[27]

Returning now from this lengthy, but I believe necessary, excursus on German academic criticism and its positivist and idealist elements, to the essays of Peter Szondi, one sees at once the difficulty confronting him as he begins to discuss the problems of philological understanding and literary criticism. These problems are summed up in his treatment of Wilhelm Dilthey. In "On Textual Understanding" and "Schleiermacher's Hermeneutics Today," Dilthey is first credited with refuting the positivist error that would equate human science (*Geisteswissenschaft*) with the natural sciences, and, by extension, philological knowledge with "objective" historical knowledge.

> The Thirty Years' War and a sonnet of Andreas Gryphius do not become objects of knowledge in the same way; indeed, in this regard the study of history appears to be closer to the exact sciences than it is to the study of literature. In literary study, even the most ancient text is present to an undiminished degree. ("On Textual Understanding")

But Dilthey's subjective theory, his insistence that one not confuse cognitive structures with objective facts, although it allows for and even necessitates a constantly renewed understanding of the relationship between the critic and the text, appears in a different light when Szondi analyzes the discourse embodied in Dilthey's *Lebensphilosophie* ("philosophy of life"). As Szondi shows, Dilthey's reading of Schleiermacher emphasizes its subjective aspects and especially the notion of empathy—intuitive understanding between kindred souls. It overlooks the critical, reflective element in Schleiermacher's theory and opens Dilthey's subjective idealism to a linkage with the Nazi ideal of a "natural bond" linking the German people.[28]

Szondi, of course, does not state these particular intertextual connections, since they are not present in the texts he is analyzing. He is true to his method here; only what is in the work is scrutinized as a possible object of knowledge. But the German reader would be expected to understand the reasons for Szondi's interest in Dilthey as well as the reasons for his "historical abstinence."[29]

The non-German reader who wishes to grasp the historical and discursive implications of Szondi's analysis should not allow the historical nexus to escape his or her attention through lack of familiarity, however. A doubling of Szondi's abstinence would simply blind the reader to his or her connections with the problematic of a critical tradition that reaches from Schleiermacher and the romantic discovery of the "divided self," though Dilthey into the postwar era.

If Szondi chooses Schleiermacher's texts as a means of deconstructing

Dilthey, it is to make clear the difference between Schleiermacher's prior theoretical assumptions and their later historical and ideological codification. For only if Szondi can demonstrate this difference can he have hope of speaking in a critical language at all. He must first wrest it from the silence of its own complicity.

We in turn can also use Schleiermacher, or at least his intellectual and historical position, as a means of discovering this demonstration in the interstices of Szondi's texts. Schleiermacher was, after all, one of the founding fathers of the modern German university, in addition to being the first theoretician of modern hermeneutics.[30] For Szondi, this turning back to Schleiermacher is much more than a nostalgic return to his critical origins. By reading Schleiermacher "anew," Szondi can reflect both on twentieth-century distortions *and* on his own relationship to them and the critical theory generated by German romantic criticism. By thus objectifying his own critical method, he can establish the distance or the space of difference from which to contemplate his own discourse as it moves in relation to its predecessors: the ideals of the critical *Geist* are held in check by self-conscious reflection. Difference replaces canonical repetition as methodological goal. This difference becomes the source of knowledge, knowledge that "can exist in the first place only through constantly confronting texts, only through continuously referring knowledge (*Wissen*) back to its source in cognition (Erkenntnis), that is to say, by relating it to the understanding of [a text]".[31]

And so, Szondi turns to Schleiermacher, Schlegel, and Hölderlin, whose texts announce the modern problematic of understanding, of the individual irrevocably separated from the "other," be it God, the past, other speaking subjects, or one's own unresolved desires. What Szondi discovers "anew" in these texts is not simply alienated desire, but a dialectic of difference and the polysemy of the text. While the polysemic nature of language inscribes the difference between subject and object, signifier and signified, idea and event in the text, a dialectical understanding of this difference allows nonetheless for a *critical* evaluation of these relationships; for knowledge is derived not from an assumed sublation of difference, but from an effort to allow the poles of difference to comment on each other. Knowledge is the possible result of this dialogue, a dialogue that traces the hope of understanding rather than asserting a closed and arbitrary "meaning." Szondi thus does away with both the referential fallacy and with a self-satisfied immanence that would allow a critic to propose his or her own empathetic "competence" as the meaning of a text.

Szondi's method can, therefore, be said to begin with these texts, although it does not have its origin in them. The term *influence* ceases to be of much value at this point, and so it is that Szondi, when discussing

Benjamin and Proust, instead of trying to "prove" lineal heritage (and submit to a critical discourse that denies difference), examines Proust's use of "memory" in order to better understand Benjamin's *different* use of the same trope.[32] This effort to establish a dialectical and critical relationship is a fundamental movement in Szondi's method, one that helps him derive a historically conditioned evaluation of an author's particular use of the general forms offered by language and aesthetic tradition. It is always the singular in a text that emerges as the starting point of Szondi's criticism since it announces the "individual process that gave rise to the passage in the first place."[33] Whenever a formal or linguistic element of a text does not fit the "rules" of style or genre that condition the poetics of an age, this gap opens the critic's eyes to the concrete process of the text itself. And this process in turn suggests the possibility of an interpretive dialogue. The "facts" uncovered by the interpretation do not, then, become hypostatized as a final "meaning." They remain "subjectively conditioned" and "accessible to understanding" only by means of subjective mediation. In this way, facts are finally perceived in their true "objectivity"—as objects of the critical agent.

Szondi's treatment of Hölderin in "The Other Arrow" stands fully within this method. He not only demonstrates the manner in which the formal process of Hölderin's writing can be elucidated through textual differences, he also shows how other critics, including Heidegger, Alleman, and Lachmann have imposed rather traditional readings on Hölderlin's work because they fail to allow the text to remain fully within the difference of its own hermetic language. By emphasizing this hermetic aspect of language as a crucial element in the development of Hölderlin's poetry, Szondi is also able to comment on the collapse of generic tradition embodied in Hölderlin's *oeuvre*. Text informs context.

This consciousness of change and the collapse of traditional genres also emerges in Szondi's essay on tragedy, "The Notion of the Tragic in Schelling, Hölderlin, and Hegel." Schelling's "discovery" of the subject, the individual ego, opens the way to an analysis of the implications for the drama of German romantic philosophy as it sought to distinguish between the "natural" world of the Greeks and the modern world of "artifice"; between fate and individual will. Schelling, Hölderlin, and Hegel mark the early history of a theory of tragedy that is no longer interested in the neoclassical problem of form, but in a theory and philosophy of the tragic itself. The discourse of neoclassical genre theory, for all its ostensible vigor, has, at this point, ceased to organize meaningful statements about the form and function of the drama. The shift from tragedy to the "tragic" reveals the historicity of genre theory itself.

Schelling's juxtaposition of the individual and nature—"the essence of *tragedy* is ... a genuine conflict between freedom in the subject and objective necessity"—provides access to two other key notions, one relevant for Szondi's method, the other as an indication of the history of an effort to resolve the problem embodied in the "tragic" conflict. As Szondi reads Schelling, Hölderlin, and Hegel, he uncovers the notion of the dialectic with which they attempt to overcome the tragedy of difference. He also establishes a distance from them by reading them as the history of a mode of thinking. His analysis becomes a critique of the history embodied in their texts. Thus, it is as a philosophy of history that much of Szondi's work must be read if one is to avoid confusing his own use of the dialectic with a return to the romantics and particularly to Hegel. Here and in Szondi's essays on Schlegel and Schleiermacher, the dialectic embodied in the recognition of difference remains part of his hermeneutic method, but this mode of arriving at cognitive knowledge remains without any announcement of a utopian synthesis.

Because Szondi's method is based in a dialectical theory of language, it also stands as a possible bridge between recent German hermeneutics and a rather critical adversary: French poststructuralism. Nowhere is this more apparent than in "The Poetry of Constancy," the final essay in this volume. In this essay Szondi links his own and Benjamin's notions of language to those of Foucault, Derrida, and Deguy. And as his reading progresses, Szondi arrives not only at a description of the difference between Shakespeare's sonnet 105 and Celan's translation, he also extrapolates a theory of postmodern poetry itself. Celan's text manifests "a determinate negation of discursiveness." This new poetic mode does not renounce traditional rhetorical figures, but is built on a different set of presuppositions. "In other words, [Celan's poem] displays a different mode of signification." It is this difference that, once recognized, becomes the basis for a possible interpretation of the poem as well as for a discussion of its historical situation. A new aesthetic mode requires a new critical mode—a mode even today being organized out of confrontation of hermeneutic and poststructuralist discourse.

Szondi's essay on Celan also brings us back to the starting point of this foreword. Tieck, like Celan, managed to "pierce the facade of linguistic performance" and in so doing, he laid bare the subject matter of critical inquiry. In the essays printed here Szondi has elucidated some recent phases in, and a method for, such inquiry. They are a concrete assertion that hope does not lie in the past or in silence, but in an effort to speak, *critically,* in the present. The full significance of this assertion can only be measured by his readers, however, since, as Szondi was so obviously aware, the statements of an other always implicate the self. To borrow a line from Proust, Szondi's texts furnish the reader with "le moyen de lire en [lui]-même."

On Textual Understanding and Other Essays

Chapter 1
On Textual Understanding

If we set out to investigate how understanding is acquired in literary study we will find this to be a "broad subject indeed."[1] The best procedure, therefore, would be to restrict it right from the start. In Schleiermacher's "Brief Presentation of Theological Studies" we find a statement that not only describes what the term "understanding" (or "cognition"—*Erkenntnis*) should encompass in literary study but that also tells us where we should look to uncover the hidden problems involved in acquiring such knowledge.* "The perfect understanding of speech or writing is an artistic achievement and requires a theory of art or a technique, which we designate by the term 'hermeneutics.' "[2] It might seem surprising that Schleiermacher, instead of relating the concept of cognition to the ideas and structure of a work of art and to its historical setting, confines it to the understanding of a text. In addition, the notion of cognition, which is a philosophical concept, might seem alien in the domain of philology. And yet this impression of strangeness indicates, at bottom, the existence of a set of epistemological problems specific to philology. Moreover, if rightly considered, it points to these problems no less insistently than does the

Written and published in 1962, in *Die Neue Rundschau*, 73rd Year, no. 1 (1962): 146-65. Originally titled "Über philologische Erkenntnis."

*Following the advice of Professor Jean Bollack, the editor of Peter Szondi's collected works and his literary executor, I have translated *Erkenntnis* as "understanding" (not "cognition") in the title of this essay and in most other instances in the text.—Trans.

3

question that immediately comes to mind when one ponders the statement quoted above: why has literary study, which should see its task in
the "perfect understanding of a text," failed to develop further the theory
that Schleiermacher called for and that he even sketched out in his theological lectures; indeed, why has it virtually closed itself off entirely from
the problems of hermeneutics? There exists no guide to the study of
German literature that attempts to acquaint the student with the theoretical questions involved in understanding a text. These questions are scarcely
ever brought up in discussions among scholars, and it is seldom realized
how often they give rise to differences of opinion.

The fact that a theoretical hermeneutics does not exist in the realm of
Germanistik might at first appear to be bound up with the former's reflexive
character. In the field of hermeneutics, scientific investigation does not ask
about its object, but rather about itself; it asks itself how it comes to attain
an understanding (*Erkenntnis*) of its object. Such understanding can, it is
true, exist without this hermeneutical consciousness. Still, there can be no
true science in the absence of self-reflection; and, in any case, this is not
something that science lacks, as can readily be seen from the methodological disputes that have continued to rage for decades now. The
reason for the absence of hermeneutics must therefore be sought elsewhere, namely in literary study's self-image. Literary scholarship's neglect
of hermeneutical problems seems to result from its tendency to consider
itself a "science" (*Wissenschaft*) and to see its defining characteristic as the
accumulation of (factual) knowledge (*Wissen*), that is, as a static *condition*.
A glance at the situation in France and in the Anglo-Saxon countries
shows that this point of view is not one that simply must be taken
for granted. The danger that this reference might be misunderstood as
praise for unscientific methods is not too high a price to pay for the recognition that "literary science" (*Literaturwissenschaft*), as the discipline
is called in Germany, cannot be the science it likes to think of itself
as being in its efforts to emulate its older, sister sciences. Indeed, this
is precisely what it cannot be if it is to maintain its own proper scientific status.

In English, scholarly concern with works of literature is called "literary
criticism": it is not a "science." And the same thing is true in French. Even
if it is no longer possible to employ the word *Kritik* to designate this
domain in German- . . . speaking countries, it would be presumptuous to
reproach the discipline's English, American, and French representatives
for being unscientific. The fact that they do not consider their profession
to be a science testifies to an awareness that understanding of works of
art requires, and makes possible, another kind of knowledge than that
recognized by the other sciences. Since Dilthey, it is no longer neces-

sary to discuss the essential difference between natural science (*Naturwis-senschaft*), at least as it was conceived in the nineteenth century, and human science (*Geisteswissenschaft*), even though literary study has not yet renounced all the criteria and methods that it borrowed from natural science and that are unsuited to its proper object of study. This very reference to Dilthey's achievement, however, makes it necessary to point out that philological knowledge is fundamentally different from historical knowledge as well. The Thirty Years' War and a sonnet of Andreas Gryphius do not become objects of knowledge in the same way; indeed, in this regard the study of history appears to be closer to the exact sciences than it is to the study of literature. In literary study, even the most ancient text is present to an undiminished degree, and this is what distinguishes it from the discipline of history. History must, and can, recover the events of the past from the distant reaches of time, bringing its object into the realm of knowledge, outside of which it is not "present." Philological knowledge, on the other hand, is always assured of the presence (and presentness) of the work of art, against which it must measure itself again and again, each time proving its validity anew. This testing, however, must not be confused with that examination of what is already known that no science, not even natural science, can dispense with. Philological knowledge possesses a dynamic aspect that is peculiarly its own. This is not simply because, like every other kind of knowledge, it is constantly being altered by new points of view and new findings, but because it can exist, in the first place, only through constantly confronting texts, only through continuously referring knowledge (*Wissen*) back to its source in cognition (*Erkenntnis*), that is to say, by relating it to the understanding (*Verstehen*) of the poetic word.

Philological knowledge has never abandoned its origin, understanding; in this area, knowledge is—or at least ought to be—perpetually renewed understanding (*perpetuierte Erkenntnis*). To be sure, this kind of return to earlier experience can also be found in the other disciplines. In the chemistry experiment, the characteristic properties of the elements and of their compounds are constantly demonstrated afresh; and in studying the sources, students are always acquiring knowledge as it was acquired historically. But neither chemistry nor history sees its goal as lying in such reconstruction, which serves mainly pedagogical purposes. The task of these disciplines, rather, is to convey knowledge of their objects, to reproduce the object once it is understood in order to make it a part of available knowledge. In literary study the situation is different. No commentary and no stylistic examination of a poem should aim at producing a description of the poem that would be considered an end in itself. Even the most uncritical reader will wish to compare such a description with the poem, and he will not truly understand the critical exercise until he has succeeded in tracing its assertions back to the perceptions from which they arose. This is particularly apparent in the extreme case of the hermetic poem. Here interpretations are ciphers. But it cannot be their job to place the deciphered image of the poem on the same level with the poem itself. To be sure, even the hermetic poem is meant to be understood—and often it cannot be understood without ciphers; all the same, the deciphering operation should allow the poem to be understood *as* written in cipher, for only then is it seen as the poem that it truly is. It is a lock that snaps shut again and again, and explanation should not try to break it open. When, however, through the intermediary of a commentary, the interpreter's knowledge (*Wissen*) is transformed into understanding (*Erkenntnis*) for the reader, then he too is able to understand the hermetic poem as hermetic.

Consequently, it is precisely for the sake of its object that philological knowledge must not be allowed to congeal into mere knowledge of the facts. Ludwig Wittgenstein's remark concerning the difference between philosophy and the natural sciences is eminently suited to describe literary study: "Philosophy," he wrote in the *Tractatus logico-philosophicus*, "is not a theory but an activity. A philosophical work consists essentially of elucidations."[3] The English and French terms for literary study seem to indicate an awareness of this difference. Rather than the accumulation of knowledge, they stress the active side of criticism, namely, analyzing and judging. In this kind of criticism one does not simply judge the quality of a work of art but also what is false and what is true in it. Indeed, criticism does not simply render judgements *about* something; it judges itself, for its essence lies in understanding (*Erkenntnis*). Hence, it is no accident that Anglo-Saxon literary criticism, in contrast to German "literary science," has always addressed itself to hermeneutical problems. I. A. Richard's *The Philosophy of Rhetoric* and William Empson's *Seven Types of Ambiguity* are examples of this abiding concern.

The absence of hermeneutical awareness in German literary study seems, therefore, to be related to the fact that it pays too little attention to the particular nature of philological knowledge, in other words, that it too easily overlooks the gulf that separates it from the other disciplines, not least from history. This impression grows stronger when one turns to the second aspect of literary study's perception of itself, namely, to the question of how the discipline conceives its own growth and development. The activity through which knowledge is enriched and transformed is called "research" (*Forschung*). The fact that this exists in literary study, as in every other discipline, does not contradict our assertion that philological knowledge usually does not seek to comprehend itself as perpetually renewed understanding, as it should, given the nature of its object. For even the concept of research betrays the inadequacy of the customary position; and here too English and French usage presents a different picture. According to the dictionaries, *Forschen* once meant "questioning" and "searching," as in the expression "an inquiring look" (*ein forschender Blick*). But the element of questioning, and thus also of understanding (*Erkenntnis*), implied by this word has steadily diminished, and research has become simply a matter of looking for items of knowledge. From the very way in which he speaks of his "research projects," the literary scholar admits that he views his efforts as consisting more in seeking out something that exists and that it is his job to discover than in cognizing and understanding. Here also more attention is devoted to knowledge than to understanding.

Naturally, this situation has its roots in the history of the discipline. Modern historical and literary studies arose in the nineteenth century as part of the reaction against the speculative systems of German idealism. Hegel's famous quip, "So much the worse for the facts," had to be atoned for, and speculative understanding (*spekulative Erkenntnis*) had to be sacrificed to factual research. The contribution of the positivist current is too great for us to lament this development. Indeed, theorists and interpreters have often expressed their gratitude to positivists both of earlier times and of the present day for research upon which they themselves could build further. As early as 1847 the historian of literature Theodor Wilhelm Danzel, in weighing up the merits of the two extreme approaches, wrote that "spiritless empiricism" "at least always [furnishes] genuine material, which can then be animated (*vergeistert*), whereas ingenious talk of things that are entirely nonexistent (*gar nicht vorhanden sind*) [is] of no use whatsoever: *ex nihilo nihil fit.*"[4] Even if one leaves aside the question of whether the category of "existence" (*Vorhandensein*) is an adequate one in discussing productions of the mind, this favoring of positivism remains an exercise in self-deception. For, to the extent that philology studies language and literature—and not extraliterary matters such as biography and the transmission of texts—, there simply is no such thing as that "spiritless empiricism" from which Danzel was sure that genuine material would be forthcoming. The gulf between objective research into the facts and subjective explanation is always narrower than either the positivist or the interpreter care to admit. The interpreter who disregards the facts also disregards the rules of interpretation (there exists no "overinterpretation" that is not false); and the positivist who abstains from understanding, decrying it as something notoriously subjective, forgoes the possibility of investigating "the facts." Dilthey's statement that "understanding" in the human sciences (*Geisteswissenschaften*) is what corresponds to explanation in the natural sciences, also holds good of factual research in philology. As soon as such research seeks, in the name of a presumed objectivity, to exclude the subject and its cognitive perceptions, it runs the danger of falsifying the facts by the use of inappropriate methods; for these facts always bear the mark of subjectivity. Furthermore, it debars itself in this way from ever becoming aware of its error. And, as a result of relying entirely upon empirical methods, research can not even make use of subjective perceptions in verifying its results.

These questions, which are of decisive importance in dealing with the epistemological problems encountered in literary study, can be profitably investigated only by means of a concrete example. A good one for these purposes is furnished by the controversy over the first strophe of Hölderlin's hymn entitled *Celebration of Peace (Friedensfeier)*. The disputed strophe reads:

> With heavenly, quietly echoing,
> With calmly modulating music filled,
> And aired is the anciently built,
> The sweetly familiar hall; upon green carpets wafts
> The fragrant cloud of joy and, casting their brightness far,
> Full of most mellow fruit and chalices wreathed with gold,
> Arranged in seemly order, a splendid row,
> Erected here and there on either side above
> The leveled floor, stand the tables.
> For, come from distant places,
> Here, at the evening hour,
> Loving guests have forgathered.

> Der himmlischen, still wiederklingenden,
> Der ruhigwandelnden Töne voll,
> Und gelüftet ist der altgebaute,
> Seeliggewohnte Saal; um grüne Teppiche duftet
> Die Freudenwolk' und weithinglänzend stehn,
> Gereiftester Früchte voll und goldbekränzter Kelche,
> Wohlangeordnet, eine prächtige Reihe,
> Zur Seite da und dort aufsteigend über dem
> Geebneten Boden die Tische.
> Denn ferne kommend haben
> Hieher, zur Abendstunde,
> Sich liebende Gäste beschieden.[5]

Among the explanatory notes of the principal edition of Hölderlin's works (known as the Stuttgart Edition), we find the following remarks concerning this strophe:

Some commentators see the metaphor of a landscape in every detail of this poetically erected and elevated space in which the gods gather together. . . . If a metaphor were actually intended, however, then it would be unexampled in all the rest of Hölderlin's work. For when he offers such metaphorical depictions, he usually employs extended similes or even explicit identifications, as in *Bread and Wine*, v. 57: "the floor is ocean and the tables are mountains" (*der Boden ist Meer! und Tische die Berge*). But the reference to what he means by the metaphor always remains clear because of his use of names. This is true even in the boldest of his transformations of image: "fragrant with a thousand tables" (*Von tausend Tischen duftend—Patmos*, later version, v. 30), where previously the subject of the phrase was "peaks" (*Gipfeln*); for in the next verse we find the name "Asia," which acts in an illustrative manner, and earlier there was a mention of the "regions" (*die Länder*—v. 24). Here [i.e., in *Celebration of Peace*], however, there is no suggestion of a . . . landscape.[6]

One of the interpretations to which this commentary takes exception states that the strophe in question:

evokes a banqueting-hall with well-arranged tables; "Full of the most mellow fruit and chalices wreathed with gold" (*Gereiftester Früchte voll und goldbekränzter Kelche*). It is, as immediately becomes clear, a landscape hall of huge proportions which is to accommodate the gods' celebration of peace, and one recalls the verse from *Bread and Wine* where, in a similar manner, the landscape is seen as the space in which the gods assemble: "Festive hall, whose floor is ocean, whose tables are mountains, / Truly, in time out of mind built for a purpose unique!" (*Festlicher Saal! der Boden ist Meer! und Tische die Berge, / Wahrlich zu einzigem Brauche vor alters gebaut!*)[7]

The issue, then, is whether or not a certain passage is intended metaphorically. This is, in general, one of the oldest problems of hermeneutics, a discipline whose origins are bound up with the theological disputes over the allegorical meaning of the Old Testament texts.[8] In Hölderlin's strophe, however, we are faced with a question that cannot be settled on theoretical, let alone dogmatic, grounds. Here it is entirely a matter of deciding whether, in this particular instance, a metaphor exists or not. In the present essay we shall be concerned less with pursuing the debate itself than with inquiring into the epistemological and methodological premises of the two ways of arguing the case.

The refutation of the metaphorical interpretation is based on the undeniable difference between the two descriptions of the hall. Nothing can be found in *Celebration of Peace* that corresponds to the explicit equation in *Bread and Wine* ("the floor is ocean and the tables are mountains"). This observation could be considered conclusive, however, only if, in the metaphorical interpretation, the passage from *Bread and Wine* were likewise called in as evidence, as it is in the counterassertion, according to which metaphors in Hölderlin are always made recognizable as such by the use of names. In point of fact, however, those who advocate the metaphorical interpretation do not rely on this citation to *prove* their case. They maintain, rather, that the reference to a landscape is "clear," appealing to what they consider to be "evident." This "evidentness" (*Evidenz*) derives, in part, from the individual details of the description itself (the fragrant cloud of joy wafts upon green carpets, and the tables stand above the leveled floor). It also derives, in part, however, from the passage in *Bread and Wine,* which, to be sure, cannot prove the metaphorical character of the strophe from *Celebration of Peace,* but which, in conjunction with the second counterexample from *Patmos* ("fragrant with a thousand tables"), does make it clear that the metaphorical connection between landscape and hall, between mountain and table, is an important element of Hölderlin's poetic language. If this much is admitted, then the question arises concerning the implication of the difference between the two descriptions of the hall with respect to the evidentness of the use of metaphor in the *Celebration of Peace* strophe. Does this difference speak against it or for it? Those who use this difference as a counterargument do not base their reasoning on the individual passage in question, and not even on the particular stylistic qualities of the poem as a whole, but rather on a catalogue of passages in which the related instances mutually support each other and, at the same time, ostracize the singular occurrence. This point of view is consistent with philology's justified efforts to achieve objectivity. Yet, in placing its hopes for objectivity exclusively in the collection of illustrative examples and in distrusting all subjective perception of evidentness, the discipline cuts itself off from the subjective component of poetry and thereby from the individual process that gave rise to the passage in the first place. And, since philology's subject matter consists of such passages, it must seek to understand them in accord with their own law if it wishes to be a science at all.

In reconstructing this process it should be remembered that (according to the Stuttgart Edition) the elegy *Bread and Wine* was begun in the autumn of 1800 or earlier and was completed in the winter of 1800–1801. The historical event that occasioned *Celebration of Peace,* which was completed in 1801 or 1802, was the signing of the peace of Lunéville in February 1801. Now, how does this sequence fit in with the philological postulate of the relevance of analogous examples in poems written at different moments in a poet's development? A consideration of the dates at which the two poems were begun, but also of the short span of time separating them, clearly shows that if we apply this postulate here, we must also assume the existence of a repetition in the poems that, from the aesthetic point of view, would have to be interpreted as a sign of weakness, indeed as a mannerism. It is true that Hölderlin, in the autumn or winter of 1800–1801, explicitly identifies both members of the comparison in his metaphorical description of Greece as a hall. Yet this fact does not rule out the possibility that, in evoking a similar vision somewhat later, he could have been satisfied with the image alone; to the contrary, it supports this hypothesis, since individual epithets like "green carpets" and "leveled floor," as well as the expression "cloud of joy," could still have suggested clearly enough the relationship to landscape.

One of the inner contradictions of the scientific approach to poetry is that, in its concern with clarity, it must consider a passage like "fragrant with a thousand tables" to be bolder and more exceptional than the equations "the floor is ocean and the tables are mountains," even though in poetry, whose essence lies much more in the unity of metaphor than in the rational dualism of comparison, it is just that explicitness that must count as exceptional. Moreover, it would be worthwhile to try to determine if such passages in Hölderlin's late work are not intended to create a poetic language capable of dispensing with comparisons and identifications altogether. Granted, the second counterexample—the verse from a later version of *Patmos* ("fragrant with a thousand tables") in which the metaphorical aspect is elucidated by two words found in the same context: "Asia" and "regions"—stems from the period *after* the composition of *Celebration of Peace*, but this does not confute the genetic interpretation proposed here. For, once again, it is not the isolated example and the degree of its explicitness that must be taken into account, but the process of composition. In the fair copy of *Patmos,* which was finished before February 1803, this passage, without the disputed metaphor, reads as follows: "Mysteriously / In the golden haze, / Quickly grown up, / With strides of the sun. / And fragrant with a thousand peaks, // Now Asia burst into flower for me, . . ." (*Geheimnissvoll / Im goldenen Rauche, blühte / Schnellaufgewachsen, / Mit Schritten der Sonne, / Mit tausend Gipfeln duftend // Mir Asia auf. . .*[9] Now, if months later, when composing a new version of the poem, Hölderlin puts "tables" in the place of "peaks," and immediately follows this with the name "Asia," this means not so much that he still considers it worthwhile to designate the metaphor as such, but rather that in the meantime the metaphorical significance of "table" had become self-evident for him. Yet, even leaving this genetic aspect aside, the discussion of *Patmos* offers no grounds for expecting that, in the

introductory strophe of the *Celebration of Peace,* names should appear in
the evocation of the landscape, if that is actually what is intended there.
Indeed, this particular hymn is governed by a stylistic rule that (with the
one exception of v. 42, "beneath the Syrian palm-tree," *unter syrischer
Palme*) permits no proper names, neither in substantivized nor in adjectival form.[10]

Meanwhile, the problems raised by the two illustrative examples from
Bread and Wine and *Patmos* should not lead us to forget that, at bottom,
the refutation of the metaphorical interpretation does not rest on these
examples but on a general claim: "If . . . a metaphor were actually intended," we are told, "then it would be unexampled in all the rest of
Hölderlin's work." Since this statement comes from the pen of the leading
expert on Hölderlin's poetry, there seems to be no point in going through
his *oeuvre* looking for a further example, especially since even two examples would count for very little in comparison with the work in its entirety.
But, in any case, what we must examine here is not the factual correctness
of the argument. The important thing to see is the argument's methodological and epistemological underpinnings; for, after all, these are what
make it possible to establish factual correctness in the first place. We must
therefore ask to what extent it is legitimate to object to a metaphorical
interpretation of a given passage on the grounds that, if the passage were
meant as a metaphor, it would be without example in all the rest of
Hölderlin's work. This kind of argumentation clearly derives from the
natural sciences, which, as a matter of principle, do not acknowledge
isolated occurrences. Founded as they are upon the specific character of
their object of study, they recognize only universal laws and seek to
explain appearances on this basis. Consequently, the unique, the unexampled, is understood either as something abnormal, which as such still
refers to the norm, or else as a miracle, as a breach in the laws of nature,
in the face of which natural science simply lays down its arms. Such an
attitude is by no means appropriate in literary study. Of course, it too can
employ this method, namely, when it is concerned with establishing generalizations. For example, if we wish to make a valid general observation
concerning metaphor in Hölderlin, we must take his entire output as our
starting point and evaluate the numerous examples of the different types
of metaphor that he uses. This is done with the aid of examples. But the
discussion of the two passages from *Bread and Wine* and *Patmos* should
have demonstrated that, in literary study, before conclusiveness can be
ascribed to any individual example, it must be interpreted in its own right
no less carefully than the passage for the interpretation of which it is to
serve as supporting or contradictory evidence.[11]

This, incidentally, casts light on the use of footnotes. They are considered an attribute of philological style, a guarantee of the solidity of the assertions in the body of the text. What usually tends to get tucked away in the footnotes, however, are illustrative examples that are not subject to any further examination and whose cogency, therefore, remains thoroughly problematical. And here we touch on one of the dangers encountered in philological work. As a result of the preference given to factualness over interpretation, which is thought to be merely subjective, every illustrative instance is automatically granted probative force simply by virtue of its existence. Now, while such force may be part of the definition of an illustrative example, the latter should not be assumed actually to possess it until this has been shown in detail. In philological demonstrations the example not infrequently plays the same role as does the evidence in certain tragedies of Shakespeare or Kleist: the piece of "evidence" stills doubt because it itself is never brought into doubt. If this were done more often, then footnotes could scarcely preserve their aura of solidity.

Yet even the unobjectionable illustrative example has its place only in the realm of general knowledge, only on those occasions when one is concerned with a rule, with regularity. As soon as literary study recognizes that its proper task is the understanding of texts, the scientific principle of "once is never" (*einmal ist keinmal*) no longer applies. For texts present themselves as individuals, not as specimens. We must try to interpret them at first in accord with the concrete process whose results they are, and not in accord with an abstract rule, which itself cannot be established without an understanding of individual passages and works.

The scientific principle cited above has entered philology as the point of view of literary history—and this is another sign that literary study, like the study of all art, is separated from history by the same gulf that divides it from the natural sciences. Literary history also tends to see the particular only as a specimen, not as an individual entity; uniqueness falls outside its purview too. Friedrich Schlegel had some harsh words to say on this score. He complained that one of the "basic principles of the so-called historical criticism [is] the postulate of commonness: Everything truly great, good, and beautiful is improbable, for it is extraordinary, and, at the very least suspect."[12] Such criticism of literary history by no means implies acceptance of the thesis that the individual, the particular work, is unhistorical. Quite to the contrary, historicity is in fact a part of its particularity, so that the *only* approach that does full justice to the work of art is the one that allows us to see history in the work of art, not the one that shows us the work of art in history. The latter point of view also has its justification: of that there should be no doubt. One of the tasks of literary study is to abstract from the individual work in order to arrive at an overview of a more or less unified period of historical development.

Moreover, it cannot be denied that a deeper understanding of an individual passage or an individual work is sometimes facilitated by this general knowledge, however problematical it may be.

Yet we must not overlook the fact that every work of art possesses a certain monarchical strain, that—as Valéry put the matter—simply by its very existence it would like to destroy all other works of art. This is not a question of personal ambition on the part of the poet or artist (something with which scholarship is not concerned) and not even of the claim to originality and incomparability, which only rarely can stand up to critical examination. No work of art claims that it is incomparable (this would be claimed, in any event, only by the artist or the critic); rather, it demands that it simply not be compared. This demand—the claim that it be treated as existing in absolute independence of all others—is part of the nature of every work of art; for every work seeks to be a whole, a microcosm, and literary study should not just set aside this demand, if its procedure is to be appropriate to its object, that is to say, if it is to be scientific. Admittedly, it must ignore this demand when it turns from the examination of individual works to that of an entire *oeuvre,* the style of a given period, or an historical development.

This overview, however, must proceed from the summation of details that have been carefully investigated in their own right; understanding of particular works must not be confused with their inclusion under historical generalizations. It would not be necessary to make a special point of this if Schlegel's harsh strictures on historical criticism, uttered long before the emergence of the discipline of literary study, had not so often proved their aptness subsequently. Historical works often give the impression that the author deliberately avoided immersing himself in the individual work of art, as if he shied away from this intimacy; and the reason for this shyness appears to be the fear that through such intimacy he might lose the distance that is supposed to be a distinctive feature of science. Yet, in this regard, literary study appears to be faced with a dilemma: it is able to grasp the work of art *as* work of art only through such immersion, and, therefore, for the sake of its scientific status (that is to say, of its appropriateness to its object) it must give up the criteria of distance and of the "once is never" principle that it has taken over from the other disciplines. The wish to avoid the false appearance of similarity to these latter is not the least of the reasons why literary study in the Anglo-Saxon countries and elsewhere refrains from calling itself a "science."

So much for the methodological aspects of the objection that holds that if a metaphor were intended in the first strophe of *Celebration of Peace,* it would be without example in the rest of Hölderlin's work. Admittedly, the inappropriateness of the argumentation does not in itself affect its factual correctness, though it does undermine the cogency that has been ascribed to it. Now, as to the question of its correctness, this must be decided by an examination of its underlying epistemological assumptions.

The claim that the description of the banqueting hall is not intended metaphorically is based on the fact that in all the rest of Hölderlin's work no other metaphor has been found in which the relationship to what is meant is not made clear by extended comparison, explicit equation, or, at the least, the use of names. The cogency of the argument, therefore, rests not on examples, but on the absence of examples. Yet, just as in the positive demonstration every passage cited as evidence must first of all prove its conclusiveness, so, too, in the negative demonstration, it must be shown that the reason for the lack of examples is not a failure to recognize passages as appropriate ones but the sheer nonexistence of such examples. It is precisely this condition, however, which remains unfulfilled in the present case. For those who assert that Hölderlin's entire *oeuvre* offers no other instance of the type of metaphor that some have seen in the opening strophe of *Celebration of Peace* have overlooked an important fact: such passages cannot be recognized simply by skimming all the poems. The metaphorical nature of the strophe can be confirmed only by passages that are not more obviously metaphorical than this strophe itself. Now, if this way of proceeding is considered insufficient, then it cannot serve, either, to distinguish the related passages from the other, nonmetaphorical material. And thus the assertion itself becomes untenable.

A demonstration that tries to keep strictly to the facts breaks down for the reason that not enough attention is given to its epistemological presuppositions, and the latter are insufficiently examined because of a blind trust in the facts. The appeal to the facts, however, does not relieve one of the obligation to consider the conditions under which they are known — any more than the act of interpretation allows one to ignore the facts furnished by the text and the history of the text. This was already pointed out years ago by E. Ermatinger. Taking issue with positivism's purely inductive approach, he objected that the latter is not a method but merely a form of self-delusion, for "if one wishes to collect and examine a body of material one must first have made up one's mind about the formal criteria to be used in the collecting."[13] This admonition seems to have been too little heeded. We may, however, go still further and ask if in literary study it is *ever* possible to establish a strict division between objective material and subjective interpretation, since the use to which the material is put is in itself an interpretation of it. The philological understanding of a text involves a much different relationship between evidence and insight than the one that was thought to exist on the basis of experience in the exact sciences.

This circumstance is attested by the hermeneutical analysis of the type of interpretation that is based on variant readings. One of the most important tasks of the scientific study of texts is to reconstruct the genesis of a text with the aid of earlier versions; and this is a task which, at the same time, serves the interests of interpretation. To proceed in this way does not mean that one ignores the postulate (which is admittedly problematical) that a work should be interpreted exclusively on the basis of itself, for the variants are part of the work; they are part of its genesis, an early state that ultimately reappears in the later stage of completion, having been "raised up" (*aufgehoben*), in the Hegelian sense of the term [i.e., at once canceled, preserved, and brought to a higher level]. Only orthodox phenomenology would think of refusing to exploit this kind of material, which it considers to be foreign to the text. But this refusal is more useful in testing the phenomenological method than in understanding a work of literature.

If one does not wish to accept the meaning of tables in the verse from the later version of *Patmos* (which reads "fragrant with a thousand tables"), he will refer back to the earlier version: "fragrant with a thousand peaks." He can substantiate the metaphorical meaning of "tables," which he is now in a position to give, by means of the text of the first version. For the fact that the word "peaks" appears there in the place of "tables" proves that in the later version tables stand metaphorically for peaks. But does it really prove this? Another hymn of Hölderlin's begins with the verses: "As on a holiday, to see the field / A countryman goes out, at morning . . . " (*Wie wenn am Feiertage, das Feld zu sehn / Ein Landmann geht, des Morgens, . . .*).[14] In the prose sketch, the beginning reads: "As the countryman goes out on a holiday to examine the field, at evening . . ." (*Wie wenn der Landmann am Feiertage das Feld zu betrachten hinausgeht, des Abends . . .* "). Now, from the fact that in the first version evening takes the place of morning, no one would conclude that in the metrical version "morning" is meant to be understood as "evening." One would assume, instead, that in the period between writing the two versions the author's way of conceiving of time had changed. This shows, however, that in the case of *Patmos* as well, one is not entitled to speak of a proof furnished by the first version. For this "proof" has implicitly been helped along by the interpreter, inasmuch as he views the change from peak to table as a metaphorical process, as a transfer, and on this basis concludes that the meaning has remained unchanged in the process. It is only in this context, which has been furnished by understanding, that fact becomes proof.

Philological proof is therefore dependent on understanding in a much different way than is, for example, mathematical proof. In philology, it is not enough simply to understand the way in which the proof is carried out. In addition, the evidential character of the facts is first revealed by the interpretation, while, conversely, the facts indicate the path that interpretation should pursue. This interdependence of proof and understanding is a manifestation of the hermeneutic circle. If we refuse to accept that a fact is capable of demonstrating the correctness of an interpretation only after it has itself first been interpreted, we falsify the circle of understanding, turning it into an ideal of a straight line that leads directly from the facts to understanding. This does not mean that we must throw up our hands in resignation, and still less that we must open the door to unscientific arbitrariness. Indeed, the ascription of objective cogency to facts in the name of a scientific ideal taken over from other disciplines is actually a much more arbitrary approach than this, since in the domain of literature the facts simply do not possess such cogency. In this area a discipline that has become aware of the conditions under which it acquires understanding—conditions that seem like limitations only from the point of view of other disciplines—will develop procedures which are more, not less, exact and which, far from becoming less compelling, will become truly conclusive for the first time.

Yet how does such a method of interpretation work, a method in which facts are indications more than they are items of evidence? Confronted with an array of facts whose organization has been destroyed by their transformation into illustrative examples, the method attempts to reproduce this organization in a dynamic fashion by reconstructing the genesis of the work. In this reconstruction, the facts help to indicate both the paths to be followed and those to be avoided. None of the facts may be ignored if the reconstruction is to attain evidentness. And evidentness is the only adequate criterion of philological understanding, the only one to which it must submit. When one has arrived at evidentness, he does not fail to hear the language of the facts, nor is he misled by their hypostatization. To the contrary, he perceives them as subjectively conditioned and as accessible to understanding only by means of subjective mediation. In this way, facts are finally perceived in their true objectivity.

This symbiosis of evidence and understanding can also be seen from an analysis of the procedure known as the method of parallel passages. This method, one of the oldest hermeneutical stratagems, is the inversion of the method of variant readings. The meaning of a word is not explained, as in the latter, with the help of other words that stand in the same place in earlier versions, but rather on the basis of other passages in which the same word occurs. Naturally, this word must have the same meaning in every case; the passages must be parallel passages in this strict sense of the term. This stipulation constitutes the method's limitation, just as the variant method is limited by the condition that the modification of the passage must not correspond to a modification in meaning as well. For this reason, the parallel passage method, like the other, must confront the question of which facts are truly capable of demonstrating the parallelism of the passages in question. Schleiermacher commented on this point in his second Academy Address on hermeneutics in 1829:

> Assuming that one establishes the rule that a word in the same context may not be explained one way in one instance and another way in another instance, on the grounds that it is improbable that the author would have used it differently in the two instances: one can nevertheless assume the validity of this rule only insofar as the sentence in which the word occurs the second time may still rightly be considered part of the same context. For in a new section many other meanings may, under many circumstances, be found to occur with as much right as in an entirely different work.[15]

With this warning, Schleiermacher offered no hermeneutical solution of the problem; he simply transferred responsibility for its solution to the field of rhetoric. He supposed that the latter would provide a guarantee for the findings of hermeneutics, inasmuch as the functioning of the parallel passage method was founded on the assumption that every text conforms to rhetoric's insistence that a word must not mean two different things in the same context and that a new section of text is always indicative of a new context. Even in Schleiermacher's time this solution was illusory, since the question of whether or not the rules of rhetoric are observed in any given case always leads discussion back to hermeneutics. And the solution is entirely irrelevant in an age that no longer feels itself bound by the rules of rhetoric. Whether a passage can be considered a parallel passage is therefore not something that can be inferred from the division of the text, nor from any other fact or group of facts; it must be decided exclusively on the basis of the meaning of the passage. Like any other presumed piece of evidence, the passage in question must first demonstrate its own cogency, and it can do this only in the process of interpretation. However valuable parallel passages may be for an interpretation, the latter may not be based on them as if they were evidence independent of it, since it is from the interpretation that they derive their probative force. This interdependence is one of the fundamental facts of philological cognition, and no ideal of science may brush it aside.

In the statement quoted above, Schleiermacher himself does not entirely escape a danger related to one of the basic epistemological problems of literary study. Namely, by assuming that the rules of rhetoric are always observed, he masks his object with an ideal image which leads him to misconstrue that object's true character. Literary study must guard against refashioning its object, which is literature, in accord with the criteria supposedly dictated by the discipline's scientific character. This danger becomes especially clear when we consider the problem of equivocation, of the double and even multiple meanings that the variant reading and parallel passage methods are designed to elucidate.

In this case we may have to deal with the ambiguity of a word, but also of syntax, that is to say, of the function of a word, in itself unambiguous, within a sentence. Consider for example, in Kleist's *Amphitryon,* the response Sosias gives to his master's question "And what about the command I gave you?"—"I went / Through an infernal darkness, as if day / Had been sunk ten thousand fathoms deep, / Consigning to all devils you and the errand, / On the road to Thebes, and the royal palace." (*"Ging ich / Durch eine Höllenfinsternis, als wäre / Der Tag zehntausend Klaftern tief versunken, / Euch allen Teufeln, und den Auftrag, gebend, / Den Weg nach Theben, und die Königsburg.)*[16] Some commentators have seen in these lines an error in grammatical case: the text, they maintain, should read: "the way to Thebes and *to* the royal citadel" (*den Weg nach Theben und der Königsburg*); and they think the grounds for the error reside in the French model [i.e., Molière's play of the same name], in which there is no declension. To this view, it may be objected that the last part of the sentence, "and the royal citadel," possibly belongs not to "I went the way to . . . " but to the participial phrase "Giving you and your command to all the devils. . . ." Sosias curses his master and the order as well as the place where the order is supposed to take him. But the question is not only which of the two is more probable: the grammatical error or the bold placing of the last phrase far from its expected position (examples of both can be found in Kleist's work, and even if one or the other alternative were unexampled, that fact would not in itself constitute a refutation). The important question to ask is whether any decision is called for here at all, i.e., whether the alternative does not lie within the subject matter itself. Just as the insertion of *und den Auftrag* ("and the command") between *Euch allen Teufeln* and *gebend* seems to play on the confusing association of *den Auftrag gebend* (i.e., "giving the order"), so too could the third object of the curse, the royal citadel, be linked to the expression *den Weg nach Theben,* in order to lure the reader so to speak, into following the wrong signpost. Such ambiguity easily strikes the philologist as scandalous. But if it is his task to perceive all the intricate internal relationships within a literary text, and to resolve the problems connected with them, then the resolution cannot consist in totally brushing aside an ambiguity that is inherent in the text. The philological solution ought not to set itself in the place of the problem; instead, a problematical utterance, such as Sosias's, must reopen the question each time it is heard. This is what is meant by the thesis that philological knowledge (*Wissen*) is perpetually renewed understanding.

The situation becomes more complicated as soon as we realize that we must give up the attempt to establish the writer's intention. Although philology does not ordinarily overlook the problem of equivocations, it nevertheless generally expects that the solution will come from recognizing which meaning (or even which meanings) were actually intended by the writer and which were not. The claim that it is capable of making such a distinction more often results in the misunderstanding than in the accurate understanding of the object. The scientific postulate that only the ambiguity intended by the writer is to be considered in understanding a work does not do full justice either to the peculiar nature of the poetic process or to the peculiar nature of the linguistic work of art, since it takes it for granted that a poetic text is the reproduction of ideas or mental images. If the word is conceived as a kind of vehicle in the service of ideas and images, then, in the case of an ambiguity, only *that* meaning (or *those* meanings) should be considered which corresponds to the idea or to the image.

Mallarmé's poem *Prose* begins with the word "Hyperbole!"—does it signify the rhetorical figure of hyperbole or the act of exaggerating, or are both viewed as one, with the hyperbole serving as the image representing the mental act? Which thought lies at the start? We are forbidden to answer this question by Mallarmé's pronouncement that poems are not made out of thoughts but out of words. It is in this strong sense that the poem may be said to begin *with the word* "Hyperbole"; it cannot have been preceded by any image or notion existing independently of the word. As soon as the word is no longer seen as simply a means of expression, it acquires its own authority; and this prevents us from putting forward any interpretation that makes it dependent exclusively on the poet's intentions. If the work of art thereby escapes from the poet also, the latter is, all the same, not the loser. And, in any case, it cannot be philology's task to go against the poet's will and perception in drawing the poem into the imaginary net of intention.

Stefan George is reported to have said that he accorded his poems "the right to exist for their own sake; [that] he could perhaps still find a meaning in them of which he was not conscious while he was writing; [and that] indeed, perhaps even later readers could do the same."[17] And Valéry wrote: "It is an error contrary to the nature of poetry and which would even be fatal to it, to assume that to every poem there corresponds a genuine and unique meaning, which conforms to, or is identical to some thought of the author's."[18] The reluctance with which the discipline accepts such insights can be seen, for example, from a recent study on Kleist, which does emphasize the art of ambiguity in this author but which also makes the following assertion: "One must not think, however, that this circumstance could justify the ambiguity of the interpretations. A work as a whole can not be interpreted in any way one likes (*ist nicht beliebig auslegbar*), but rather is meant unequivocally."[19] The error of this statement lies not merely in the assumption that a work of art as a whole is intended to possess an unequivocal meaning—an assumption which, by the way, raises the question of what conception of the structure of the work of art could permit one to maintain that the work is meant unambiguously as a whole despite the existence of ambiguity in the details. In addition, it presents a false alternative: if a work is not "unequivocally intended" then it "can be interpreted in any way one likes." This alternative plainly suggests the motivation behind such a point of view, namely, the justified desire to minimize arbitrariness in interpretation—the reasonable claim of every discipline that it is able to submit its results to examination. But this examination ought not to be undertaken using a criterion that falsifies the object under study more than it unmasks false interpretations. This criterion also falsifies the conditions of philological understanding. For the assumption that a work is not intended unequivocally in no way signifies that, as a result, *all* interpretations are justified. Quite to the contrary, it is only when one advances beyond this false alternative that the real difficulty, but also the authentic task, of textual understanding becomes discernible: to distinguish between false and true, between what is alien to the meaning of the work of art and what is related to its meaning. In carrying out this task, though, one must not, in the name of a presumed unambiguousness, impinge upon the richness of meaning residing in either the (sometimes) objective ambiguity of the individual word or the (virtually ever-present) ambiguity of the theme.

The problem of equivocations that are valid even though not intended by the poet appears to be bound up with the development of the modern lyric, as can be seen from the examples cited above: Mallarmé, George, Valéry. To be sure, similar ideas were set forth in earlier times. For instance, we find the following passage in a book published in 1742, Chladenius's *Einleitung zur richtigen Auslegung vernünftiger Reden und Schriften* ("Introduction to the Correct Interpretation of Reasonable Speech and Writing"): "Since men are not able to survey everything, it may happen that their words, speech, and writing mean something that they did not wish to say or write"; and thus "in attempting to understand their writings, one can justifiably think of things that did not cross the minds of the authors."[20] Naturally, this idea should not be applied unhistorically to earlier periods. But, at the same time, it is impossible to imagine how we in the twentieth century would go about understanding poetry if deprived of the insights of symbolism; hence literary study has equally little right to minimize these insights by considering them merely the manifestation of an historical phenomenon that has no bearing on its methods and criteria. It would be worth investigating whether the conception of language developed by Mallarmé and his followers is of heuristic value at least for those periods of literary history that are generally classified as mannerist, and whether, in similar fashion, the rationalistic conception corresponds to the poetics of those classical works whose classicality exists at the expense of the so-called mannerist elements.

Once again, we see that the epistemological problems confronting literary study stem from the temptation to submit its perceptions (*Erkenntnis*) to criteria which, far from assuring its scientific status, place that status in doubt since they are inadequate to the object it studies. Literary study, or "science" (*Literaturwissenschaft*) must not forget that it is a study, or "science," of art, which should elaborate its methodology on the basis of an analysis of the poetic process. It can hope to arrive at genuine understanding only if it immerses itself in the works themselves, in the "logic of their existence as the results of a productive process" (*die Logik ihres Produziertseins*).[21] At the same time, of course, literary study must demonstrate anew in each of its efforts that with this approach it does not necessarily fall prey to the arbitrariness and uncontrollable element of what it sometimes calls—with a remarkable disdain for its object—the "poetic" sphere. By confronting this danger straight on, however, instead of seeking shelter in the methods of other disciplines, it makes good its claim to be a science.

Chapter 2
The Other Arrow:
On the Genesis
of the Late Hymnic Style

In discussions of Hölderlin, the term "late works" generally refers to those hymns in free rhythms of which *Patmos, The Only One* (*Der Einzige*), and *Celebration of Peace* (*Friedensfeier*) are among the most famous. Is this expression justified? And why should it be applied to hymns rather than to other poems? For one thing, the hymns are the work of someone only thirty years old. Moreover, in the last years before the onset of the mental derangement in which he was to live for more than forty years, Hölderlin composed other poems belonging to different genres, specifically odes and elegies. And yet this term, and the precedence accorded to these poems, is justified. It is true that in the years 1801 and 1802 Hölderlin wrote not only the hymns *At the Source of the Danube* (*Am Quell der Donau*), *Celebration of Peace,* and *The Only One,* but also the elegies *Bread and Wine* (*Brot und Wein*) and *Homecoming* (*Heimkunft*), as well as the odes *The Blind Singer* (*Der blinde Sänger*) and *The Poet's Courage* (*Dichtermut*). All the same, in the internal chronology of his literary endeavors, the hymns belong to a later period than do the other lyric genres.

Evidence for this assertion comes, to begin with, from the impression made by *As on a holiday . . .* (*Wie wenn am Feiertage . . .*), the first of the hymns inspired by Pindar (and here we are speaking only of these, not of the early rhymed songs in the style of Schiller). When compared to

Written in 1962 and published in 1963 (Frankfurt am Main). Originally titled *Der andere Pfeil: Zur Entstehungsgeschichte von Hoelderlins hymnischem Spaetstil.*

Hölderlin's earlier work around the turn of the century, it appears as something entirely new. The odes and elegies, by contrast, reach back uninterruptedly to the beginnings of his poetic creativity. And this continuity exists, at least in the case of the odes, not merely at the level of the genre, but often at the level of the individual poem as well. For Hölderlin expanded many of the odes of the Frankfurt period (most of which consisted of one or two strophes) into longer poems after 1800, thus in the years of the late hymns. Comparison of the various versions of these odes or of the two versions of the elegy *Menon's Lament for Diotima,* provides further indications that the hymns occupy the final position in Hölderlin's work before his mental breakdown.

Transformations of structure and transformations of meter and diction enable us to conclude not only that the hymns evolved from the metric form of the odes,[1] but also that the odes and elegies tend toward the hymnic form. As an example of transformation of structure, consider the poem *Elegy;* it was not divided into strophes until the second version, retitled *Menon's Lament for Diotima,* which dates from the period in which Hölderlin was finding his way to the Pindaric form of the strophe. As an example of transformation of diction, compare the two versions of a strophe that at first formed the epigrammatic ode *The Course of Life* and then, after 1800, became the introduction of a poem with four strophes. The first version reads:

> High my spirit aspired, truly, however, love
> Pulled it earthward; and grief lower still
> > bows it down.
> > So I follow the arc of
> > Life and return to my starting-place.

> Hoch auf strebte mein Geist, aber die Liebe zog
> Schön ihn nieder; das Leid beugt ihn gewaltiger;
> > So durchlauf ich des Lebens
> > Bogen und kehre, woher ich kam.[2]

That which distinguishes the second version from the first is also entirely characteristic of the hymnic style of the later period. The tone becomes more personal and simultaneously, more impersonal. The text of the first version gives "my spirit" (*mein Geist*), an expression to which the following verse refers twice ("love / Pulled *it* earthward; and grief lower still bows *it* down"—*die Liebe zog / Schön* ihn *nieder; das Leid beugt* ihn *gewaltiger*); in the second version this is replaced by an instance of direct self-address: "More you also desired" (*Grössers wolltest auch du*). But immediately afterwards the limits of the individual are transcended, the familiar second person form (*du*) is dropped, and the text now reads "every one of *us* / Love draws earthward" (*die Liebe zwingt All* uns *nieder*). Even more characteristic is the gnomic element, the strain of proverbial wisdom taken over from Pindar's hymns, which is strengthened by the omission of the personal pronoun in the third sentence: instead of "grief lower still bows it down" (*das Leid beugt ihn gewaltiger*), it now is filed down to the more aphoristic phrase "grief bends with still greater power" (*das Leid beuget gewaltiger*). The change in the second half of the strophe, made with the verses added in the second version in mind, is also reminiscent of the style of the hymns. Whereas the first version is satisfied with an observation ("So I follow the arc of / Life and return to my starting-place"—*So durchlauf ich des Lebens / Bogen und kehre, woher ich kam*), the second, in contrapuntal fashion, rises to the level of making a judgment, confident of having perceived not only the arc of life but also its significance. In addition to this striving toward the universal, the succeeding strophes share with the hymns a hymnic aspect in the strict sense of the term, that is, the invocation of gods. In the second version of the poem, *The Course of Life,* the first strophe reads

> More you also desired, but every one of us
> Love draws earthward, and grief bends with
> still greater power.
> Yet our arc not for nothing
> Brings us back to our starting-place.

> Grössers wolltest auch du, aber die Liebe zwingt
> All uns nieder, das Leid beuget gewaltiger,
> Doch es kehret umsonst nicht
> Unser Bogen, woher er kommt.[3]

Doubts as to whether the hymns in free rhythms ought to be designated Hölderlin's "late works" can perhaps be dispelled by the remarks we have made so far concerning the stylistic changes in the odes and elegies. On the other hand, the objection that the poems of a thirty-year-old ought not to be called late works could only be refuted by a careful elucidation of this notion, which is usually employed in stylistic criticism rather than in biographical studies, as well as by an analysis of the hymns themselves. To this end, it would be necessary to show how Hölderlin's hymnic language—in contrast to the last poems of his madness—displays that paradoxical interlacing of extreme resoluteness and wavering, of boldness and humility, and of strength and weakness that is characteristic of the late works of those artists who do not seek to attain a limpid serenity, but rather, with an unworldly obstinacy, struggle to leap over a shadow which is not only their own but also that of their time. What emerges in such cases is usually understood only generations later. One thinks of Beethoven's late quartets, of Cézanne's last pictures—and of Hölderlin's hymns. Such works display neither the arrogance of youth, which entertains no self-doubt in its rebellion against the status quo, nor the calm of middle age, which aims at the reconciliation of the ego and the world, of the new and the old. Here harmony is not the supreme value, though rebellion against it is considered of equally little importance. The artist is alone with his work: he now struggles only against the temptation which originates in himself, against his own doubts, against his own weakness. ("To One alone, however, / Love clings. For this time too much / From my own heart the song / Has come; if other songs follow / I'll make amends for the fault. / Much though I wish to, never / I strike the right measure." [*Es hänget aber an Einem Die Liebe. Diesesmal / Ist nehmlich vom eigenen Herzen / Zu sehr gegangen der Gesang, / Gut machen will ich den Fehl / Wenn ich noch andere singe. / Nie treff ich, wie ich wünsche, / Das Maas*].)[4] If one succeeded in adequately characterizing the diction of such verses and their cadence—a cadence in which the poet's judgment upon himself and his confidence in his own knowledge have become intertwined and in which despair unites with enthusiasm—one would be nearer the secret of the hymns and would at the same time know why they are experienced as "late works."

We have set ourselves a more modest goal in this essay. Rather than attempt to examine Hölderlin's late work as a whole, we shall try to discover the path that led to it. For this purpose we shall examine a complex of poems—the first of the Pindaric songs and a short poem derived from it—that seems to offer a kind of gateway into the realm of the hymns.

The hymn *As on a holiday . . . (Wie wenn am Feiertage . . .)* is a poem about the poet and his work. The motif that runs through it from beginning to end, however, is another, belonging to the twofold sphere of nature and myth; all the hymn's pronouncements on poets and poetry ensue from it with the logic peculiar to metaphor. The motif is that of lightning, the "heavenly fire" (*himmlisches Feuer*). In a letter to his friend Böhlendorff, Hölderlin said of this fire: "among all the things I can see of God, this has become for me the chosen sign."[5] The lightning motif gives rise to the metaphorical joining of poetry and wine, which, at the high point of the hymn, makes it possible to illustrate the genesis of poetry through the birth of Dionysus. The hymn's origin secretly lies in this myth, for its first draft begins where the opening of Hölderlin's translation of Euripides' tragedy *The Bacchae* left off:

I come, the son of Zeus, here to Thebes Dionysus, born of Cad-
mus! daughter Semele, impregnated by Thunder's fire . . .

Ich komme, Jovis Sohn, hier in Thebanerland Dionysos, den
gebahr vormals des Kadmos Tochter Semele, geschwängert von
Gewitterfeuer . . .[6]

Still veiled, as befits the tone of the first strophe (which according to
Hölderlin's theory of modulation of tones would have to be called "naive"),
this metaphor is already present in the great landscape image of the
introduction:

> As on a holiday, to see the field
> A countryman goes out, at morning, when
> Out of hot night the cooling flashes had fallen
> For hours on end, and thunder still rumbles afar,
> The river enters its banks once more,
> New verdure sprouts from the soil,
> And with the gladdening rain of heaven
> The grapevine drips, and gleaming
> In tranquil sunlight stand the trees of the grove:
> So now in favourable weather they stand . . .

> Wie wenn am Feiertage, das Feld zu sehn
> Ein Landmann geht, des Morgens, wenn
> Aus heisser Nacht die kühlenden Blitze fielen
> Die ganze Zeit und fern noch tönet der Donner,
> In sein Gestade wieder tritt der Strom,
> Und frisch der Boden grünt
> Und von des Himmels erfreuendem Regen
> Der Weinstock trauft und glänzend
> In stiller Sonne stehn die Bäume des Haines:
> So stehn sie unter günstiger Witterung . . .[7]

"They" means the poets.[8] It is necessary to guard against a misapprehen-
sion right at the start. The significance of the linking of vine and poetic
word is obscured if one supposes that in this landscape it is the countryman, going out to see his field on a holiday morning, who corresponds to
the poet.[9] For the poets stand under "favourable" skies; they stand—
according to a much-cited verse that comes later in the poem (v. 57)—
"bare-headed beneath God's thunderstorms," as the vine and the trees of
the grove stood in the night, out of which the cooling flashes fell to earth.

In the next strophes, the thunderstorm motif appears in an altered
form. These lines speak of storms

that are in the air, and others
That, more prepared in the depths of time,
More full of meaning and more audible to us,
Drift on between Heaven and Earth and amid
the peoples.

die in der Luft, und andern
Die vorbereiteter in Tiefen der Zeit,
Und deutungsvoller, und vernehmlicher uns
Hindwandeln zwischen Himmel und Erd und unter
den Völkern.[10]

Nature's stormy weather is linked to historical storms, to wars. In them—that is, in the revolutionary wars and wars of the coalitions at the end of the eighteenth century—Hölderlin discerns more than mere human activity: their effects are felt not only "amid the peoples" but also "between heaven and earth." From the two poems, the ode Peace (Der Frieden) and the fragment Die Völker schwiegen, schlummerten . . . ("The peoples were silent, they lay slumbering . . ."), one can conclude that Hölderlin expected something more from the wars than just a change in historical and social relationships. (It is these wars that he also has in mind in As on a holiday . . . when he speaks of the awakening of nature "amid the clang of arms"—mit Waffenklang.) He also hoped for a fundamental transformation, a metanoia, in the relationship of man to the divine, an awakening out of the slumber of the night which is that of the remoteness of the gods and of isolation.

In the thunderstorm the god speaks to men. According to a phrase from the hymn that has usually been misunderstood due to the incorrect punctuation found in all editions, the tempests are "thoughts of the communal spirit" (des gemeinsamen Geistes Gedanken), or, according to the prose draft, "thoughts of the divine (göttlichen) spirit."[11] They are the thoughts of the same communal spirit that in the poem The Archipelago (Der Archipelagus) is yearned for as a counterimage to the godless darkness.[12] And, in another passage, this spirit is linked with Bacchus, the god of wine.[13] Bacchus was engendered by Zeus and Semele, by the supreme god and a human being, or else, according to the original legend, by the sky and the earth. Similarly, according to a verse from Hölderlin's tragedy Empedocles, the vine grew "drenched with hot sun out of the dark ground" (getränkt / Von hoher Sonn aus dunklem Boden) and thus gives evidence "of the earth and heaven" (von Erd und Himmel).[14] And again, in a similar fashion, in the fifth strophe of the hymn, the song grows "from the sun of day and from warm soil" (der Sonne des Tags und warmer Erd), as well as from those storms that Hölderlin conceives as thoughts of the divine spirit and that quietly come to rest in the poet's soul,

So that quickly struck and long familiar
To infinite powers, it shakes
With recollection and kindled by
The holy ray, that fruit conceived in love, the
                    work of gods and men,
To bear witness to both, the song succeeds.
So once, the poets tell, when she desired to see
The god in person, visible, did his lightning fall
On Semele's house, and the divinely struck gave
                    birth to
The thunderstorm's fruit, to holy Bacchus.

Dass schnellbetroffen sie, Unendlichem
Bekannt seit langer Zeit, von Erinnerung
Erbebt, und ihr, von heilgem Strahl entzündet,
Die Frucht in Liebe geboren, der Götter und
                    Menschen Werk
Der Gesang, damit er beiden zeuge, glückt.
So fiel, wie Dichter sagen, da sie sichtbar
Den Gott zu sehen begehrte, sein Blitz auf
                    Semeles Haus
Und die Göttlichgetroffne gebahr,
Die Frucht des Gewitters, den heiligen Bacchus.[15]

Here, at the latest, when Hölderlin invokes the Semele myth in order to illustrate the origin of poetry, he must have confronted the question: could the poet—could he himself—withstand the heavenly fire? Might not the poet, too, have to pay Semele's price and be turned to ashes by this fire? The later Hölderlin increasingly experienced the destructive force of the divine light, until it drove him insane following his journey in the scorching heat of Southern France in 1802; there can be no doubt that he would not have dared to hope for a different end. In the hymn *As on a holiday* . . . , however, he still seems to believe in the possibility that the poet can be touched by the "heavenly fire" and remain unharmed. One indication of this confidence is that in recounting the Semele myth he avoids any expression that alludes to her death.[16] "Divinely struck" (*göttlichgetroffen*) she bore Bacchus, just as the poet's soul was "quickly struck" (*schnellbetroffen*) by the divine lighting flash. Hölderlin's trust is even more clearly expressed in the verses that follow the Semele strophe:

And hence it is that without danger now
The sons of Earth drink heavenly fire.
Yet, fellow poets, us it behoves to stand
Bare-headed beneath God's thunderstorms,

To grasp the Father's ray, no less, with our
                                own hands.
And, wrapping in song the heavenly gift,
To offer it to the people.
For if only we are pure in heart,
Like children, and our hands are guiltless,

   The Father's ray, the pure, will not sear our hearts
And, deeply convulsed, and sharing his sufferings
Who is stronger than we are, yet in the far-flung down-rushing
                                storms of
The God, when he draws near, will the heart stand fast.

   Und daher trinken himmlisches Feuer jetzt
Die Erdensöhne ohne Gefahr.
Doch uns gebührt es, unter Gottes Gewittern,
Ihr Dichter! mit entblösstem Haupte zu stehen
Des Vaters Strahl, ihn selbst, mit eigner Hand
Zu fassen und dem Volk ins Lied
Gehüllt die himmlische Gabe zu reichen.
Denn sind nur reinen Herzens,
Wie Kinder, wir, sind schuldlos unsere Hände,

   Des Vaters Strahl, der reine, versengt es nicht
Und tieferschüttert, die Leiden des Stärkeren
Mitleidend, bleibt in den hochherstürzenden Stürmen
Des Gottes, wenn er nahet, das Herz doch fest.[17]

    The hymn ended with these verses when it was published for the first time in 1910, more than a hundred years after its composition. This was in the second edition of an anthology of the poetry of the age of Goethe whose editors were Stefan George and Karl Wolfskehl.[18] The poem then appeared in the same form in 1916, in what was the most distinguished and fruitful of all the publications of Hölderlin's works that had appeared up to that time (1916), namely, the fourth volume of the first historical and critical edition. This book, containing the late poems, was edited, as were the hymns in George's anthology, by Norbert von Hellingrath.[19] The two most important interpretations of the hymn, one of which is Martin Heidegger's, also seek to demonstrate that the verses cited above should be considered the poem's conclusion.[20] Meanwhile, in the appendix to his edition, Hellingrath had already printed several further verses which, he maintained, constituted the "continuation that [Hölderlin] never really abandoned." Thereafter, Zinkernagel, the editor of another critical edition begun around the same time, transferred these fragmentary final verses from the variant readings into the text itself, attaching them to the last strophes of the hymn.[21] As a result, the conclusion is now formed by seven verses and the beginning of an eighth, and the typographical layout (as well as the manuscript) leaves extra space between each of the first four lines, indicating that something is missing in each case. Now, what is it that is said in these verses that has led to their being rejected again and again? In the most recent critical edition, edited by Friedrich Beissner, they read:

> But, oh, my shame! when of
>
> My shame!
>
> And let me say at once
>
> That I approached to see the Heavenly,
> And they themselves cast me down, deep down
> Below the living, into the dark cast down
> The false priest that I am, to sing,
> For those who have ears to hear, the warning song.
> There
>
> Doch weh mir! wenn von
>
> Weh mir!
>
> Und sag ich gleich,
>
> Ich sei genaht, die Himmlischen zu schauen,
> Sie selbst, sie werfen mich tief unter die Lebenden
> Den falschen Priester, ins Dunkel, dass ich
> Das warnende Lied den Gelehrigen singe.
> Dort[22]

It is understandable that the early editors were reluctant to place these verses at the end of the hymn solely out of respect for philological truth. With the disparate phrasing and with the isolated "There" (*Dort*) of the last line they destroy the closed and coherent shape of the hymn. What is more, they signify the intrusion of despair into that trust which allows the poet "to stand bare-headed beneath God's thunderstorms." Finally, they give the reader no way of perceiving the grounds for this *peripeteia*, let alone of reconstructing them in his mind. And yet the verses are far from being incomprehensible. For what is missing in the blank intervals can be found in the prose draft. Naturally, we have no right to complete the fragmentary final verses on the basis of this first draft; but there is just as little justification in refusing to draw on the prose draft in attempting to discover the original train of thought. And we can then go on to ask why, in seeking to transpose his ideas into metrical form, Hölderlin came up against obstacles that ultimately resisted all efforts to complete the hymn. Accordingly, we must first try to establish the meaning of the prose draft.

The last portion, corresponding to the verses of the hymn just cited, reads as follows:

> For if only we are pure in heart, if, like children, we are guiltless or [if] our hands are purified of sacrilege, then the holy does not kill, does not consume, and, deeply convulsed, the inner heart remains steadfast, suffering the sufferings of life, the divine wrath of nature, and its raptures, which thought does not know. But when of a self-inflicted wound my heart is bleeding, and deeply lost is peace of mind, and freely modest contentment, And when unrest and deficiency drive me to the superabundance of the banqueting table of the gods, when round about me . . .

> and even if I say at once I would have   approached to see the Heavenly, they themselves cast me / down under all the living, / the false priest, in order that out of the night I may sing / the warning anxious song / to the inexperienced.

> Den sind wir reinen Herzens nur, den Kindern gleich sind schuldlos oder gereiniget von Freveln unsere Hände, dann tödtet dann verzehret nicht das Heilige und tieferschüttert bleibt das innere Herz doch fest, mitleidend die Leiden des Lebens, den göttlichen Zorn der Natur, u. ihre Wonnen, die der Gedanke nicht kennt. Aber wenn von selbgeschlagener Wunde das Herz mir blutet, und tiefverloren der Frieden ist, u. freibescheidenes Genügen, Und die Unruh, und der Mangel mich treibt zum Überflusse des Göttertisches, wenn rings um mich

> und sag ich gleich, ich wäre genaht, die Himmli <schen zu> schauen, sie selbst sie werfen mich / tief unter die Lebenden alle, / den falschen Priester hinab, dass ich, aus Nächten herauf, / das warnend ängstige Lied / den Unerfahrenen singe.[23]

The first sentence explains why the poet, unlike other men, should bear the divine without mediation, without attenuation of the words that veil it, as well as why and when he is able successfully to withstand this testing. Here too the storm comparison is retained. In the metrical version, "the holy" (*das Heilige*) that does not kill the poet is called "the Father's ray" (*des Vaters Strahl*): it is lightning. The poet's heart, which opens itself to this ray, is "deeply convulsed" (*tieferschüttert*). In the convulsion, his heart suffers the "sufferings of life" (*die Leiden des Lebens*), "the divine wrath of nature and its raptures" (*den göttlichen Zorn der Natur, u. ihre Wonnen*). These expressions show that what the metrical version enigmatically calls "the sufferings of a God" (*eines Gottes Leiden*), and then "the sufferings of the stronger" (*die Leiden des Stärkeren*), should not be understood as some kind of suffering in the human sense. Hence this compassion (*Mitleiden*) should not be interpreted as a feeling of pity (*Mitleid-Haben*), but rather as the experiencing of the convulsion which, in the god's wrathful nearness, should waken the universe and herald a new presence of the gods. What is required is an openness, a receptivity that disregards the ego. This must be what is meant by the lines that speak of a pure heart and of hands that are guiltless or purified of sacrilege. The child is pure and guiltless because it is not centered upon itself, because it has not yet excluded itself, in the form of a rigidly fixed ego, from the divine, cosmic unity. This, however, is man's sacrilege. In the poem *The Archipelago,* the invocation of the One Spirit that ought to be common to all men is followed by the elegiac lament:

> Ah, but our kind walks in darkness, it dwells as in Orcus, Severed from all that's divine. To his own industry only Each man is forged, and can hear only himself in the workshop's Deafening noise . . .

> Aber weh! es wandelt in Nacht, es wohnt, wie im Orkus, Ohne Göttliches unser Geschlecht. Ans eigene Treiben Sind sie geschmiedet allein, und sich in der tosenden Werkstatt Höret jeglicher nur . . . [24]

Compassion for the sufferings of life is the exact opposite of the attitude in which one hears only oneself. In Hölderlin's conception, the poet is able to withstand God's thunderstorms because he is not "forged to his own industry" but rather is receptive to the cosmos; he does not hear himself, but the thunder in which the god speaks to him.

Yet scarcely is this ideal set forth when the poet is overcome by doubts. The next sentence of the prose draft begins with the words "But when" (*Aber wenn*), and this "when" (*wenn,* in German, can mean either "if" or "when") clearly does not signify merely an imagined possibility; it derives from real experience. The prose draft at first contained the words "My shame" (or, "Woe is me!" *Weh mir!*); this lament was subsequently struck out, however, and a more objective tone was sought. But the exclamation stubbornly returns in the interval of the manuscript page before the words "and even if I say" (*und sag ich gleich*) and then is struck out a second time only to be restored in the metrical version. And even at this point the matter is not settled, for the expression reappears in the poem that evolved from the fragmentary conclusion of the hymn. After *Weh mir* was crossed out, the beginning of the second sentence of the prose draft became: "But when of a self-inflicted wound my heart is bleeding" (*Aber wenn von selbgeschlagener Wunde das Herz mir blutet*).

Earlier studies have taken scarcely any notice of these two expressions. This is all the more remarkable in that the metrical version breaks off for the first time at just this point, which is in fact where the decision is made that the hymn will not be concluded in accordance with the train of thought developed so far. How are these expressions to be understood? We already indicated the gist of our interpretation above, when, in analyzing the preceding lines, we referred to that passage of *The Archipelago* which states that men, who live far from the gods, are forged to their own industry and hear only themselves. The poet's heart bleeds from another arrow—but from which other arrow? By which arrow may the poet be struck? Indeed, by which should he be struck? The hymn already gave the answer: by lightning, by heavenly fire. In the decisive years from 1800 until his collapse, Hölderlin used the word arrow (*Pfeil*) four times in his poetry.[25] On three occasions it designates the sun's rays or lightning, and in a variant reading of *The Course of Life* (*Lebenslauf*) it even replaces the word "lightning" (*Blitz*), which was written down previously. The fourth time it appears, however, is when the poet mentions the "other arrow" (*von anderem Pfeile*). This phrase is later corrected to read "of a self-inflicted wound" (*von selbgeschlagener Wunde*). The change sacrifices the connection with the thunderstorm in order to make clearer what is meant by this term "other." The "other arrow" comes not from the god but from man himself: it is man who has inflicted this wound on himself. Instead of having compassion for the sufferings of the stronger god, who nevertheless needs men,[26] he suffers on account of himself, on account of his own weakness.

All the same, this is not the cause of the poet's undoing. Presumption enters the picture only when the poet, suffering on account of his own self and dissatisfied with his own lot, turns to the gods—at the time, when in the words of the prose sketch, "deficiency (*Mangel*) drives [him] to the superabundance of the banqueting table of the gods" (*der Mangel treibt [ihn] zum Überflusse des Göttertisches*). Here one is reminded of Tantalus and of the confession which, in Hölderlin's letter to Böhlendorff mentioned above, follows the evocation of lightning: "earlier I could rejoice over a new truth, over a better view of that which is above us and which surrounds us; now I fear that I might end up like old Tantalus, to whom more of the gods was given than he could digest."[27] Despite this analogy, we must not overlook the fact that the two passages are based on different presuppositions. The letter, written about two years after the holiday hymn, is not concerned with any offense nor with any outrage; the Tantalus myth stands simply for the notion of destructive abundance. Here we can already detect a premonition of that misfortune which Hölderlin expressed in the following terms after his trip to Southern France: "and as one says of heroes, I can well say of myself that Apollo has struck me."[28] In *As on a holiday* . . . the threat is conceived differently, for the hymn is born of the trust that the poet can take the risk of exposing himself to the heavenly fire—a trust which is foreign to the later Hölderlin.[29] In the hymn too he is aware of the danger, but in this case it is personally motivated; the poet's offense lies in the fact that he approaches heaven not as a servant but as one driven by his own "deficiency" (*Mangel*). In contrast to the letter to Böhlendorff, when the hymn speaks of the "superabundance of the banqueting table of the gods" (*Überfluss des Göttertisches*), it is not with reference to man's incapacity to deal with it; the problem, rather, is that it tempts man, who is not satisfied with his own portion, into an encounter he ought to seek only for the sake of the gods, not on account of his own lack, that is, only as a servant and not as a sufferer. This is the law against which the poet sins when he is driven to the divine table by a "self-inflicted wound"; for then, in the final words of the prose draft, he becomes a "false priest" and is thrust back into the darkness of night in order that he might "sing the warning anxious song to the inexperienced" (*das warnend ängstige Lied den Unerfahrenen singe*).

At this point, having reached the end of the train of thought that can be discerned in the prose draft, we are confronted by the following question: are the ideas we have found also pertinent to an analysis of the fragmentary final verses? Or does the metrical version differ so greatly from the prose draft that the draft may no longer be considered its starting point? Why did the final verses of the metrical version remain incomplete: does this signify that it is based on entirely different conceptual presuppositions, or rather that the very ideas of the prose draft blocked the way?

First of all, let us note the changes revealed by a comparison of the two versions: in the metrical version the word "guiltless" (*schuldlos*) is no longer followed by the phrase "or purified of sacrilege" (*oder gereiniget von Freveln*); the verb "sears" (*versengt*) replaces the group "then kills, then consumes" (*dann tödtet dann verzehret*); "the Father's ray" (*des Vaters Strahl*) appears in place of the original word "the holy" (*das Heilige*); and the expression "sharing the sufferings of life, the divine wrath of nature, and its raptures, which thought does not know" (*Mitleidend die Leiden des Lebens, den göttlichen Zorn der Natur, u. ihre*

Wonnen, die der Gedanke nicht kennt) becomes "sharing the sufferings of the stronger . . . in far-flung down-rushing storms / The God" (*die Leiden des Stärkeren / Mitleidend . . . in den hochherstürzenden Stürmen / Des Gottes*). Neither these changes nor the transitional stages, such as they can be seen in the variant readings of the metrical version, point toward a fundamental transformation between the two versions which, as some have supposed, would have prevented the poet from incorporating the last sentence of the prose draft into the hymn.[30] Further comparison shows that the metrical version breaks off at just the place which in the prose draft indicates the offense that the poet may possibly have committed. Twice it begins with the lament "my shame" (*weh mir!*), but the text is not taken over from the prose draft, nor is anything else put in its place. It is as if Hölderlin was no longer satisfied with the text of the prose version, without however being able to find another solution. Accordingly, he at first left blank a large space, one of the intervals that still fissure the end of the hymn, and wrote down the conclusion of the prose draft in verse form, making only a few changes. The prose draft seems to end with the words: "in order that out of [the darkness] of the night I will sing the warning anxious song to the inexperienced" (*dass ich, aus Nächten herauf, das warnend ängstige Lied den Unerfahrenen singe*). Hölderlin wished to pursue this idea beyond the text of the draft, an indication perhaps of a desperate effort on his part to overcome a powerful resistance. In the metrical version a new sentence begins with the word "There" (*Dort*)—as if Hölderlin hoped to be able to depict the punishment rather than the outrage, the false priesthood. Yet this new start, too, fails to lead any further; those lines that appear next on the page, following the several sketches of a conclusion to the hymn, no longer belong at all to the hymn itself. They lead beyond it to two other sketches, one of which is the preparation for the poem *The Middle of Life (Hälfte des Lebens).*

With this observation we could conclude our analysis of the last fragments of the holiday hymn, adopting the view of Eduard Lachmann. He thinks that once Hölderlin took a portion of those verses that formed the conclusion of the hymn in the draft and used them in another poem, it is no longer justifiable to speak of a continuation that was never abandoned.[31] In the first place, however, Hölderlin's decision does not mean that the hymn actually ends with the verse " . . . will the heart stand fast" (*bleibt . . . das Herz doch fest*). And second, it would be more in keeping with the poetic process to avoid an approach that is concerned only with "technical" factors and whose criterion is the use to which material is put. Instead, we ought to investigate, on the basis of the work's genesis, whether the poem that grew out of the uncompleted hymn and that is itself complete can help us to understand why the hymn in fact remained unfinished.

This genesis can be reconstructed on the basis of the manuscript—specifically, page 17 verso of the so-called Stuttgart Foliobuch, illustrated here [not included in present volume]—which Friedrich Beissner describes as follows:

> First, this is how the end of the poem *As on a holiday* . . . looks in the draft. About 10 cm under the upper edge we find the words: "Woe is me" (*Weh mir!*)—5 cm lower: "And even if I say" (*Und sag ich gleich*)—and 2 cm lower still: "that I came nearer in order to look at the Celestial Ones" (*Ich sei genaht, die Himmlischen zu schauen*), etc. Then, after the attempt to complete the draft has been abandoned, three titles appear one next to the other at the upper edge; they are written with a sharper quill and in a more negligent hand: "The Rose" (*Die Rose*). "The Swans" (*Die Schwäne*). "The Stag" (*Der Hirsch*). Under the first of these, and obviously written at the same time, we find *holde Schwester* ("gracious sister"). This draft is later continued, with a broader quill and in a more tightly controlled hand: around and under the words "Woe is me", *Weh mir!* (so that the line *Und sag ich gleich* is partly covered over and had to be crossed out), an idea is set down that is clearly influenced by the final lines of the draft of *As on a holiday* . . . (which are written down immediately underneath): *Wo nehm ich, wenn es Winter ist / Die Blumen, dass ich Kränze den Himmlischen / winde? / Dann wird es seyn, als wüsst ich nimmer von Göttlichen, / Denn (1) wenn (2) von mir sei gewichen des Lebens Geist; / Wenn ich den Himmlischen die Liebeszeichen / Die Blumen im [nackten] kahlen Felde Suche / u. dich nicht finde.* (It is the rose which is being addressed.) In the middle "column" of the page, under the title "The Swans", there appear the following lines, again written at a later time, with an unwieldly quill and in a darker ink: *und trunken von / Küssen taucht ihr / das Haupt ins hei- / lignüchterne kühle / Gewässer.* These themes thus fuse into a poem that was initially given the title *Die letzte Stunde* ("The Last Hour").[32]

The resulting poem, later entitled *The Middle of Life (Hälfte des Lebens)*, reads as follows:

> With yellow pears the land
> And full of wild roses
> Hangs down into the lake,
> You lovely swans,
> And drunk with kisses
> You dip your heads
> Into the hallowed, the sober water.

But oh, where shall I find
When winter comes, the flowers, and where
The sunshine
And shade of the earth?
The walls loom
Speechless and cold, in the wind
Weathercocks clatter.

Mit gelben Birnen hänget
Und voll mit wilden Rosen
Das Land in den See,
Ihr holden Schwäne,
Und trunken von Küssen
Tunkt ihr das Haupt
Ins heilignüchterne Wasser.

Weh mir, wo nehm' ich, wenn
Es Winter ist, die Blumen, und wo
Den Sonnenschein,
Und Schatten der Erde?
Die Mauern stehn
Sprachlos und kalt, im Winde
Klirren die Fahnen.[33]

In image and contrasting image the two strophes convey the particular poet's mood from which they arise. This is the feeling of darkness, of the remoteness of the gods, of the absence of love; it is the experience of isolation, whose expression is the absence of language and whose image is the absence of the shadow that once mediated between sun and earth. The longed-for mediation is presented in the first strophe as an image, as alien reality. The land and the swans unite with the water, the swans being "drunken with kisses" and the water being "hallowed and sober." Here, love and religion, the essence of both of which is union, are seen by the longing glance as joined together in one in nature. The mood of the poet (for whom this reconciliation is an alien process in which he does not participate) is no other than the one that is found in the prose draft of the holiday hymn: "when my heart of a self-inflicted wound is bleeding and deeply lost is peace of mind" (*wenn von selbgeschlagener Wunde das Herz mir blutet, und tiefverloren der Frieden ist*). There exists a direct link between this sentence, which the poet was never able to bring to a conclusion and upon which the metrical version foundered, and the second strophe of *The Middle of Life*. And the changes and deletions that the poet made in going from one to the other show why the holiday hymn could not be completed. It is the relationship to the divine that is sacrificed now.

In the hymn, unrest and lack drive the poet, suffering from a self-inflicted wound, to the abundance of the gods' table and turn him into a false priest. The poem *The Middle of Life* reveals that the offense is not merely a danger, which is how the prose draft presents it; it is the actual state of mind in which Hölderlin wrote the poem.[34] If this hypothesis is correct, then it follows that Hölderlin failed in the metrical version because he should have intensified the truthfulness of the verses, because he should have recognized that what he had previously presented as possibility was in fact reality. As a result, however, he pronounced judgment on his turning toward the divine, a movement that he should have brought to realization in the poem itself. With its fragmentary final verses, the hymn *As on a holiday . . . ,* which seeks to establish the poet's position with respect to the sphere of the gods,[35] stands before an abyss, at a point beyond which it must not go, where it must in fact abolish itself. The poet's meeting with the Celestial Ones and his exalting of his encounter in song become an outrage when his heart is bleeding of a self-inflicted wound.

This view is confirmed by the verses that form the transition between the hymn and the poem *The Middle of Life:*

Where will I find, when winter comes,
The flowers, that I may make wreaths for the Celestial Ones?
Then it will be as though I never knew of the divine,
For (1) when (2) may life's spirit leave me;
When I seek love tokens of the Celestial Ones
The flowers in [naked] barren field and do not find you.

Wo nehm ich, wenn es Winter ist
Die Blumen, dass ich Kränze des Himmlischen winde?
Dann wird es seyn, als wüsst ich nimmer von Göttlichen,
Denn (1) wenn (2) von mir sei gewichen des Lebens Geist;
Wenn ich des Himmlischen die Liebeszeichen
Die Blumen im [nackten] kahlen Felde suche u. dich nicht finde.[36]

There is no longer any hope here of a meeting with the divine, as there was in the prose draft. But the verses still lament the deficiency that compels renunciation; they still lament the impossibility of the hymnic, an impossibility that finds its image in the absence of the flowers from which wreaths were to be made in honor of the Celestial Ones. And, as if the very mention of the gods were an offense, Hölderlin incorporates in the poem itself only the words "But oh, where shall I find / When winter comes, the flowers" (*Weh mir, wo nehm ich, wenn / Es Winter ist, die Blumen*); the recipients of the flowers—"that I may make wreaths for the Celestial Ones" (*dass ich Kränze den Himmlischen winde*)—are no longer mentioned. In fact, the divine sphere is left aside altogether; it appears only in the blissful union evoked in the first strophe, in the image of nature.

The hypothesis suggested by a consideration of the phrases "of another arrow" and "of a self-inflicted wound," as well as by a study of the drafts of the metrical version of the hymn and of the poem *The Middle of Life,* becomes increasingly plausible when one turns to another poem that seems to be intimately associated with the notions linking the hymn and the poem *The Middle of Life.* The first version of this poem, entitled *Elegy (Elegie),* was probably begun in 1799, at about the same time, therefore, as the sketch of the holiday hymn. The biographical background of the elegy is underscored by its subsequent title: *Menon's Lament for Diotima (Menons Klagen um Diotima).* It is Hölderlin's lament for his lost love Susette Gontard.

In the first strophe the poet compares himself to a wounded animal who flees to the woods:

> Yet his green lair no longer now can refresh him or soothe him,
> Crying and sleepless he roams, cruelly pricked by the thorn.

> Aber nimmer erquickt sein grünes Lager das Herz ihm,
> Jammernd und schlummerlos treibt es der Stachel umher.[37]

These lines recall the injury incurred by the poet through "the other arrow," just as the comparison with the animal refers to the title *The Stag (Der Hirsch).*

The fourth strophe looks back in an elegiac manner to the poet's former happiness with Diotima:

> Meanwhile we—like the mated swans in their summer contentment
>   When by the lake they rest or on the waves, lightly rocked,
> Down they look, at the water, and silvery clouds through that mirror
>   Drift, ...

> Aber wir, zufrieden gesellt, wie die liebenden Schwäne
>   Wenn sie ruhen am See, oder, auf Wellen gewiegt,
> Niedersehn in die Wasser, wo silberne Wolken sich spiegeln,[38]

—this is the image from *The Middle of Life.* Then the North Wind appears, "the enemy of lovers" (*der Liebenden Feind*). This same hostility is depicted in the two antithetical strophes whose final verse reads "in the wind / Weathercocks clatter" (*im Winde / Klirren die Fahnen*).

The fifth strophe of the elegy begins with the verses:

Celebrate—yes, but what? And gladly with others I'd sing now,
    Yet alone as I am nothing that's godlike rings true,
This, I know, is it, my failing, . . .

Feiern möcht'ich; aber wofür? und singen mit Andern
    Aber so einsam fehlt jegliches Göttliche mir.
Dies ist's, dies mein Gebrechen, . . .

His "failing" is the deficiency referred to in the lines that constitute the transition between the hymn and *The Middle of Life:* "Then it will be as if I no longer knew anything of the divine ones" (*Dann wird es seyn, als wüsst ich nimmer von Göttlichen*).

The next strophe again recalls in elegiac fashion the time when men sat together with the gods "at the blessed table" (*an seligem Tisch'*). The prose draft of the hymn, it will be remembered, speaks of the "superabundance of the banqueting table of the gods," to which the poet was driven by lack and by unrest.

At the end of the elegy, however, a sudden change occurs: despair turns into hope and lament into exaltation. It is almost as if the elegy seeks to surpass itself and become hymnic:

Come, it was like a dream, bloodied wings have already
    Healed, and rejuvenated all the old hopes rise up.
Let him serve in Orcus, whom it pleases! We, fashioned by quiet
    Love, we seek the path to the gods.

Komm! es war, wie ein Traum! die blutenden Fittige sind ja
    Schon genesen, verjüngt wachen die Hoffnungen all.
Dien' im Orkus, wem es gefällt! wir, welche die stille
    Liebe bildete, wir suchen zu Göttern die Bahn.
                           (1st version)[39]

Karl Viëtor's essay on *Menon's Lament for Diotima* concludes with this statement: "Hölderlin's love lament fades away in the mediation and prophecy of his late poetry. The yearning for withdrawal and the chiliastic vision of salvation found in the Menon elegy flow into the "pathos" of one who has sacrificed his personality to the divine mission."[40] It is precisely this transformation that is illuminated by the relationship between the holiday hymn, the elegy, and the poem *The Middle of Life*. The light that the hymn sheds on this transformation, however, does not reveal it as being primarily a "fading away"; the elegiac spirit does not simply "flow into" the hymnic poetry. This light shows us something different. In the hymnic domain, once the poet really takes the path leading to the gods (which is the one prescribed in the final strophe of the elegy and which exists beyond the elegiac domain) that which becomes evident are its difficulties and dangers. And, according to the insight of the prose draft, only he may venture upon this path whose own wound has healed and whose own suffering has become but a dream. The elegiac, therefore, does not really flow into the hymnic: a qualitative jump separates the two forms, the jump from the lyric of personal experience (*Erlebnislyrik*) to the selfless exaltation of the gods. For Hölderlin, he who enters into the hymnic realm without first having entirely cast off the remnants of the elegiac is a "false priest." Clearly, at the end of the holiday hymn he recognized that he himself was still in the grip of the elegiac and was still bound to his own suffering; he knew that the wound that "the other arrow" had inflicted upon him had not yet healed. The close connection between the end of the hymn and the elegy leaves no doubt concerning this point: the poet's self-inflicted wound stems from the loss of his loved one, from the loss of Diotima.

It is this element of personal suffering that is banished from the hymnic realm, which recognizes the poet only as "servant."[41] When Hölderlin began to write *As on a holiday* . . . , he still had not entirely freed himself of this element, as is evident from the fact that at the end of the poem it is just this suffering that interrupts the hymnic ego and demands its rights. This, then, is the reason why the poem could not be completed. But its fragmentary final verses gave rise to a poem in which, more than in any other, justice is done to personal suffering.[42] Only after this failure, a failure that simultaneously yielded understanding and purification, could Hölderlin begin his real hymnic poetry, his real "late work." This poetry is no less personal than the odes and elegies, but the ego whose voice it carries no longer recognizes any arrow other than the god's.

Chapter 3
The Notion of the Tragic in Schelling, Hölderlin, and Hegel

Schelling

It has often been asked how Greek reason was able to bear the contradictions of its tragedy. A mortal fated by destiny to become a criminal fights *against* this destiny, and in spite of this he is horribly punished for a crime that is the work of fate! The *reason* for this contradiction, that which made it bearable, lay deeper than the level at which it has been sought: it lay in the conflict of human freedom with the power of the objective world, a conflict in which the mortal necessarily had to succumb when that power was a superior power—a *fatum*; and yet, since he did not succumb *without* struggle, he had to be *punished* for this very defeat. The fact that the criminal succumbed only to the superior force of fate and yet was *punished* all the same—this was the recognition of human freedom, an *honor* owed to freedom. It was by *allowing* its hero to *struggle* against the superior power of fate that Greek tragedy honored human freedom. In order not to transgress the bounds of art, tragedy was obliged to have the mortal *succumb*; yet, in order to compensate for this humiliation of human freedom imposed by art, it also had to allow him to undergo punishment—even for a crime committed on account of *fate* . . . It was a *great* idea to have man willingly accept punishment even for an *inevitable* crime; in this way he was able to demonstrate his freedom precisely through the loss of this freedom, and to perish with a declaration of free will.[1]

Originally published as part of *Versuch über das Tragische* (Frankfurt am Main, 1961).

This interpretation of *Oedipus Rex* and of Greek tragedy in general marks the beginning of the history of a theory of the Tragic which, unlike previous theories, is not concerned with the effect of the Tragic on the audience but aims, rather, to understand the phenomenon itself. The text cited above comes from the last of the *Philosophical Letters on Dogmatism and Criticism* that Schelling wrote in 1795 at the age of twenty. In this work he contrasts the theories of Spinoza and of Kant, which Fichte had earlier called the only two "entirely coherent systems."[2] At the same time, Schelling seeks to prevent the critical philosophy itself from turning into a new dogmatism. In a letter to Hegel written at this time he observes that "The real difference between critical and dogmatic philosophy seems to me to reside in the fact that the former starts out from the absolute Ego (which is not yet conditioned by any object), and the latter from the absolute Object or Non-Ego."[3] This difference is paralleled by the opposite meanings that the two theories attribute to the notion of freedom, in which Schelling sees the "essence of the Ego," "the beginning and the end of all philosophy."[4] In dogmatism, the subject pays for the choice of the absolute as the object of its knowledge with "absolute passivity." Criticism, in contrast, which places everything in the subject and thus negates everything of the object, is a "striving after immutable self-sufficiency, unconditional freedom, and untrammeled activity."[5]

Schelling himself seems to have perceived that neither of these possibilities sufficiently recognized the power of the Objective, since even where the Objective is triumphant, due to the absolute passivity of the subject, it owes its victory to the subject. Thus he has the fictitious recipient of his letters indicate a third possibility. This possibility, however, does not derive from the presuppositions of some philosophical system, but from life and its depiction in art. "You are right," the tenth letter begins, "one thing still remains—to *know* that there is an objective power which threatens to destroy our freedom and, with this firm and certain conviction in our hearts, to fight *against* it, to summon up all our freedom and to perish in this way."[6] Yet, almost as if he shied away from this recognition of the Objective, the young Schelling allows the struggle a place only in tragic art, but not in life itself. This struggle, he states, "could not become a system of action for the simple reason that such a system presupposes a race of Titans, in the absence of which it would undoubtedly have the most ruinous consequences for humanity."[7]

Schelling thus subscribes to the idealistic belief that the Tragic can be mastered and that it is acceptable since one can discover a meaning in it. This meaning is the affirmation of freedom. Accordingly, he views the tragic course of events in *Oedipus Rex* as meaningful only in the perspective of its *telos*. Schelling's account nevertheless brings to light the structure peculiar to this course of events. In his interpretation, the tragic hero does not simply succumb to the superior force of the Objective. He is also punished for the very fact of having succumbed, that is to say, for having undertaken the struggle in the first place. As a result, the positive value of his attitude—the will to freedom that is "the essence of his Ego"—turns against him. Like Hegel, we may call this process dialectical.[8] Schelling, it is true, has in mind the affirmation of a freedom obtained at the price of the hero's downfall: the possibility of a purely tragic course of events was alien to him. Let us recall, however, his observation that "it was a *great* idea to have man willingly accept punishment even for an inevitable crime; in this way he was able to demonstrate his freedom precisely through the loss of this freedom." This sentence underlies all philosophical attempts to deal with the problem of the Tragic. Here we may detect that somber refrain which, when it reappears later, is no longer muted by a belief in the triumph of the sublime. It is the theme of the awareness that something very great was destroyed by the very agency which should have saved it.

> The essence of *tragedy* is . . . a genuine conflict between freedom in the subject and objective necessity—a conflict that does not end with the defeat of one or the other but rather when both of them simultaneously become conquerors and conquered in the perfect Indifference (*Indifferenz*).[9]

> The conflict of freedom and necessity truly [exists] only where the latter undermines the will itself, and where freedom is fought on its own ground.[10]

The interpretation of tragedy that Schelling proposes in the *Lectures on the Philosophy of Art,* first delivered in 1802–3, explicitly refers to the early book on dogmatism and criticism. Its starting point here, however, is no longer a third type of relationship between subject and object reserved especially for art and standing alongside the two other theoretically possible types. It is developed, rather, from the principles of Schelling's philosophy of identity and occupies a central position in the aesthetic theory that he based on that philosophy. Whereas Schelling posits God as "infinite ideality comprising all reality in itself,"[11] he defines beauty as the "unification" (*Ineinsbildung*) of the real and the ideal," or, in other terms, as the "Indifference of freedom and necessity contemplated in a real entity."[12] He considers the three poetical genres to be different manifestations of this identity. In the epic, Schelling perceives "a kind of state of innocence, where everything is still together and united which later will exist only dispersed or which only will become one again after passing through a state of dispersion. As culture advances, this identity flares up in the antagonism of the lyrical poem; and it was only with the ripest fruit of later culture (*Bildung*) that, on a higher level, unity was reconciled with the antagonism and that the two became one again in a perfect formation. This higher identity is the drama."[13] Thus Schelling's entire system, whose essence is the identity of freedom and necessity, culminates in his definition of the tragic course of events as a restoration of this Indifference through conflict. Once again the Tragic is conceived of as a dialectical phenomenon, for the Indifference of freedom and necessity is possible only at a certain cost: in other words, the conqueror must also be the conquered, and vice versa. Moreover, the setting of the conflict is not an intermediate zone that remains external to the struggling subject; on the contrary, it is transposed to the very realm of freedom, which, now at odds with itself, becomes its own adversary.

Hölderlin

The significance of the tragedies is most easily grasped by means of a paradox. Because all power is distributed justly and equally, everything that is original appears not in its original strength but, properly (*eigentlich*), in its weakness. Hence the light of life (*das Lebenslicht*) and appearance quite properly (*recht eigentlich*) belong to the weakness of every whole (*jedes Ganzen*). Now, in the Tragic, the sign is in itself insignificant or without effect, but the original is openly revealed. That is to say, the original can properly appear only in its weakness; but insofar as the sign in itself is posited as insignificant $= 0$, then the original, too, the hidden ground of everything in nature (*jede Natur*) can reveal itself. If nature properly reveals itself in its weakest gift, then, when it shows itself in its strongest gift, the sign $= 0$.[14]

This fragment, which was written between 1798 and 1800, along with the two other Homburg texts on the Tragic (the *Grund zum Empedokles* and the essay *Über das Werden im Vergehen*) takes as its starting point the concept of nature. Like these other writings, it arises in a desire to grant man, face to face with nature, a place which not only indicates that he is her servant, but which also reveals nature's dependence on man. In a letter written to his brother on 4 June 1799, Hölderlin speaks of the "paradox ... that the artistic and formative drive (*Kunst-und Bildungstrieb*), with all its modifications and unusual aspects (*Abarten*), is a genuine service that men perform for nature."[15] This is the paradox that the fragment employs to explain the meaning of tragedy. The same basic idea appears in a letter to Sinclair of 24 December 1798, in which Hölderlin states that the fact that "there exists no monarchic power in heaven and on earth" is "the first condition of all life and of all organization."[16] Accordingly, since "all power is distributed justly and equally," that which is original by its very essence, i.e., nature, is not able to appear "in its original strength." "Properly" it can appear "only in its weakness." (Here "properly," *eigentlich,* means in conformity with its own possibility, through its own power.) This dialectic, in which the strong can appear by itself only as weakness and requires something weak in order that its strength may appear, establishes the necessity of art. In art, nature no longer appears "properly"; instead it is mediated by a sign. In the tragedy this sign is the hero. Unable to prevail against the power of nature, which ultimately destroys him, he is "insignificant" and "without effect." But, in the downfall of the tragic hero, when the sign $= 0$, nature shows itself as conqueror "in its strongest gift," and "the original is openly revealed." Hölderlin thus interprets tragedy as the sacrifice man offers to nature so that it can appear in an adequate manner. Herein lies the tragic aspect of man's situation: this service, which gives his existence meaning, is one he can perform only in death, when he becomes a sign that is "in itself insignificant $= 0$". According to Hölderlin, this conflict between nature and art (whose goal, in fact, is their reconciliation) comes to a head in tragedy. Indeed, he makes this the explicit theme of *Empedocles,* the tragedy that he composed at the same time as his theoretical writings on the subject. In Hölderlin's view, Empedocles is "a son of the violent antagonisms between nature and art in which the world appears before his eyes. [He is] a man in whom those contradictions unite so inwardly that they become *one* in his person."[17]Yet, his situation is still tragic since he must perish for the sake of that very reconciliation he embodies—indeed *because* he embodies it, that is, represents it in the domain of the senses. For, as the *Grund zum Empedokles* argues, the reconciliation only becomes recognizable as such when that which was previously joined in an inner unity undergoes separation through conflict. On the other hand, the physical union must be merely apparent and temporary, and it must be annulled and surpassed; "otherwise the universal would be submerged in the individual and . . . the life of a world would die out at a particular point."[18] Empedocles is thus "the victim of his time,"[19] a victim whose "perishing," however, makes possible a "birth" (*Werden*). And this fate is not his alone; as Hölderlin insists, it is "more or less" the fate of all "tragic figures."[20]

> The representation of the tragic is mainly based on this, that what is monstrous and terrible in the coupling of God and man, in the total fusion of the power of Nature with the innermost depth of man, so that they are one at the moment of wrath, shall be made

intelligible by showing how this total fusion into one is purged by their total separation.[21]

The "Remarks on Oedipus" and the "Remarks on Antigone," both written in 1803, closely follow the late hymns, just as the Homburg essays accompany *Empedocles.* The definition of tragedy contained in these remarks substantially agrees with the earlier one, but its proximity to the hymns gives it a new significance. An external sign of this change is that Hölderlin no longer bases his reflections on the Tragic on his own writing, but rather on his translations of the two Sophoclean tragedies. The tragic solution of the antagonistic relationship between nature and art—which in the late Hölderlin appears in a more absolute manner, becoming the relationship between God and man—is no longer the theme of his own lyrics. To be sure, Hölderlin does not turn away from the tragic dialectic that he sought to portray in the *Death of Empedocles.* But, in his notion of the relationship between God and man, the Tragic has become as it were immanent, by virtue of the notion of "divine faithlessness." Hölderlin, looking at the matter from the perspective of the philosophy of history, sees both the age in which the action of *Oedipus Rex* is set and his own age as intermediate periods, as a night in which "God and man, in order that the course of the world have no lacunae and that *the memory of the Celestial Ones will not come to an end, reveal themselves in the all-forgetting form of faithlessness,* for divine faithlessness is what is best remembered."[22]

This dialectic of faithfulness and faithlessness, of remembrance and forgetting is the basic theme of Hölderlin's late poems, poems that both define and fulfill the poet's mission in an age in which the only way the gods can be close is by remaining at a distance. In the night that Hölderlin pictures, the gods are far away and yet they are present in the only manner possible without destroying man. Hölderlin is determined to persevere in this night and to prepare the future coming of the gods. This determination is what gives his poems, such as *Celebration of Peace* (*Friedensfeier*), their utopian structure and their extremely intense rhythm, in which each word resists the longing to which Empedocles yielded when he threw himself into Mt. Aetna. In Sophoclean tragedy, too, according to Hölderlin's interpretation, the tension is not resisted but discharged. The chiliastic future in which the gods will be near erupts prematurely within a present not yet able to bear it: a spark flashes, and in the fire kindled by it the night turns into searing day. In Hölderlin's view, by "interpreting the words of the oracle *too infinitely,*"[23] that is, as a religious command and then carrying out this command, Oedipus forces the union with God. But this "boundless unification," the "Remarks" tell us, must turn into "boundless separation," if the monstrous act that it represents is to become knowable. The day, having been forced, turns tragically into intensified night: into the darkness of the blinded Oedipus.

Hegel

Tragedy resides in the fact that the moral nature (*die sittliche Natur*), in order not to become entangled with its inorganic (*unorganische*) nature, separates the latter from itself as a fate, and places it over against itself; and, through the recognition of this fate in the course of the battle, it is reconciled with the divine being, which is the unity of both.[24]

This, Hegel's earliest interpretation of tragedy, is found in a work entitled "On the Scientific Ways of Treating Natural Law," which appeared in 1802–3 in the *Kritische Journal der Philosophie* that he edited jointly with Schelling. Like the journal as a whole, this essay was directed against Kant and Fichte. Hegel here deals with questions in the field of ethics, but the dispute is actually motivated by differences over fundamental principles; it is a confrontation between the emerging dialectic, just then becoming conscious of itself, and the dualistic formalism characteristic of the philosophy of that time. What Hegel objects to in Kant's *Critique of Practical Reason* and in Fichte's *Foundations of Natural Law* is the rigid opposition they maintain between law and individuality, between the universal and the particular. According to Hegel, Fichte considers "all the action and being of the individual as such to be overseen, known, and determined by the universal, which stands opposed to him, as well as by the [process of] abstraction."[25] Hegel, for his part, proposes the "absolute idea of morality (*Sittlichkeit*)," which contains within itself "as perfectly identical (*schlechthin identisch*)" the "state of nature" and the "majesty and divinity of the whole state of law . . . which are alien to the individuals."[26] Hegel seeks to replace the abstract notion of morality with a real notion that displays the universal and the particular in their identity, thereby surmounting the opposition created by formalism's abstract point of view.[27]

Real, absolute morality, as Hegel understands the notion, "is immediately a morality of the individual; conversely, the essence of a morality of the individual [is] nothing less than real morality and is hence universal and absolute."[28] Yet, in contradistinction to Schelling, Hegel directs his attention not only to the identity, but also to the perpetual conflict of the powers grasped in their identity and to the movement inherent in their unity; it is this movement, moreover, which makes it possible for the identity to become a reality. The conflict between inorganic law and living individuality, between the universal and the particular, is thus not eliminated: it is dynamically surpassed and absorbed into the heart of the notion of identity. Anticipating his discussion in the *Phenomenology of Mind,* Hegel here sees this process as a division of the self, as a sacrifice:

> The force of the sacrifice lies in the contemplation and objectivation of the entanglement with the inorganic;—contemplation undoes the entanglement and brings about the separation of the inorganic, which, having been recognized as such, can now be incorporated in the Indifference (*Indifferenz*); the Living (*das Lebendige*), however, inasmuch as it places in this same inorganic that which it knows to be a part of itself, thus sacrificing that part to death, has simultaneously recognized the rights of that part and cleansed itself of it.[29]

Hegel illustrates this process, which he equates with the tragic process as such, with the conclusion of Aeschylus's *Orestia.* In the conflict between Apollo and the Eumenides, the latter are the "powers of the right that exists in the Difference (*Differenz*)," that is to say, the inorganic part of ethics. This conflict takes place "before the moral organization (*die sittliche Organisation*), the people of Athens," and ends with the reconciliation brought about by Pallas Athene. The Eumenides are henceforth revered as divine powers, "so that their wild nature may delight in the contemplation of Athene sitting on her throne high on the citadel opposite their own altar, which is erected down in the lower city, and in this way be calmed."[30]

By interpreting the tragic process as the self-division and self-reconciliation of the moral nature, Hegel makes its dialectical structure immediately apparent for the first time. In Schelling's definition of tragedy, the dialectical aspect had not yet been elucidated, for Schelling advances too quickly toward the stage of harmony. (Later, in the preface to the *Phenomenology,* Hegel reproached him in veiled terms for this haste.) In Hegel, by contrast, the Tragic and the dialectic coincide. This identity is not just an afterthought, but goes back to the origin of both of Hegel's formulations, as can be seen from his early work known under the title of "The Spirit of Christianity and Its Fate," which dates from the years 1798-1800. It is significant that the origin of the Hegelian dialectic is to be found in a work devoted to the history of the origins of the dialectic.

Hegel first expressed his disagreement with Kantian formalism in the framework of a theological and historical study in which the dispute appears to lie within the subject matter itself, that is, in the form of the opposition between Christianity and Judaism. The young Hegel defines the spirit of Judaism in the same way that he later describes the formalism of Kant and Fichte. This spirit is characterized, he asserts, by a rigid opposition of the human and the divine, of the particular and the universal, of life and the law, between which no reconciliation is possible. The relationship is marked, in each case, by the domination of one term and the submission of the other. This strict dualistic spirit is opposed by the spirit of Christianity. The figure of Jesus spans the chasm separating man from God: the son of God and the son of man, he incarnates reconciliation, the dialectical unity of the two powers. Likewise, his resurrection makes him a mediator between life and death. In the place of the objective command to which man must submit, Jesus introduces a subjective disposition in which the individual is at one with universality.

In this early work, however, Hegel does not view the identity as a stable harmony, any more than he does later in his essay on natural law. Quite to the contrary, he considers it to possess an inner movement, and this is none other than the process which, in the *Phenomenology,* will assume its definitive form as the dialectic of mind. The early work labels the two stages of self-division and of reconciliation found in the advance from being-in-itself to being-in-and-for-itself: they are "fate" and "love." Judaism, according to Hegel, does not admit the notion of fate, recognizing domination as the sole bond linking God and man. It is the spirit of Christianity that establishes the possibility of fate. Fate is "not something alien, like punishment," for the latter belongs to the alien law; it is "consciousness of self, but as something hostile (*als eines Feindlichen*)."[31] In fate, absolute morality splits up within itself. It does not find itself faced with an objective law that it might have transgressed. What it confronts, rather, in the form of destiny, is the law that it itself has established in the course of some action.[32] As a result, morality is capable of being reconciled with fate and thus of restoring the lost unity, whereas in the case of objective law, absolute opposition persists beyond the punishment. Hegel's early work is thus not restricted to the study of the fate of Christianity, as the title given it by the editor seems to indicate. It is also concerned with the genesis of fate in general, which for Hegel coincides with the genesis of the dialectic, which occurred in the spirit of Christianity.

Still, in the Christian realm, too, "fate" for Hegel means tragic fate, as can be seen from his definition of tragedy in the work on natural law, where it signifies the moment of self-division in the moral nature. The manuscript pages of the "Spirit of Christianity" contain quotations pertaining to *fatum* in the *Iliad*;[33] and the peculiar character fate assumes when exteriorized by an individual subject is illustrated by the tragedy of *Macbeth.* After the murder of Banquo, Macbeth is faced by no alien law independent of himself. In Banquo's ghost he beholds the injured life itself, which is not something alien; it is, in fact, also his "own forfeited life." "Now, for the first time, the injured life confronts the criminal as a hostile power, ill-treating him as he once ill-treated it; thus, the punishment in the guise of fate is the equally strong reaction to the criminal's own deed; [it is the] reaction of a power that he himself has armed, of an enemy that he himself has created."[34] Since it was the criminal "who originally established this law," however, "the separation that he has brought about" through his own efforts—as opposed to what is purely and simply separated by the law—can "be reunited," and "this reunification occurs in love."[35] Hegel accordingly offers the following interpretation of Mary Magdalene's fate (ascribing the responsibility for her delinquency to the spirit of Judaism): ". . . the period in which her people lived was no doubt one of those in which the beautiful soul (*das schöne Gemüt*) can not live without sinning, but in this period, as in every other, it could return through love to the most beautiful consciousness (*zum schönsten Bewusstsein*)."[36]

Although the words "tragic" and "tragedy" do not occur in Hegel's essay on religion, the definition of the Tragic found in the essay on natural law does derive from that early work, which also contains the origin of the Hegelian dialectic. For the young Hegel, the tragic process is the dialectic of morality, which he first sought to demonstrate in the spirit of Christianity and which he later postulated as the foundation of the new moral philosophy. The dialectic is that of morality, "of the motive force (*Beweger*) of all human things,"[37] which, in fate, divides within itself but then returns to itself in love; whereas, in the world of law, the rigid division persists unchanged through sin and punishment.

> The proper theme of the original type of tragedy is the Divine; not, however, the Divine as the object of the religious consciousness as such, but as it enters the world and individual action. Yet in this actual appearance it does not lose its substantive character, nor does it see itself there as inverted into the opposite of itself. In this form the spiritual substance of will and accomplishment is the concrete ethical order [*das Sittliche*]. . . . [But,] everything that forces its way into the objective and real world is subject to the principle of particularization; consequently the ethical powers [*die sittliche Mächte*], just like the agents, are differentiated in their domain and their individual appearance. Now if, as dramatic poetry requires, these thus differentiated powers are summoned into appearance as active and are actualized as the specific aim of a human "pathos" that passes over into action, then their harmony is canceled and they come on the scene in *opposition* to one another in reciprocal independence. In that event a single action will under certain circumstances realize an aim or a character that is one-sidedly isolated in its complete determinacy, and therefore, in the circumstances presupposed, will necessarily rouse against it

the opposed "pathos" and so lead to inevitable conflicts. The original essence of tragedy consists then in the fact that within such a conflict each of the opposed sides, if taken by itself, has *justification*; while each can establish the true and positive content of its own aim and character only by denying and infringing the equally justified power of the other. The consequence is that in its moral life [*in ihrer Sittlichkeit*], and because of it, each is nevertheless involved in *guilt*.[38]

Two decades separate this definition, which appears in Hegel's *Aesthetics,* from the one given in the essay on natural law. The Tragic is still conceived here as the dialectic of morality. But something essential has changed. To be sure, the tragic hero's fate—the fact that his "pathos" leads him to act rightly and wrongly at the same time and thus incur guilt through his very morality—is still viewed in the same metaphysical context, one that is founded on the entry of the divine into a reality governed by the principle of particularization. Yet this relation is here much looser than it was in the essay of 1802. The Tragic is no longer an essential part of the idea of the divine, since in the religious consciousness the divine lies beyond the Tragic. The self-division characteristic of morality is inevitable, but in its concrete manifestation it is determined by the prevailing circumstances and is thus contingent with respect to its content. In contrast to the first definition, the present one does not appear to stem directly from a philosophical system; this accords with the fact that it occurs in an aesthetic theory in which it seeks to encompass the full range of possible tragic actions and situations.

The remarks on historical development in the *Aesthetics,* which follow the passage quoted above, make it clear that Hegel broadened his definition only reluctantly, and that basically he preferred to retain but a single form of tragic "collision." The aspect of chance that enters into his definition here obviously derives from the portrayal of the Tragic found in modern literature, whose heroes stand "in the midst of a wide range of fortuitous relationships and situations . . . allowing them to act in various different ways."[39] Their behavior is determined by their individual characters, which do not inevitably embody a moral emotion, as was the case in antiquity. For this reason, Hegel admits the legitimacy of modern tragedy only with reservation. Even within ancient tragedy, however, he clearly favors one among the possible "collisions." It is the type which he finds in *Iphigenia in Aulis,* in the *Orestia,* and in Sophocles' *Electra,* but which he thinks is most fully developed in *Antigone,* that "most excellent and most satisfying work of art among all the splendors of the ancient and modern worlds."[40] The collision involved here is that of love and law as they confront each other in the characters of Antigone and Creon. Thus, behind the apparent lack of precision in the definition given in the *Aesthetics,* there still stands the one form of the Tragic that Hegel had analyzed in the *Phenomenology of Mind.* Naturally, we must not overlook the fact that in the latter work Hegel does not view the Sophoclean tragedy as a tragedy and that he offers no definition of the Tragic. The terms "tragic" and "tragedy" are in fact not used in the *Phenomenology.* Rather, in the course of this account of the dialectical process of the mind, Hegel arrives at the stage of "true mind" (or "true spirit," *wahre Geist*), which he defines as "morality" (*Sittlichkeit*) and which he views as being divided into two separate essences: divine law and human law. The former is fulfilled in woman and in the sphere of the family, the latter in man and in the life of the State. In *Antigone,* Hegel sees a clash of these two manifestations of morality and therefore, in the last analysis, he sees in it the clash of Absolute Spirit in the process of returning to itself.

In contrast to the *Aesthetics,* and in accord with the work on natural law, the *Phenomenology* places the Tragic (though without calling it by that term) in the center of the Hegelian philosophy, interpreting it as the dialectic governing morality, that is to say, as the spirit in its stage of "true spirit." Although a comparison of Hegel's early theological work, the essay on natural law, and the *Phenomenology* (and even the *Aesthetics* as a formalized echo of the latter), reveals their similarities, it also brings to light all the more clearly the essential difference between them, allowing us to infer a hidden change in Hegel's conception of the Tragic. In the writings preceding the *Phenomenology,* the Tragic is the characteristic sign of a world of morality that divides in two through the workings of fate and is reconciled in love, whereas the Tragic cannot exist at all in the antithetical world of the law, which rests on a rigid opposition between the universal and the particular. In the *Phenomenology,* on the other hand, the tragic conflict arises precisely between the world of the law and the world of love. It would seem, therefore, that in Creon we behold a figure in whom the spirit of Judaism and of formalistic ethics, which had previously been excluded from the tragic realm, appears in the form of a tragic hero whose actions are as justified as those of his adversary, Antigone, who is the embodiment of love.

This change in Hegel's conception, which is further underscored by the fact that he pleads for the moral pathos of Creon, is bound up with a change in the meaning of the dialectic. In the years between the essay on natural law and the *Phenomenology,* the dialectic ceases to be an historical and theological phenomenon (in the spirit of Christianity) and a scientific postulate (for the reconstitution of moral philosophy) and becomes rather the law of the world and the method for arriving at cognitive knowledge. In this way the dialectic, which is at the same time the Tragic (and the means of transcending the Tragic), goes beyond the limits assigned to it in the two early works to embrace even the sphere of the law, from which it had previously been so strictly separated. Raised to the status of a world-principle, the dialectic permits no realm to be closed to it. Hence the fundamental tragic conflict is now seen as one necessarily arising between the origin of the dialectic and the field from which it set itself off in the very process of its emergence. In this manner, the opposition between Judaism and Christianity is surpassed in Hegel's image of antiquity.[41]

The unification of these two worlds that were previously so sharply differentiated from each other was already being prepared in Hegel's early theological work. Even before he called it by that name, the dialectic was exercising its rights, behind his back as it were. This can be seen from the remarkable circumstance that Hegel uses the same tragedy to characterize both Judaism and Christianity. A few pages before the scene between Macbeth and Banquo's ghost (which is meant to display the dialectic of subjective fate) we find the sentence which consigns Macbeth to the harsh confrontations that must be endured in the world of objective reality: "The fate of the Jewish people is the fate of Macbeth, who stepped beyond the bounds of nature, clung to foreign beings (*Fremde Wesen*) and thus, in their service, had to trample upon and kill everything holy in human nature, and who, abandoned by his gods (for they were objects and he was a slave), was finally crushed because he held on to this belief."[42] The twofold interpretation and twofold use of the figure of Macbeth, which are themselves evidence of the Hegelian dialectic, anticipate (contrary to the intentions of the early work but in the spirit of Hegel's later writings) the synthesis that Hegel achieved in the *Phenomenology* with his interpretation of Antigone.[43]

Chapter 4
Friedrich Schlegel and Romantic Irony, with Some Remarks on Tieck's Comedies

The ideas of the young Friedrich Schlegel derive their unity from a philosophy of history that informs all his thinking. Every such philosophy is based on the belief that the course of history is governed by laws and that every period possesses a particular value by virtue of its position within a process of sequential development. Consequently, any given period can be correctly understood only as a definite stage in this development. Schlegel's own conception of the philosophy of history has three sources: his profound knowledge of antiquity, his anguish in the face of the gulf he perceived between that age and his own, and his belief in the coming of the Kingdom of God. Classicism, a critique of contemporary conditions, and eschatology unite to form a coherent, tripartite whole encompassing the three temporal dimensions of past, present, and future. From the standpoint of intellectual history, it could be said that Schlegel prepared the way for the Hegelian dialectic, since in his conception of history this triadic scheme is animated by a dialectical process. Earlier writers, such as Winckelmann, who were less deeply historical in their thinking, considered antiquity a model to be imitated (though Winckelmann himself viewed the period as one rooted in history). Its thoroughgoing historicization began with Herder. Although he accepted the notion that antiquity,

Written in 1952 and originally published in 1954 as "Friedrich Schlegel und die romantische Ironie: Mit einer Beilage über Tiecks Komödie," in *Euphorion* 48 (1954): 397-411. A new version was published in *Satz und Gegensatz: Sechs Essays* (Frankfurt am Main, 1964), pp. 71-78.

as a natural and perfect age, was historically unique, Herder, at the same time, considered it to be the first stage in the historical evolution of the human mind and referred to it as a kind of paradise.[1] He therefore rejected the possibility of reproducing antiquity in the present; indeed, he thought that the latter, as a second age, was the antithesis of the first and thus had to be left in its state of negativity. On the other hand, in Herder's scheme antiquity becomes important for the future, although what lies ahead is not, to be sure, its repetition. Hence the future will not be a natural totality but rather a spiritual one, evolving from within the heart of the modern age. This spiritual harmony, Herder believed, determines its own destiny, since its foundation is freedom—or, to use Schlegel's favorite term, "arbitrariness" (*Willkür*). In this harmony the isolation of the mind is overcome, while the spiritual element itself is dialectically surpassed: the harmony thus turns out to be a synthesis.

Schlegel, in his essay "Über das Studium der Griechischen Poesie" (1795), distinguishes between the concepts of antiquity and modernity—or, in terms of the philosophy of history, between the first and second ages.[2] In this work, which dates from his preromantic phase, antiquity and modern times are analyzed as strictly antithetical periods. This recourse to the past in interpreting the present stems from the author's neoclassical outlook. At the same time, however, it reflects an essential trait of modern philosophy of history: the notion of time as an interval, as a "no longer" and a "not yet." The negativity of this interval, he holds, can be seen as meaningful only through the remembered thesis of the past and the foreseen synthesis of utopia. Schlegel's basic perception in this essay is that antiquity was a natural formation (*natürliche Bildung*), whereas the modern age is an artificial one (*künstliche Bildung*). In the former, "the first and original source of activity" is "an indefinite longing," whereas in the latter it is "a definite purpose." In antiquity, understanding, "even at its highest point of development," was "only the servant and interpreter of inclination; the complex will (*Trieb*) in its totality, however, [was] the sovereign legislator and it determined the course culture took." In modern times, "to be sure, the motive, executive power, is also the will; the ruling, *legislative power,* on the other hand, is the *understanding.* It is, so to speak, a supreme *governing principle,* one that directs and leads the blind force, determines its orientation, decides the arrangement of the entire mass, and separates and joins the individual parts ad libitum."[3] The emancipation of the understanding lies at the origin of modern times. Its activity consists in separating and mixing, and that is why Schlegel labels his age a chemical one. All relationships have been destroyed or at the least have become questionable and subject to reflection.

In Schlegel's view, the essence of antiquity was its cohesion whereas that of modernity is its dismemberment. This dichotomy finds its parallel in that characteristic phenomenon of modern aesthetics wherein the "beautiful" gives way to the "interesting." "The isolating understanding (*isolierende Verstand*) starts out by separating and dividing the wholeness of nature into isolated elements. The direction that art everywhere takes under its lead, therefore, is toward the faithful imitation of the particular. With the advent of higher intellectual culture, the goal of modern poetry naturally became *original and interesting individuality*."[4] Schlegel attributes this penchant for the "interesting" to the loss of finite reality, to the destruction of the notion of perfect form, and to the striving for infinite reality. The opposing terms of ideal and real, infinite and finite, subjective and objective are torn asunder; their dialectic is destroyed. Hence it is no longer possible to achieve a synthesis through decision and deed—something that in the aesthetic realm was attained with the classic hero and with the action of the drama.

In a letter he wrote to his brother August Wilhelm in 1793, Friedrich Schlegel made the following remarks concerning *Hamlet:*

The subject and the effect of this play is heroic despair, that is to say, an infinite derangement of the very highest powers. The source of Hamlet's inner death lies in the greatness of his understanding. If it were less great, he would be a hero. For him, it is not worth the trouble to be a hero; if he wanted to be, he would find it easy. He surveys an innumerable quantity of relationships—hence his indecisiveness. But if one seeks truth in *that* way, nature grows dumb; in the face of *such* a will (*solche Triebe*), of such strict examination, the world is nothing; for our fragile existence can create nothing that satisfies our divine demands. The very innermost heart of his existence is a fearful nothingness, contempt for the world and for himself.[5]

And in the essay "On the Study of Greek Poetry" he writes:

As a result of an extraordinary situation all the vigor of his noble nature is compressed into his understanding, but the active force is entirely destroyed. His mind is divided, as if torn apart in opposite directions on the rack; it collapses and sinks into the abundance of his idle understanding, which weighs down upon him even more painfully than upon those who surround him. There is perhaps no more consummate representation of the inalterable disharmony that is the real theme of philosophical tragedy than the boundless disproportion, in Hamlet's character, between the thinking force and the active force.[6]

Schlegel interprets Hamlet's situation as representative of his own and that of his time. His early work is an attempt to grasp and to overcome the negativity that this futile notion of the understanding engenders in the isolated individual. While the essay on Greek poetry of 1795 is still devoted primarily to analysis and criticism, the *Lyceum* fragments show that a reversal of values has already occurred by 1797. Consider the following passage:

> There exists a negative feeling (*Sinn*) which is much better than zero, but which is also much rarer. One can love something passionately precisely because one does not possess it; this gives at least a premonition of it without a conclusion. Even outright incapacity of which one is fully aware, or which may indeed be mixed with strong antipathy, is wholly impossible in the case of complete lack, and it presupposes at least a partial capacity and sympathy. Like the Platonic Eros, therefore, this negative sense is no doubt the son of abundance and poverty. It is born when one has only the spirit without the letter; or, conversely, when one has merely the materials and forms, the dry hard shell of the productive genius without the core. In the former case, the results are pure tendencies, projects that are as vast as the blue sky, or, at most, sketches of fantasies; in the latter, there arises that harmoniously elaborated artistic triteness of which the greatest English critics are such classic examples. The hallmark of the first type, of the negative mental sense, is this, that one must always want [to do something] but never can, that one always wants to hear but never can understand.[7]

Here the writer merely alludes to the two factors that he will later call upon in an effort to turn negativity into something positive, even though these factors themselves constitute part of the negative realm. They are (1) a clear recognition of incapacity and (2) an openness to the future that expresses itself in "presentiment" and "projects." We may call them *reflection* and *utopia*.

These two aspects of Schlegel's thought cannot be understood, however, without a clear awareness of their underlying tendency, which is what stamps them as romantic. The essence of the modern age is division; its central thrust is towards unification. The desire to overcome oppositions and to unify that which is separated inspires Friedrich Schlegel's most varied pronouncements. It appears explicitly in his definition of romantic poetry, that is to say, the novel.*

---

*On this point see "Friedrich Schlegel's Theory of Poetical Genres," this volume, n. 52.—Trans.

Romantic poetry is a progressive, universal poetry. Its vocation is not merely to reunite all the separate genres of poetry and to put poetry in touch with philosophy and rhetoric. It also seeks, rightly, sometimes to mix and sometimes to melt together poetry and prose, genius and criticism, the poetry of art (*Kunstpoesie*) and the poetry of nature (*Naturpoesie*); it rightly seeks to make poetry lively and sociable, to make life and society poetical, to poeticize wit, and, finally to fill and saturate the forms of art with every sort of genuine cultural material (*Bildungsstoff*) and animate them with the vibrations of humor. It embraces everything that is in any way poetic. . . .[8]

Schlegel already made the same demand in *Lyceum* fragment no. 115: "The entire history of modern poetry is a continuing commentary on this short philosophical text: 'All art should become science and all science should become art; poetry and philosophy must be united.' "[9]

It may be useful at this point to review Schlegel's opinions on several related subjects. About philosophy he writes: "Most thoughts are only profiles of thoughts. They must be turned upside down and synthesized with their antipodes."[10] About aesthetics: "In every good poem all must be intention, all must be instinct. This is what renders it ideal."[11] And, "Beautiful is that which is at once charming and sublime."[12] About ethics: "In order to be moral, sentiments must not be merely fine, but also be judicious, serve a purpose within the totality of one's sentiments, and be proper in the highest sense of the term."[13] On the problem of the relationship of the individual ego to the world: "Only he who is at one with the world can be at one with himself."[14] On the notion of love: "In accord with its origin, true love should be entirely arbitrary and entirely fortuitous, and yet it should seem both necessary and free; in accord with its character, it should be both vocation and virtue, and yet it should seem a secret, and a miracle."[15] On the question of evaluating intellectual systems: "It is equally fatal for the mind to have a system and to have none. One must therefore decide to adopt both positions."[16] Finally, on the definition of what it means to philosophize: "To philosophize is to seek omniscience together with others."[17] The basic thrust of Schlegel's thought is thus to strive for unity, communication, universality, and infinity. This orientation can be understood only by reference to the early romantic notion of the ego, wherein the subject is the isolated ego, thrown back upon itself and become an object for its own contemplation. The ego's destiny is consciousness; and Schlegel finds the consummate depiction of this destiny in the figure of Hamlet.

The isolated subject, however, is conscious primarily of his own being. And thus there arises the problem of *reflection,* understood here in the

sense of self-consciousness, self-relatedness, and self-mirroring. The decisive influence of this conception can be inferred from the following two
definitions of grace. For Schiller, grace is "the beauty of form animated
by freedom." For Schlegel, "Grace is the proper conduct of life; [it is]
sensuousness that contemplates itself and gives itself form."[18] Schiller
distinguishes between the object affected (form) and the effect (beauty),
specifies the modality (freedom), and presupposes the existence of an
active subject. Schlegel's formulation recognizes only one factor, a sensuousness constantly in the process of reflecting upon itself.

The problem assumes a more central position in Schlegel's work on
those occasions in which he draws upon the ideas of Kant and Fichte. The
critical philosophy inaugurated by Kant is one that adopts a critical stance
toward itself, calling even its own foundations into question. The first
fragment of the *Athenaeum* asserts, characteristically, that "There is nothing they philosophize less about than philosophy." And in fragment no.
238, Schlegel applies Kant's ideas to poetry.

> There exists a poetry whose primordial concern is the relationship
> between the ideal and the real and which, therefore, by analogy to
> philosophical terminology, should be called transcendental poetry.
> It begins as satire with the absolute divergence between the ideal
> and the real, hovers in the middle as elegy, and ends as idyll with
> the absolute identity of both terms. But we would accord little
> value to a transcendental philosophy which was not critical,
> which did not represent the producer along with the product, and
> which did not include, in the system of transcendental thoughts, a
> characterization of transcendental thinking. And the same thing is
> true of this kind of poetry: it should unite the transcendental ma-
> terials and preliminary exercises for a poetic theory of literary
> creativity (both of which are often found in modern poetry) with
> the artistic reflection and beautiful self-mirroring that appear in
> Pindar, in the lyric fragments of the Greeks, in the ancient elegies,
> and, among the moderns, in Goethe; this poetry should describe
> itself in every one of its descriptions, and everywhere be simulta-
> neously poetry and the poetry of poetry.[19]

In the present essay we cannot examine the relation between Schlegel's
definition of transcendental poetry and Schiller's theory of sentimental
poetry. It is essential, however, to underscore what may be termed the
critical moment, that is to say, the moment of reflection. Schlegel calls for
a poetry which writes poetically not only about its explicit object or theme
but also about itself, which takes itself for its theme, and which, through
this inner division into subject and object, gains in intensity and becomes
a poetry of poetry. The same view is set forth in the fragment on romantic

poetry (no. 116), in which this kind of writing is called "a progressive, universal poetry." Continuing his characterization of it there, Schlegel writes:

> It can become so lost in what is depicted that one might be tempted to think that its sole and entire aim was to characterize all the various poetical individuals; all the same, no other form exists yet that is capable of expressing so fully an author's mind: so that many an artist who wanted to write just another novel has accidentally wound up depicting himself. Only it [i.e., the romantic novel] can become, like the epic, a mirror of the entire surrounding world, a portrait of its age. And yet, since it is free from all real and ideal interests, it can also, more than any other form, hover on wings of poetic reflection between the depiction and the author of the depiction, perpetually intensify this reflection, and multiply it as in an endless series of mirrors.[20]

With this important first step toward a theory of the novel (which was subsequently elaborated by Georg Lukács), this form appears as the modern equivalent of the epic. The epic was the depiction of the entire world in a presubjectivist period whose wholeness was never questioned and which was unaware of the split between the ego and the world. In the modern age, which has been marked by this split at least since Kant, the reconciliation of the subjective with the objective in the work of art has seemed impossible. Once again, the demands Schlegel places on romantic poetry express a quest for synthesis, a synthesis achieved through that "hovering" stance which, as we have seen, is characteristic of reflection.

The preceding remarks should help to illuminate the dialectic of reflection. As relationship-to-self, reflection expresses the individual subject's isolation and seems to keep him permanently in this isolated state. Yet, in becoming an object for himself, the subject also gains a certain distance with respect to himself; he contemplates both himself and the world and through this synopsis eliminates the split that reflection has produced. In this synthesis, however, the world exists only as appearance. Moreover, the inner split resulting from the transformation by which the subject becomes an object for himself can be overcome only by a second reflection. Since the latter, too, "does not turn out right," the process continues in a "perpetual intensification of reflection." The existence of the world and of oneself becomes more and more one of mere appearance, and reflection becomes ever emptier.

The second fundamental aspect of Schlegel's thought is a concern with *eschatology* and *utopia*. *Athenaeum* fragment no. 222 announces that "The revolutionary wish to realize the Kingdom of God on earth is the elastic point of progressive culture, the beginning of modern history. Whatever is entirely unrelated to the Kingdom of God possesses only minor significance in this culture."[21] If the modern age is capable of interpreting itself, it owes this capacity to anticipation.

> How would it be possible to understand and punctuate the present period of the world correctly, if one could not foresee at least the general character of the immediately following one? On the analogy of the ideas set forth above, an organic age will follow our chemical one, and then the inhabitants of the earth in the next solar cycle may well have a far less high opinion of us than we ourselves do, and consider much that now causes astonishment as merely the useful exercises of mankind in its youth.[22]

But the early romantic is not satisfied with knowing what the next period will be like. He adopts as his own the negative judgment that the later age will make and that the coming synthesis renders valid; he thereby anticipates, as it were, a retrospective view. Reflection is set in a temporal framework, and through this self-mirroring process the subject comes to be temporally ahead of himself. *Athenaeum* fragment no. 139 asserts that "from the romantic point of view, even the unusual forms of poetry, even the eccentric and the monstrous, furnish valuable raw materials and preparatory exercises for universality, provided they possess a least some content, provided they are original."[23]

The act of relativizing the present by comparing it with the future is, like reflection, an inherently dialectical process. Negative insofar as it conceives modern poetry as a preliminary exercise, as a merely provisional stage, it becomes positive when it introduces a progressive aspect into the definition of this kind of poetry. *Athenaeum* fragment no. 116 makes this point explicit:

> Romantic poetry is a progressive, universal poetry. . . . Other literary genres now stand ready and can be fully analyzed. The romantic genre is still in the process of becoming; indeed this is its real essence, that forever it can only be becoming and can never reach perfection. No theory could ever exhaust it, and only a divinatory criticism could have the audacity to characterize its ideal.[24]

Schlegel also reevaluates the fragmentary nature of the modern age from this perspective. His perception that "many works of the Ancients have become fragments [and that] many works of the Moderns are such right from their creation"[25] has a conciliatory effect; for in the fragment it is possible to glimpse the dimension of the future. The fragment is conceived as a project, as the "subjective seed of a nascent object," as preparation for the desired synthesis. What Schlegel finds in the fragment is no longer the unachieved, that which has remained in a partial state, but rather anticipation and promise. The fascination with fragments and projects is revealed as a stage in the quest for synthesis. It must be set, according to Schlegel, in the context of the relationship between the ideal and the real, and it can thus be termed "the transcendental component of the historical spirit."[26]

It is not solely in this explicit form of anticipation, however, that the future appears. It is also implied in the dialectical conception of history. According to Schlegel's scheme, the third period will neither repeat the first nor be entirely new; rather, it will develop, through a dialectical reversal, out of the very heart of the modern age, out of the latter's negative traits themselves. This same vision is embodied in Schlegel's aesthetics, for example, in the thesis that "The excessive emphasis on the individual leads . . . by itself to [an] objective [form of art]; the interesting is the preparation for the beautiful; and the ultimate goal of modern poetry can be none other than *supreme beauty,* the maximum of objective aesthetic perfection."[27] It is also evident in the prediction that "The supremacy of the interesting is only a *temporary crisis* of taste, for ultimately it will destroy itself."[28] As early as 1794, in the essay "On the Limits of the Beautiful," Schlegel, after sketching the characteristic traits of antiquity, makes the following remarks:

> This coherence as against our dismemberment, these pure masses as against our endless mixtures, this simple resoluteness as against our petty confusion—this is why the *Ancients* appear to have a more elevated style. Yet we should not envy them as favorites of an arbitrary good fortune. Our failings are also our hopes; for they arise from the supremacy of the understanding, whose perfection, though it be slow, knows no bounds. And when it has completed its task of securing for a man a solid foundation and of determining an immutable direction, one will no longer be in doubt as to whether man's history returns eternally upon itself like a circle, or advances infinitely toward the better.[29]

Knowledge of the future makes it easier to live with negativity, since the latter is seen as a transitory state. The idea that it is immanent, that it is subject to movement brought about by a dialectical reversal, makes possible its reevaluation. It is for this reason that the early romantics do not renounce understanding and reflection. They believe that by having completely rethought what they had previously perceived as negative, they have arrived at something positive: their very failings are their hopes.

So far we have sought to discover the presuppositions of romantic irony without naming the concept and without attempting to define it. For it was our hope that in this way we might resist the temptation to which so many scholars have succumbed—to cite or paraphrase Schlegel's definitions and leave the matter at that. It is perhaps not fortuitous that the most illuminating remarks on romantic irony are to be found in the writings of authors who either had no knowledge at all of Schlegel's theoretical texts, like (presumably) Kierkegaard, or else who did not set out with the specific intention of interpreting them, like Lukács in his *Theory of the Novel*. Still, we will not have demonstrated the value of an exposition that leaves out the term "romantic irony" until we have shown that it elucidates not only the meaning of Schlegel's seemingly disparate definitions and descriptions of irony but also their inner necessity and interdependence.

The appearance of irony in the relationship of the romantic author to his work is discussed in *Lyceum* fragment no. 37:

> In order to be able to write well about a subject, one must no longer be interested in it. The idea that is to be expressed with deliberateness must already be completely past; it must no longer really exercise the mind. As long as an artist is still inventing and is still inspired, he finds himself in an illiberal state at least with respect to communication. He will then want to say everything, which is an error of young geniuses, and a true prejudice of old bunglers. And hence he fails to recognize the value and dignity of self-restraint, which for the artist as well as the man is really the first and the last, the most necessary and the highest thing. The most necessary: for everywhere that a man does not restrain himself, the world restrains him; and thus he becomes a slave. The highest: for a man is capable of self-restraint only in those areas and in those respects where he possesses infinite power—self-creation and self-destruction.[30]

Directness of expression has given way to self-consciousness. The call for self-restraint manifests a renunciation of the world. Self-restraint is preferable to restraint imposed by the world, for it presupposes, and thereby demonstrates, the individual subject's potential infinity. The subject's knowledge of this fact eliminates the negative aspect of self-restraint. In the interplay between self-creation and self-destruction there occurs that "hovering" which, in the eyes of the early romantics, is the anticipation of a synthesis.

In the *Discourse on Poetry* (1800) we read:

> Every poem should be truly romantic, and every poem should be didactic in that broader sense of the word that designates the tendency toward a deep and infinite meaning. We make this demand everywhere, even when we do not employ the term. Even in the most popular forms, such as the theater, we demand irony; we demand that the events, the men, in short, the whole game (*Spiel*) of life really be conceived and represented as a game.[31]

Life is contemplated from the perspective of a "deep and infinite meaning" that is not immanent to it. This circumstance gives rise to the notion of the game or of play (*Spiel*). Play is life that is lived and interpreted from an Archimedean point external to it. By "playing" his life, the early romantic believes he can transcend it and thus, despite everything, share in the harmony that history has denied him. The didactic element in this passage lies in its allusion to infinity. Anticipation is implicit here, too, as is shown by *Athenaeum* fragment no. 249: "The didactic poem should be prophetic, and it has everything it needs to become so."[32]

With regard to irony in the work of art, Schlegel writes:

> There are ancient and modern poems that throughout, in the whole and in all the parts, breathe the divine breath of irony. A truly transcendental buffoonery dwells within them. Inside [there is] a mood which surveys everything and rises infinitely above all that is contingent, even above its own art, virtue, and genius; outside, in the execution [there is] the mimic style of a good ordinary Italian *buffo*.[33]

Once again we observe an internal division and the elimination of the self, the destruction of the contingent. This time it appears in the form of a mood, as buffoonery in the gap opened between the ideal and the real.

In his essay on Goethe's *Wilhelm Meister* (1798) Schlegel writes:

> It is fine and necessary to abandon oneself entirely to the impression produced by a poem and to let the artist do with us as he will, though one might also wish to confirm one's feeling by reflecting on the details, elevate it to the level of thought, and, where this feeling still gives rise to doubt or dispute, to decide and complete it. This is the first, and the most crucial point. But it is no less necessary to be able to rise above all the details, to grasp the universal in a state of hovering (*schwebend*), to survey the entire mass, to maintain a firm hold on the totality, and, finally to seek out even the most hidden elements and link together even the most remote. We must rise above our own love and be able to destroy in thought that which we adore; otherwise, regardless of our other capacities, we will lack a feeling for the infinite and with it a feeling for the world.[34]

The critic's ironic attitude creates a distance between himself and all that is limited; and the destruction of the latter is the price that must be paid for this "hovering" perception of the totality.

Let us conclude with a late formulation of Schlegel's: "Irony is the clear consciousness of eternal agility (*Agilität*), of the infinitely full chaos."[35] Eternal agility characterizes the man of modern times, who lives in chaos.

In raising his chaotic existence to the level of consciousness, in living it consciously, he is adopting an ironic attitude toward it.[36] This notion, too, has its utopian orientation, as is shown by a neighboring fragment that also contains the word "chaos": "Only that confusion out of which a world can arise is a chaos."[37]

It is clear, then, that in the romantic conception of irony the subject is the isolated man who has become his own object, from whom the ability to act has been taken away by consciousness. He longs for unity and infinity; the world appears to him riven and finite. Irony, then, is his attempt to endure a painfully difficult position by means of a renunciation and an inversion of values. Through ever more intense reflection he seeks to reach a standpoint outside himself and to eliminate, on the level of appearance, the cleft between his ego and the world. He cannot overcome the negativity of his situation through an action leading to a reconciliation of the contingent and the necessary. Nevertheless, by anticipating the future unity in which he believes, he declares this negativity to be temporary, whereby it is both preserved and reevaluated. The reevaluation renders his existence tolerable and induces him to dwell in the realm of the subjective and the virtual. Irony, however, by preserving the very negativity that it was designed to overcome, is itself transformed into negativity. Tolerant of completion only in the past or in the future, whatever irony encounters in the present it measures against infinity and thus destroys it. Acceptance of his own incapacity prevents the ironist from respecting what has nevertheless been accomplished—therein lies its danger for him. The fact that through this acceptance he himself bars the way to perfection, while at the same time this acceptance continuously proves to be unbearable, finally leading nowhere—this is his tragedy.

On Tieck's Comedies

Two of the essential elements of romantic irony play an important role in the ironic structure of Tieck's comedies: provisionalness and self-consciousness.

Romantic irony conceives of reality as merely provisional and, in turn, it produces works that are likewise no more than provisional. This accounts for the function assigned to the prologue, the one dramatic form that by its very nature signifies provisionalness. As a way of representing the latter, Tieck uses the "inversion method" described by Günther Anders in his *Kafka—Pro und Contra*. In order to illustrate the ephemeral nature of life, the author presents a prologue that turns out to be definitive. This procedure implicitly raises a question: is the meaning of reality immanent to it, is reality by nature serious? or, is it, rather, only a curtain raiser, a prelude, something provisional, best endured by treating it as a game? This question, however, is not dealt with in a concrete context. Instead, the starting point is itself a prologue. The very fact that Tieck's use of this form is not without ambiguity suggests that he does not intend the prologue to serve as an announcement or an introduction. He employs it, rather, in a reflective mood; it is designed to raise questions about itself and to comment on itself. The brief comedy entitled *A Prologue* (1796) is set in the orchestra section of a theater where a few early arrivals are waiting for the performance to begin. Four of them engage in the following conversation:

Michel:	Oh look, look at all the people!
	What kind of a play is being put on today?
Melantus:	Heaven knows, I cannot discover it,
	Perhaps a comedy of errors.
Peter:	How one's eyes grow bright!
Melantus:	So it goes with all things on earth.
Michel:	Methinks, you speak quite sadly;
	What's amiss, if it please you to say?
Melantus:	Ah, my good man, I have many cares,
	In the end, we sit here in the dark,
	I'm getting dumber and soft in the head,
	And meanwhile I do not even believe in an art.
	It may be that we're waiting for nothing,
	And then, good friend, we are really proper fools.
Peter:	Yes, surely, that would be a bad joke.
Michel:	By your leave, would you be so good and explain that.
Melantus:	Look, who can assure us,
	That we are really going to see anything here?
	Possibly we hope for luminaries in vain,
	Perhaps there is neither director nor playwright;
	Are they going to raise the curtain?
Anthenor:	Neighbors! By your leave, I am sorry,
	But you are all not very clever,
	I would not, of course, rob you of your hope,
	But still it all seems to me mere superstition.
	See here, I swear on my head
	There never has been a director,
	How should there be a play, then?
	The idea, I admit, is quite pretty;

> But who is going to carry it out?
> We pay our dues, I reckon,
> And then sit here and compose and aspire;
> And that already counts as a play.
> Have you ever met a director?

Peter: Good God, you know I come from the country.

Anthenor: Could you define a director for me?

Peter: I think the fellow wants to vex us.

Anthenor: What is then a *directeur*?
> You think and conjecture this way and that,
> Wander about hither and thither,
> and in the end all that comes of it is—

Melantus: Oh don't finish up all too quickly!

Anthenor: That when one considers it in depth,
> In the back no director either moves or stirs,
> That *behind* the curtain nothing stirs,
> A play is put on *before* the show
> By us, we who as true apes insist
> That everything be created only
> To serve a goal in the future
> And therefore throw away the present.[38]

The very solution of the problem is itself ironic. The indignant optimists chase the skeptic, Melanthus, and the pessimist, Anthenor, from the theater, but even absent these two have the last word. For the prologue is in fact not followed by a play; it *is* the play. By ending the text at this point, the author gives symbolic expression to the fact that provisionalness, if reflected upon explicitly, is incompatible with a truly dramatic style. This is so because in a play every speech is binding, irrevocable, and fraught with consequences.[39] The drama is the genre of "presentness," in both senses of the word: the *present* and *presence*. It is also the form most suited to convey immanence of meaning. To be sure, it is possible, given a secure transcendental standpoint, to compose plays in which reality is described as being, in metaphysical terms, provisional. Theater of this kind, however, would lack genuine dramatic form. Consider, then, a situation where such a transcendental point of view has not yet been attained and where, furthermore, the very necessity of seeking one is subject to doubt. In this case, all possibility of true drama would be lost. Consequently, the form best suited to the romantic artist is not the drama but the novel, whose essence is reflection and questing.[40]

The problem of self-consciousness is raised in a dialogue from *Prince Zerbino.*

King: Ah, as it is said: who knows what lies ahead for us!
        A relentless fate directs us.
Fool: Could I say what I really feel inside?
King: Nothing else, as long as the gods protect us.
Fool: Well, I think it is not so much fate
        As the caprice of the playwright, as he
        Calls himself, he who keeps changing his whole play around,
        And leaves no man with his healthy good sense.
King: Ah, friend, what a string you start strumming there!
        How sad I become, when I even consider
        That we utterly do not exist at all.
        The idealist is a miserable fellow,
        But he is always forced to assume,
        That his existence is something true;
        But we, we are still less than air,
        Children of a strange imagination,
        Whom it directs according to willful caprice.
        And indeed none of us can know,
        What that quill will still mete out to us.
        Oh the woeful destiny of dramatic characters![41]

As is well known, it is essentially by destroying illusion in this manner that romantic irony came to assume such importance in romantic comedy. In studies on Tieck, for example, it is frequently noted that this "stepping out of the role" is a stock comic device found in every period and in every literature since the time of Aristophanes, and that, consequently, its excessive use is the only peculiarly romantic thing about it. Yet it is necessary to make a distinction here. The remarks usually made about this device pertain to the actor and focus on the reduction of the dramatic figure, of the role, to the person of the actor. In Tieck, however, something different occurs. The role speaks about itself as a role. It is aware that its own existence is only relative, subordinate to the requirements of dramaturgy. But the role is by no means diminished thereby; to the contrary, it is strengthened. Through its self-consciousness, the role becomes objective to itself, on the model of the divided ego of the early romantic writers, of which it is the aesthetic projection. This transposition of self-consciousness to the aesthetic realm is not without effect on the dramatic structure. In his role, the character is conscious not so much of his specific existence as it is revealed in the play, as he is of the very nature of this existence, which is a dramatic one. Here the romantic writer's peculiar relationship to the drama becomes particularly evident. This genre is a form of expression that does not come easily to him. What leads him to try his hand at it is the special attractiveness of the world of the theater, a world which is absolute but which, since it is produced, can also be transcended. In the drama, the early romantic author can express his ironic relationship to the world in a concrete manner; in real life he can only aspire to this relationship, which is the union of "being-in-the-world" and "standing-beyond-the-world."

The dramatic figure's self-consciousness is not, however, simply the aesthetic equivalent of early romantic reflection. It also furnishes a comic strain within the comedy. This is well illustrated in a scene from *The World Turned Upside Down (Die verkehrte Welt)*.

> *Innkeeper:* Few guests lodge here now, and, if this keeps up, in the end I'll simply have to take down my sign. —Ah, yes, once things were good: there was scarcely a play then without its inn and innkeeper. I still can recall the hundreds of plays in which splendid intrigues were prepared right in this very room. Sometimes it was a prince in disguise who ate up all his money here, sometimes a minister, or at least a rich count, and they all kept on the lookout in my inn. Even better—in all the plays translated from English I was able to earn my share of money. Occasionally, of course, one had to swallow a bitter pill and disguise himself as a member of a band of thieves, for which one was thoroughly abused by persons of upright character. Still, at least one was active. —But now! Even if a rich foreigner stays over on a journey, he thinks it's smart to find quarters with some relative and wait for the fifth act to reveal his identity. As for the others, one gets to see them only on the street, as if they didn't live in honest lodgings. All this, it is true, serves to keep the spectators in a wonderful state of curiosity, but it deprives people like us of our only livelihood.[42]

Once again, there is no sign at all of an actor. It is not the actor who steps out of his innkeeper role; it is rather the latter which, through reflection, surpasses itself. The comical element thus produced is one of character-comedy, although only in the specific sense that the term has in Tieck's formalism, in which "character" refers to dramaturgical and not to psychic structure. Another comic aspect here is the transgression of the norm; it is the innkeeper's having "one eye too many" (*das Auge zuviel*),[43] his self-consciousness, which is the source of the comical element. All the same, genuine situation comedy is also possible in this realm, as can be seen in the succeeding passage, which contrasts the refracted figure of the innkeeper with the simple figure of a stranger inquiring about a room.

Stranger: Good morning, innkeeper.

Innkeeper: Servant, your servant, my lord. Who in the world are you that you are traveling incognito and come to me for a room? You are surely from the old school; isn't that right? a man of the old stamp, perhaps translated from the English?

Stranger: I am not a lord, nor am I traveling incognito. Can I lodge here today and tonight?

Innkeeper: My house stands entirely at your disposal. But, seriously, don't you wish to make some family here in the area unexpectedly happy: or suddenly get married: or look for a sister?

Stranger: No, my friend.

Innkeeper: Then you really are just traveling, like an ordinary traveler?

Stranger: Yes.

Innkeeper: Then you will have little success.

Stranger: I believe the fellow is mad.[44]

In Tieck's writing, therefore, we encounter a phenomenon which, strictly speaking, does not require the character to step out of his role, but which results rather, from the representation of self-consciousness on the aesthetic level. Accordingly, this phenomenon is not related to romantic irony merely through the vague categories of "subjective arbitrariness" and "destructive drive," as is too often maintained. Time and time again the humor of Tieck's comedies derives from the difference between one level and another within reflection. What we savor in our laughter is the distance that the comedy establishes by reflecting on its own dramatic structure.

Chapter 5
Friedrich Schlegel's Theory
of Poetical Genres:
A Reconstruction from the
Posthumous Fragments

1. The Critique of Poetical Reason

When one recalls the first *Athenaeum* fragment, it does not seem surprising that Friedrich Schlegel addresses the following question: under what conditions is it possible to formulate and systematize concepts of poetical genres? For in that fragment he observes, not without a note of reproach and contempt: "About no subject is there as little philosophizing as about philosophy."[1] Schlegel was certainly no orthodox Kantian; the most important stimuli in his philosophical development came from Fichte's *Wissenschaftslehre* and, no doubt, from Schelling's early work on *Dogmatism and Criticism*.[2] All the same, the orientation of his philosophical and aesthetic reflections was determined by Kant's approach. While it is true that Schiller, in developing his views on the sublime and on the play character of art, was inspired by a number of Kantian notions, it was not he but Schlegel who applied Kant's "critical" method to aesthetics.

It was a rather unusual application. The result was neither an exhaustive "critique" in the Kantian sense nor a system of poetics established in accord with the tenets of "criticism." In the fragments, Schlegel is

Written in the winter of 1966-67 and presented in a lecture given in French at the Collège de France. First published under the title "La Théorie des genres poétiques chez Fréderic Schlegel," in *Critique* 250 (March 1968): 264-92. A somewhat revised version appeared as "Friedrich Schlegels Theorie der Dichtarten: Versuch einer Rekonstruktion der Fragmente aus dem Nachlass," in *Euphorion* 64 (1970): 181-99.

generally satisfied with questions and affirmations. Often, though, it is difficult to know whether the questions are raised in earnest or are really meant as affirmations; and the affirmations frequently leave one in doubt as to how he would have gone about proving them. In Schlegel, Kantian criticism often appears in the form of skepticism, even nihilism. But if one does not turn away in indignation, as Hegel did,[3] it is possible to discern the deeper motive behind this programmatic questioning and annihilation—that same urge to prepare the future which led him to outline, in *Athenaeum* fragments 116 and 252, not just a new art but also a new poetics. It is solely for this reason that Schlegel could consider his fragments as projects.[4] As early as 1797, in the first collection of fragments that he published (in the journal *Lyceum der schönen Künste*), Schlegel writes: "We already have so many theories of poetical genres. Why do we not yet have a concept of poetical genre? Perhaps we should then have to get along with a single theory of poetical genres."[5] Here are three sentences, each one in a tone characteristic of Schlegel. First comes the slightly contemptuous observation of a large quantity that necessarily entails its own condemnation. ("We already have so many theories of poetical genres"); then the provocative, critical question, which simultaneously suggests the reason for this excessive quantity ("Why do we not yet have a concept of poetical genre?"); finally, the ominous premonition of the possible consequence of answering the question ("Perhaps we should then have to get along with a single theory of poetical genres"). This fragment is important for Schlegel's "critique of poetical reason" because it indicates the necessity of raising questions about the very concept of poetical genre and not merely about the division of poetical works into genres (for the latter is what Schlegel means when he speaks of "theories" of poetical genres, of which there are already so many). Only a theory of genres that is based on a critique of the underlying concept itself and replaces all the contending theories could be considered a genuine *poetics* of genres.

The concept of poetical genre, which Schlegel rightly considers to be the underlying premise of a poetics of genres, is left essentially undefined in the fragments. There is one exception, however. It is fragment no. 1880 in *Fragments on Literature and Poetry* (*Fragmente zur Literatur und Poesie*), in which Schlegel writes: "All *poetical genres* are original—poetry of nature (*Naturpoesie*)—a definite poetry, tied to a place, individual. (There can be an infinity of poetical genres.) The individual element persists in them even after the transformation wrought by the artists. The forms are capable of infinite transformation. All the Greek and all the romantic forms are lost in the darkness of time and are not made by artists."[6]

When Schlegel compares a poetical genre and a particular artist (or more precisely, a particular work), it is not to the latter that he applies the notion of "individual character." On the contrary, he emphasizes the individuality of the various poetical genres, viewing them in their historical determinateness (hence his remark that they are "tied to a place"). For this very reason—and in agreement with Herder's ideas—he holds that they are not the work of particular artists. In the essay "On the Study of Greek Poetry" (*Über das Studium der griechischen Poesie*), Schlegel finds that modern poetry or artificial poetry (*Kunstpoesie*) differs from classical poetry or the poetry of nature (*Naturpoesie*) chiefly because it bears the stamp of individuals and is dispersed in individual *oeuvres,* whereas Greek poetry, as he is never tired of pointing out, must be considered as a whole, as a "mass."[7] Similarly, he asserts here that all poetical genres are original and are poetry of nature.

The fragment in question stems from the years 1798–1801 and is thus subsequent to Schlegel's distinction between ancient and modern poetry (which he presented in the essay "On the Study of Greek Poetry" and in the preface accompanying its publication).[8] We may therefore conclude that the poetical genres, if they are truly poetry of nature, are valid only for classical poetry and not for modern poetry. In other words, a theory of the poetical genres must be historical in nature and limit itself to classical poetry. It is likewise evident that a concept of modern poetry must make do without a division into genres, or to put the matter more precisely, it must coincide with the concept of a single genre that unites all the others within itself. These two consequences point toward the topics that we shall discuss in detail in sections 2 and 3 below: (a) the union of the poetics of genres and the philosophy of history and (b) the advance beyond the poetics of genres, on the one hand, and the resulting theory of a single modern genre, namely that of the novel, on the other.*

In stating that there can exist infinitely many poetic genres, Schlegel does not seem to be asserting anything really new. His father, Johann Adolf Schlegel, in his translation and adaptation of Batteux's treatise *Les beaux arts réduits à un même principe,* had previously compared, with the enthusiasm of a second Columbus, the discovery of further poetical genres with the discovery of unknown continents. [9] He thereby broke with classi-

---

*Peter Szondi did not ignore the objections that were raised against his inclusion of the novel in the genre that Schlegel defined as objective/subjective (see p. 136 of Fr. ed. = p. 51 of *Schriften*, and especially against his linking of the two oppositions poetry of nature / artificial poetry and Antiquity / Modernity. In a reply to Jost Schillemeit on 13 April 1971 Szondi said that he intended to reflect further on the first point and to reexamine the second. [Note added in the French edition, *Poésie et poétique de l'idéalisme allemand* (Paris, 1975), p. 120.—Trans.]

cist poetics,* which had never raised the question of *possible* genres, an inherently critical question, concerning itself instead only with the existing genres created by the Greeks, with a view to encouraging their imitation. The young Schlegel's statement in his essay "On the Study of Greek Poetry," in which he defines Greek poetry as "an *eternal natural history of taste and of art,*" is still very much a part of this classicist tradition[10] — except that in this essay the thesis of the possibility of infinitely many poetical genres is linked with a conception of modern poetry and leads to the postulate of a single genre.

Yet, it is not this utopian point of view alone that distinguishes Friedrich Schlegel's thesis of infinitely many poetical genres from that of Enlightenment poetics, as formulated, for example, by his father. For the younger Schlegel makes the thesis a subject of reflection and gives it a "critical" foundation. In this perspective, the laconic *Lyceum* fragment 113 is extremely important: "A classification is a definition that contains a system of definitions."[11] The various Enlightenment poetics are still preoccupied with classification: they arrange the existing works in classes on the basis of similarities in form and content. The categories are merely juxtaposed, forming a series which displays no principle and which cannot be terminated. Schlegel, in contrast, maintains that the very act of classification itself constitutes a definition of the poetical genre. Unlike the simple descriptions characteristic of the Enlightenment theories, definitions (as the term itself indicates) mark the boundaries between things and, hence, presuppose a knowledge of the relationships between the different genres. But Schlegel goes one step further. He does more than just state that the existence and definitions of the other genres are implicit in the definition of each individual genre. He also affirms that if one is dealing with a true definition, the connection between the genres cannot be fortuitous but must be founded upon a principle; indeed, it must be reducible to a principle. In a word, for Schlegel, the elements of a genuine definition constitute a system. The sentence that begins with the word "classification" and leads to the word "system" is not merely a theoretical proposition: it itself completes the transition of poetics from the Enlightenment to German idealism, from a pragmatic to a philosophical theory of the poetical genres.

In completing this transition, however, Schlegel simultaneously called into question its principal result: the possibility of deducing the poetical

---

*We have preserved the distinction made in German between *klassisch*, meaning "paradigmatically classical," and *klassizistisch*, meaning "in conformity with the classical style of the works of art of antiquity" (a conformity characteristic of art produced at the end of the eighteenth century and the beginning of the nineteenth, and often called "neoclassical" in English). [Note adapted from the French edition. — Trans.]

genres, that is to say, of constructing a closed system of genres. For the logic of the problems involved led him to raise the question of the historicity of the genres and, at the same time, to assert that their systematization presupposed their historicity. The fifth of the *Fragments on Literature and Poetry* reads: "Only the wholly valid poetical genres (*die ganz gültigen Dichtarten*) can be deduced in *pure* poetics. —The epic only in *applied* poetics, and the same thing is true for everything that is valid *only* in classical or only in progressive [i.e., modern] poetry."[12] Schlegel thus does not merely distinguish between two epochs, antiquity and the modern age, or, in the terminology of the essay "On the Study of Greek Poetry," between two formative principles, natural formation (*natürliche Bildung*) and artificial formation (*künstliche Bildung*). In other words, he does not simply make a distinction between poetical genres which belong to one epoch and those which belong to another, for example, between the epic and the novel. He also takes into account whether a genre is indigenous to only one of the two epochs or to both of them. Those that can exist in both epochs are termed "wholly valid" genres, and it is only these that are called deducible. Now, this does not mean that Schlegel abandoned the historical approach halfway along, and that he views only certain genres in a historical perspective and not others. When he speaks of poetical genres that occur not *only* in "classical" or not *only* in "progressive" poetry, he does not mean that these genres are ahistorical but rather that their historicity entails a transformation within the boundaries of the genre and not the emergence of a new genre (as in the case, say, of the epic realm, where the novel replaces the epic). Examples of such enduring genres are the lyric and the drama. We might add here that Georg Lukács in his *Theory of the Novel,* which is strongly influenced by Schlegel's notions, revived this idea of differentiating genres according to their mode of historical transformation, although in 1914 he could not have been familiar with the posthumous fragment cited here.[13]

It is yet another distinction, however, which constitutes the thesis of this fragment, a distinction which, in the spirit of "criticism," concerns not so much the object of study as the conditions under which it is possible to know it. This is the distinction Schlegel makes between pure and applied poetics. The twenty-fourth of these same *Fragments on Literature and Poetry* reads: "In a pure poetics perhaps *no* genre would exist; poetics [is] therefore *both* pure and applied, both empirical and rational."[14] This statement contradicts the one just cited, correcting it in a polemical fashion. Schlegel recognizes that it is correct to distinguish between a pure (deductive) aspect and an applied (pragmatic-inductive) aspect of poetics; but he rejects the division of poetics into separate (pure and applied) branches. There are not two poetics; to the contrary, poetics should be (and Schlegel underscores the word) *both* pure and applied, that is, both empirical (i.e., inductive) and rational (i.e., deductive). While this insight, which corrects the earlier statement, represents an advance in Schlegel's critique of poetic reason, it also renders matters more complex. For the boundary no longer divides poetical genres, but has been incorporated into the concept itself of a poetics of genres, in the form of an inescapable constitutive antinomy. This explains Schlegel's polemic against Goethe's treatment of the subject. Referring to a passage in the latter's *Wilhelm Meister's Apprenticeship,*[15] Schlegel, in no. 115 of the *Fragments on Literature and Poetry,* observes that Goethe, "in his search for the spirit of the poetical genres, proceeds *empirically;* but the character of this particular genre [i.e., of the novel] cannot be discovered in a full and exact manner by the empirical method."[16]

After abandoning his original thesis of two types of poetics, Schlegel constantly seeks to arrive at a clearer notion of the interdependence of empirical knowledge and speculative theory, in other words, of induction and deduction in the poetics of genres. Thus, in no. 224 of the *Fragments on Literature and Poetry* he writes: "Deduction in art must be preceded by an empirical or historical datum that provides the basis for classification in logic, poetry, and ethics."[17] In his efforts to eliminate the boundaries between individual disciplines and areas of life, Schlegel often reflects in his notebooks on the manner in which the various systems (poetics, logic, ethics) relate to each other. Sometimes, as in the sentence just cited, he postulates an element common to all of them; sometimes he maintains that the concepts derived from the genres in the form of adjectives ("the epic," "the lyrical," "the dramatic") are "applicable" outside the realm of poetry as well. For example, he defines morality as *lyrical philosophy,*[18] and, on one occasion, he even asserts that "each of the sciences classified— ethics, poetics, politics, history—if treated . . . progressively, is universal and thus embraces all the others."[19] This theme must be viewed in the perspective of the utopian synthesis of the individual disciplines and fields of activity sketched in *Athenaeum* fragment no. 116.

More important in the present context, however, is that Schlegel here attempts to resolve the antinomy resulting from the twofold nature of poetics by means of chronology, namely, by the assertion that deduction is preceded by an empirical or historical fact. The fragmentary character of the utterance could easily lead to misunderstanding. One might imagine that the empirical and historical presupposition is conceived as a philosophical premise of the deduction; but this would be incompatible with the essence of deduction, in which concepts are paramount and experiential data irrelevant. The way we are to interpret this sequence, in which empirical and historical observation precedes deduction, is indicated by several other fragments, for example, no. 193 of the *Fragments on Litera-ture and Poetry* and the conclusion of *Athenaeum* fragment no. 252. (Inci-dentally the latter text is obviously derived from the former, and a comparison of the two illustrates how Schlegel reworked his notes into "fragments.") In the sketch we read: "One should philosophize about art, for one should philosophize about everything; but one must already know something about art. —Of course, everything that one has learned about art only becomes knowledge through philosophy. It is not *through (aus)* philosophy that one knows that the ancients are classics, for Goethe knows that too; but certainly it is only *with (mit)* philosophy that one knows it."[20] *Athenaeum* fragment no. 252, which establishes a twofold vocation and a twofold program for a (pragmatic) "aesthetics of poetry" and for a (speculative) "philosophy of poetry," concludes with the following decla-ration: "Only he who knows or has mastered a subject can employ philos-ophy when treating it; he alone will be able to grasp what philosophy wishes and intends. Philosophy cannot inoculate or magically procure experience and senses. But, in any case, it should not want to do so. He who already knows a subject will not learn anything new from philosophy; yet it is only through philosophy that this knowledge becomes knowledge and thereby receives a new form."[21] There is no mention here of an empirical starting point for a deduction of the genres; and, in any case, that would contradict the essence of such a deduction. Schlegel is concerned only with understanding deduction, or more precisely, with making it comprehensible, an operation that requires empirical data drawn from history.

The problem of deductive poetics is not satisfactorily solved, however, as long as one must refer to its opposite pole, induction, in order to understand it. Even though the opposition between induction and deduc-tion is not one of contradiction within the deductive process, both mo-ments are nevertheless external to one another. The problem of the mediation of the universal and the particular was first solved by Hegel; and this is no less true in the case of the system of poetical genres, which, as a system, is simultaneously the history of the genres. In Hegel, induc-tion and deduction are mediated by each other, because the concepts are not considered as existing beyond the empirical realm but are posited, rather, as first becoming what they potentially are only in this realm and thus in the course of history.

Schlegel's proposition that poetics must be both pure and applied, both empirical and rational, that is, simultaneously inductive and deductive, did not lead, in Schlegel's own writings, to a solution anticipating Hegel's, or indeed to any other solution. Schlegel recognizes the problem, and this in itself prevents him from accepting the poetics of genres in its traditional inductive-descriptive form; but he leaves the problem unsolved. One may regret this fact, or one may view it as an accurate expression of Schlegel's place in the development of German aesthetics—that of a pioneering thinker who early abandoned a promising course. Finally, one may wonder whether his choice of the fragmentary form is not simply a sign that Schlegel recognizes his inability to solve these problems. In any event, the title of Helmut Kuhn's book, published in 1931, *Die Vollendung der klassischen deutschen Aesthetik durch Hegel* [*Hegel's Completion of Classical German Aesthetics*] is an apt one; but this completion is (as the German word *Vollendung* indicates) also an end.[22] The only way to go beyond it is to go back behind it. For this reason, the innovations that were made in the poetics of genres did not come in the wake of the Hegelian system (not, for example, by F. T. Vischer). On the contrary, it was necessary to return to the foundations of Hegelianism, to the unsystematic insights, that is to say, to the early romantic conception of the philosophy of history and its connection with the poetics of genres. This is the lesson of Benjamin's *Origins of German Tragic Drama* and of Lukács's *Theory of the Novel,* which was written a decade earlier. Lukács and Benjamin both wrote their books after intensive study of Friedrich Schlegel.

Schlegel's rejection of systems was not, however, a matter of principle; nor was it the consequence of the nihilism of which he has so often been accused. In the posthumous *Philosophical Fragments* (*Philosophische Fragmente*), for example, he writes "it is not true that individuals possess more reality than the genres."[23] And *Athenaeum* fragment 234 asserts the necessity for a literary work to belong to a definite genre. "All the genres are good, says Voltaire, except the boring genre. But which is the boring genre? It may be larger than all the others and many paths may lead to it. The shortest is probably when a work does not know to which genre it wishes or ought to belong. Did Voltaire never take this path?"[24]

As we have seen, Schlegel speaks of genres (and thus of the division of poetry into genres, of the system of poetic genres), but he scarcely ever does so without raising the question of their historicity, and thereby implicitly casting doubt on the status of the genres and of their system. In asserting that "the subdivisions of the genres are often [neglected] to the great disadvantage of the theory of genres," the fourth *Athenaeum* fragment only seems to assert the need for a system.[25] For it goes on to say: "Thus the poetry of nature, for example, may be divided into natural poetry and artificial poetry, and folk poetry (*Volkspoesie*) into folk poetry for the people (*das Volk*) and folk poetry for people of rank and the learned."[26] The subdivision presented here has two aspects. The first is historical, and it characterizes the contrast between antiquity and the modern age as one between the poetry of nature and the poetry of art, between natural and artificial formations, thus challenging the traditional classifications by showing their historical character. The second is ahistorical, for in introducing (in the form of a subdivision) art poetry into the domain of its opposite, natural poetry, it undermines the original historically based division. And this reversal is carried out in the spirit of the dialectic, which asserts that every thesis contains its antithesis. Schlegel's thinking thus approaches Hölderlin's theory of the mirror symmetry of Greek and Hesperian poetry, whose respective starting points and orientations correspond in a crosswise fashion. In stating his thesis, Schlegel's aims respecting artistic politics are, to be sure, different from Hölderlin's. Whereas Hölderlin wishes to surpass classicism with the air of classical Greek poetry—as can be seen from his first letter to Böhlendorff of 4 December 1801—Schlegel looks forward to a poetry of the future that is to be a synthesis of ancient and modern poetry.[27] In the essay "On the Study of Greek Poetry," Schlegel prepares the way for this synthesis, which he calls "objective" poetry,[28] by rejecting the sharp contrast between an ancient poetry of nature and a modern poetry of art and by acknowledging that artificial poetry exists already within the poetry of nature. This view was made possible by the progress achieved in classical philology in Schlegel's time especially at Göttingen, where he was studying, and by the new, more accurate insights into the nature of Greek poetic works, in particular, the odes of Pindar and the tragedies of Sophocles.

It was in reflecting upon philosophical systems, even more than in his study of the various systems of poetics, that Schlegel came to realize the need to adopt an historical point of view. Thus, in the *Philosophical Fragments* we read: "Genuine classification is historical, as much from the point of view of knowledge (*principio cognoscendi*) as from the point of view of existence (*principio existendi*). All the divisions into a *definite number (bestimmt Viele)* are historical. —Kant [is] always for either *one only* or the *definite number;* Fichte more for the *infinite number.*"[29] And a few lines later: "Kant's moral theory and Fichte's theory of natural law show how meager all systems must turn out if they are not historical as well as philosophical."[30] Although the former fragment still leaves open the possibility that Schlegel does not include systems when he describes classificatory schemes as historical, the latter speaks explicitly of "systems." (The former also refers to systems, but only implicitly, with the mention of Kant and Fichte.) And in the following fragment, from the same collection, Schlegel entirely divorces his insight from the extraaesthetic field represented by Kant's theory of ethics and Fichte's natural law. For this fragment, which attributes the rise of the critical approach to literature to the transformation of philosophy into art, begins with the general proposition that: "As soon as philosophy becomes science, there is history. All systems are historical, and vice versa. (*Alles System ist historisch und umgekehrt.*).[31]

Athenaeum fragment 434, which offers the most concentrated discussion of all the questions we have discussed so far, combines the rejection of Enlightenment poetics with the bold sketch of a new theory of poetical classification—a theory that formulates the "laws of motion" of poetic writing together with the law of its historical transformation. In holding that this transformation is susceptible to calculation, Schlegel breaks with his earlier essays on literary history. History cedes its place to the philosophy of history:

> Should poetry be purely and simply divided? or should it remain one and indivisible? Or should it alternate between separation and union? Most conceptions of the poetic world-system are still as rough and childish as the ancient conception of the astronomical world-system before Copernicus. The usual divisions of poetry are only inert latticework designed for a limited horizon. What someone can do, or simply what happens to be in style, is taken for the motionless earth in the center. In the universe of poetry, however, nothing remains still, everything is becoming, is in process of transformation, and moves harmoniously; even the comets move according to immutable laws. But until we can calculate the orbit of these stars, until we can predict their return, we will not have discovered the true world-system of poetry.[32]

This was written around 1798. Twenty years later, in the notes to *East-West Divan*, Goethe wrote a passage on the "Natural Forms of Poetry" in which the history of poetry is represented as forming a circular pattern reminiscent of Schlegel's astral orbits. But in the preceding two decades, idealist aesthetics had undergone a profound change. Although it still retained the ideals of a system and of the possibility of calculating the course of history, it had definitely given up its belief in the possibility of reproducing what had once existed or had once been created, and this change amounted to an abandonment of that identification of art and nature on which Winckelmann had based this belief.

2. The Poetics of Genres and the Philosophy of History

In a note to the fragment "On Homeric Poetry" published in 1796, Schlegel intimates that his explanation of Homeric epic presupposes a philosophically based theory of the division of poetical genres according to type.[33] A year later, in entry no. 190 of his *Fragments on Literature and Poetry,* he writes: "*How* we ought to classify is something that we often learn from the Ancients; but we ourselves must add the basis for the classification in a mystical way."[34] Inasmuch as Schlegel makes systematization an integral part of his definition of "classification," he does more than simply reject the theories of the Enlightenment. It appears that he wishes to leap over the theories of the Renaissance and the Baroque as well and to revive the theories of Plato and Aristotle. At the same time, he maintains that a systematics of genres must be erected on a "mystical" foundation, that is to say, one provided by speculative philosophy. In the same notebook of the *Fragments on Literature and Poetry* he states (in no. 256) that *"True philosophy of art is only pure mysticism and pure polemics."*[35] By "mysticism" he means the idealist philosophy that Fichte and Schelling were formulating at just this time, and by "polemics," literary criticism of the type that appears in his own essays on Goethe, Lessing, and Forster. Schlegel's study of Fichte cannot be dealt with in detail here. The crucial point for us is that Fichte's work entitled *Grundlage der gesamten Wissenschaftslehre* (*The Foundation of the Entire Science of Knowledge*), which appeared in 1794–95, furnished Schlegel with the philosophical concepts which, along with those he borrowed from Schelling's *Briefe über Dogmatismus und Kritizismus,* enabled him to lay the philosophical foundations of the poetics of genres.

Schlegel thus seeks to establish the poetical genres with the aid of the concepts of "subjectivity" and "objectivity." In the course of this enterprise, he sometimes contradicts himself. (It may be remarked that in each case his insights are set out in single sentences that can scarcely be called "fragments" in the early romantic meaning of the word.) For example, in a note to which the editor assigns the date 1799, Schlegel writes: "Epic = objective poetry, lyric = subjective poetry, drama = objective-subjective poetry."[36] A year later he asserts that "Epic = subjective-objective, drama = objective, lyric = subjective."[37] We shall not attempt here to evaluate the grounds for preferring one of these series of definitions over the other. It may simply be recalled that in these pronouncements we see the reappearance of the Platonic division of the expository modes into two fundamentally different types, as well as into a third one formed by their union, viz., the *genus mixtum,*[38] although Schlegel elevates the distinction from the level of poetic technique to that of speculative philosophy. Two questions must be asked at this point. First, how are we to understand the change in Schlegel's thinking that leads him to favor the epic over the drama as the genre which realizes the desired synthesis and which, therefore, is the supreme genre? Second, how should we go about determining in what larger context to place the notion of the superiority of the epic, which, it may already be said, represents Schlegel's real view of the matter?

The sequence epic—lyric—drama (i.e., the conception of the drama as a return to the objectivity of the epic, but on a higher level, on which that first, epic objectivity is mediated by the subjectivity of the lyric) corresponds to the historical development of Greek poetry in which the tragedy follows the epic. Moreover, it anticipates Hegelian aesthetics, whose essential classicism appears in the privileged position accorded to Greek tragedy. The anticlassical aspect of Schlegel's preference for the epic is not so much that it disregards the actual development of Greek poetry as that it leads him to raise the epic's modern counterpart, the novel, above the tragedy.

To answer the question of whether, for Schlegel, it is the drama or the epic that ultimately represents the synthesis of the objective and the subjective, we have to consider more than just the chronological point of view. It has, indeed, been established that the two sequences correspond to two periods in the young Schlegel's biography, the one to the classicist phase and the other to the early romantic phase; yet, among the *Fragments on Literature and Poetry,* there exists a fragment from the year 1797 that not only seems to anticipate the later version but also places it in the service of early Romanticism—specifically, in the service of a theory of the novel. The fragment, no. 828, reads: "In all the forms of the novel (*Romanarten*) everything subjective must be made objective; it is an error to think that the novel is a subjective genre."[39] Granted, there is no mention here of objective thesis, subjective antithesis, and objective-subjective synthesis, nor of the problem of the succession of genres. Yet, if one recalls that for Schlegel and his contemporaries the novel is the most recent genre and, in the pregnant sense of the word, the "modern" genre, then it becomes clear that in this fragment the novel is already conceived of as an objectivized form of subjectivity, as that notion is understood in the later fragment (no. 2065), where it is applied to the epic. At the same time, however, in this fragment Schlegel places the novel, as a modern genre, above its classical equivalent, the epic. To do so, he finds it necessary to reject the thesis, widespread in the age of Goethe and ultimately incorporated by Hegel in his system, that the novel is a subjective epic.

Let us recall that the concretization of the sequence objective—subjective—objective-subjective (or subjective-objective) as epic—lyric—drama corresponds to the classicist position, while its concretization as drama—lyric—epic corresponds to the early romantic position. These pairings signify that while the chronological sequence epic—drama is derived from literary history, and specifically from Greek literary history, which was the first subject Schlegel studied, the reverse order, drama—epic, contradicts the historical facts. It can be justified historically only if, instead of being applied to two epochs of Greek poetry, it is referred to

the succession from classical to modern poetry, as this succession is analyzed in the essay "On the Study of Greek Poetry." This means, however,
that in giving the genres a philosophical foundation (with the help of the
concepts "subjective" and "objective"), Schlegel is led to incorporate the
genres into his philosophy of history, whose pivotal point is the difference
between antiquity and the modern age, between natural formation and
artificial formation. As long as Schlegel is writing a history of Greek
poetry, the different genres (epic, lyric, drama) can be linked with various
periods of Greek history. In the famous sentence from the essay on Greek
poetry asserting that the latter constitutes "an *eternal natural history of
taste and of art,*"[40] Schlegel is not thinking of a history determined by
natural law but, like Pliny, of an order, of a natural system. He insists on
the fact that in Greek poetry "the *entire cycle of the organic development
of art* is closed and completed"; and it is this alone that allows him to
speak of a system in the strict sense.[41]

By abandoning the classicist position (which he had set out to defend
when he began writing the essay on Greek poetry) in favor of self-under-
standing and of a self-justification of the modern age, Schlegel explodes
the system based on the history of Greek poetry. The new system includes
artificial (i.e., modern) as well as natural (i.e., classical) formations. The
sequence dramatic—epic reflects the opposition between classical tragedy
and the modern novel, two forms in which, for Schlegel (although not
only for him), the respective periods found their most characteristic
expression.

By giving the genres a speculative foundation, which is inseparable
both from the understanding he had of his own time and from his philosophy of history, Schlegel arrives at the following correspondences between
genres and historical periods: "*Three dominant genres.* (1) *Tragedy* among
the Greeks. (2) *Satire* among the Romans. (3) The *novel* among the moderns."[42] The meaning of the term "dominant" can be gathered from *Athenaeum* fragment no. 146, which begins with the following observation:
"Just as the novel colors all of modern poetry, so satire—which, despite
all the transformations it underwent, remained among the Romans a
classical universal poetry, a social poetry by and for the center of the
civilized world—colors (*tingiert*) all of Roman poetry, indeed all of Roman
literature, and as it were sets its tone (*gibt den Ton an*)."[43] The genres that
are said to characterize each of the individual historical periods are not
dominant merely in the sense that their importance surpasses that of the
other genres; more significantly, they have an effect beyond their own
boundaries and determine the character of the other genres, imparting to
them their own distinctive tones. The two expressions "to color" and "to
set the tone" already point to the topic that we shall treat in detail below:

the transcendence of the poetics of genres by the elimination of the bound-aries between the genres, along with the subsequent transformation of genres into "tones," paralleled by the transformation of their formerly substantivized conceptualizations into adjectives, the substantive *Epos* becoming the adjective *episch.*

Schlegel's recasting of the theory of genres, which was prepared by his earlier essays on literary history, is effected by a transposition of the philosophical concepts "subjective" and "objective" to the realm of the philosophy of history, where they serve to establish the nature of the three genres. *Athenaeum* fragment no. 90 does not explicitly refer to the history of poetry, but Schlegel doubtless was thinking of this field too when he stated that "The subject of history is the realization (*Wirklichkeitswer-den*) of everything that is practically necessary."[44] The sentence summa-rizes the thesis of the essay "On the Study of Greek Poetry," according to which the history of Greek poetry is a system of poetical genres, but it removes this perception from its classicist framework by presenting the declaration as a pronouncement about history in general. Now, to say that in history only that which is necessary becomes real, is to imply that what becomes real in history is what is deducible from concepts. Deduction and induction are thus mediated by one another.

Surely this is what is meant by no. 1374 of the *Fragments on Literature and Poetry,* whose much less incisive formulation is no doubt due to the fact that (as the editor assumes) it is not a fragment in the early romantic sense of the term but rather the program of a projected book: "The history of modern poetry perhaps [lies] in *aesthetics.*"[45] A glance at the table of contents of Hegel's *Aesthetics* reveals that Schlegel anticipated a good portion of what today is considered to be the *completion of classical aesthetics;* but it also reminds us of the great number of insights he never elaborated. The book that he wanted to write was written (or at least given as lectures) by Hegel.

A fuller indication of Schlegel's views can be found in no. 322 of the *Fragments on Literature and Poetry,* which touches on several basic ques-tions pertaining to a poetics of genres based upon a philosophy of history: "There exists an epic *form,* [a] lyrical *form,* [and a] dramatic *form* without the spirit of the ancient poetical genres that bore these names, but [sepa-rated from each other] by [a] definite and eternal difference. —As *form,* the epic obviously is at an advantage. It is subjective-objective. —The *lyrical* form is merely *subjective,* the *dramatic* form merely *objective.* — The ancient epic alone lends itself to romanticization. In the drama, only the new comedy can be romanticized. —The poetry of nature is either subjective or objective. An equal mixture is not possible for the natural man (*Naturmensch*)."[46] Thus, epic, lyrical, and dramatic forms can exist without the spirit of the ancient genres called by these names, but marked by a definite and eternal difference. This means, in the first place, that the epic, the lyrical, and the dramatic forms continue to exist in the modern age, too, though they do not coincide with their Greek models (as the supporters of the classicist position assume). It also signifies that while individual genres may be dominant during certain periods (the tragedy in the classical age and the novel in the modern age) the three persist as separate forms, although not necessarily as genres. Schlegel is here attempting to solve the problem of how the generic differences can be incorporated into a poetics that is concerned solely with the difference between two epochs, the classical and the modern. No. 287 of the same set of fragments states: "For the artist, the only pragmatic theory of art [that which is to take the place, therefore, of the *ars poetica,* of the *Kritische Dichtkunst* that had reigned, in many different forms, for centuries] is the theory of the classic and the romantic."[47]

The problem is resolved by means of an apparently unhistorical concept of form. Yet Schlegel does not seek to create a theory of forms that ignores history; he merely wishes to take into account the formal and technical aspects of the work of art. Now, these aspects are inherently historical and separated from each other by an "eternal difference,"[48] but through their concretization in the individual work of art they participate in the latter's historicity, and, in every case, they exist in a particular, historically conditioned functional context. In the middle portion of fragment no. 322 we again find the definitions: lyrical = "merely *subjective,*" dramatic = "merely *objective,*" epic = "subjective-objective";[49] but here the synthetic character of epic poetry is seen not merely as an indication that it belongs to the modern age, but also as a mark of excellence. If, among the forms of Greek poetry, it is only the ancient epic (and not the tragedy or the lyric) that can be "romanticized," this is because the epic corresponds to the novel, which has given the modern age its name: the romantic period. In the area of dramatic poetry, only Menander's "new comedy" has found a modern equivalent, namely, the Enlightenment *Lustspiel.* The synthetic character of a form thus proves to be more than simply a marker in the domain of the philosophy of history, for it also ensures the form's elasticity through time. Accordingly, the fragment continues with the remark that the poetry of nature is "either subjective or objective."[50] The mixture of the subjective and the objective, on the other hand, is not possible in a natural formation.

Fragment no. 322 is an attempt to solve an antinomy that arises in any poetics founded upon a philosophy of history. But the concept of form that it introduces in making the solution possible simultaneously produces a decisive transformation in the conception and structure of the work of art. For it now appears divided into two moments that Schlegel calls form and spirit, the form being ahistorical and the spirit historical. Form is what differentiates works of art of the same period, while spirit makes the work of art what it is, namely, an historically conditioned phenomenon belonging to a definite period. It might seem as if Schlegel was simply taking over the old distinction between form and content, still accepted by Goethe and Schiller, according to which form is governed by classical norms, while content alone bears the mark of history.[51] Yet the following fragment makes it clear that Schlegel's analysis of the work of art is actually much more complex. Indeed, the analysis itself is historical inasmuch as the concepts it employs vary according to whether the period of the work in question is ancient or modern. Thus, in no. 843 of the *Fragments on Literature and Poetry,* we read: "In the forms of the novel, *manner, tendency,* and *tone* are determined. In the classical genres, on the contrary, [it is] *form, content (Stoff),* and *style.*"[52] What Schlegel is investigating here is not the relationship between form and content in the classical and in the modern genres; nor is it the distinction between the spirits of the respective epochs. His point, rather, is that the three aspects into which the classical work of art is customarily divided, namely, form, content, and style, are matched by three other aspects of the novel (or of romantic writing in general): manner, tendency, and tone. Further texts of Schlegel's as well as texts of other authors (for example, Goethe's essay on "Simple Imitation of Nature, Manner, Style" ["Einfache Nachahmung der Natur, Manier, Stil"] 1789), allow us to determine the content of the following pairs of concepts: (1) form and manner, (2) content and tendency, (3) style and tone. Alternatively, we may consider another configuration, which is based from the outset on an interpretation of the concepts: (1) form and tendency, (2) content and tone, (3) style and manner. The opposition style—manner is Goethean. The pair form—tendency yields the contrast between the fully achieved classical figure and the progressive aspect, the unfinished, fragmentary nature of the modern work of art. Finally, the opposition content—tone expresses the contrast between the sensuousness and plastic character of ancient works and the musical, intellectual, and reflective character of modern works.[53] It is in this perspective that the concepts ought to be tested for their value as historical indices. In other words, we should determine whether they can contribute to an analysis capable of differentiating ancient from modern works of art.

3. The Transcendence of the Poetics of Genres and the Origins of the Theory of the Novel

This terminological distinction is important for the poetics of genres because it presupposes reflection upon the historical transformation of the genres and upon what Lukács, in his *Theory of the Novel*, calls the "historico-philosophical dialectics" of "artistic forms."[54] But Schlegel's distinction between "form" and "spirit" (that is to say, between "form" as characteristic of ancient poetry and "tendency" as characteristic of modern poetry, or again, between "content" as characteristic of ancient poetry and "tone" as characteristic of modern poetry) impinges on the poetics of genres in another way as well. In making these distinctions, with the aid of which he distinguishes the different literary "tones," Schlegel employs the names of the traditional genres in their adjectival forms, as did Schiller at the end of his essay "On Naive and Sentimental Poetry" ("Über naive und sentimentalische Dichtung"), in which Schiller affirmed that these terms designate ways of writing and of feeling.[55] Schlegel's procedure is also related to the one that Hölderlin adopted in presenting his theory of the modulation of tones, which are likewise derived from generic concepts.[56] Schlegel used the term "tone" to convey a similar meaning, but, unlike Hölderlin, he considers the concept to be historically limited, since its ancient counterpart is called "content."[57]

The generic concepts appear in adjectival form in no. 1063 of the *Fragments on Literature and Poetry:* "Among the novels, too, there is a lyrical genre—an epic genre—and a dramatic genre."[58] This sentence illustrates perfectly the use of the three genre concepts within a single genre and thus also illustrates a typical early romantic procedure: the elevation to the second power of the traditional division into three genres; it is equally significant that the example chosen is not a classical but a modern genre, the novel. From the division of the novel into lyrical, epic, and dramatic forms, it is but a step to the thesis of *Athenaeum* fragment no. 116, which affirms that romantic poetry (that is to say, the novel)[59] is destined to "reunite all the separated genres of poetry."[60] This precise meaning of the word *romantisch* is also clear from another fragment, which shows, at the same time, how the reformulation of the genre concepts as adjectives makes possible not only the differentiation of a single genre such as the novel, but also—again recalling Hölderlin—the distinction between two aspects of the same work of art, each derived from a different genre. Finally, it is evident from the same text (no. 1063) that Schlegel ascribes this distinction, which is immanent in the work of art, only to modern or postclassical literature. In the *Philosophical Fragments* of the year 1797 we read: "In Shakespeare's tragedies the form is dramatic, the spirit and purpose romantic [i.e., in the manner of a novel, epic]. The separation of comedy from tragedy is either a vestige or a step toward classicism."[61] Here Schlegel contrasts the "pure" comedies and "pure" tragedies of French and German classicism with Shakespeare's blending of the two genres. The latter was not only Schlegel's own preference; it had already been seen by the writers of the Storm and Stress movement as a source of the English playwright's greatness.

Schlegel did not, however, confine his adjectival use of the genre concepts to the epic, the lyric, and the drama. He treated numerous such genre concepts in the same way, reminding us that this triad became established very late in Germany, and still later in France.[62] Here are two examples of his adjectival use of other concepts of genre: "Is there not also . . . epic, lyrical, dramatic, idyllic, satirical, epigrammatical prose?"[63] And, "In the *absolute* poetic drama nothing should be unrefinedly (*roh*) epic or lyrical; rather, everything should fuse together. Nor should anything be unrefinedly elegiac or idyllic."[64] In this fragment, written in 1797, the concepts "elegiac" and "idyllic" refer to Schiller's essay "On Naive and Sentimental Poetry," which had appeared the previous year. Another fragment influenced by Schiller is no. 426, also from 1797: "[The] *sentimental* is the union of the *elegiac* and the *idyllic*."[65] These three concepts are taken from Schiller's essay, but their specific application here reflects a different analysis of the work of art, one that anticipates Hölderlin's conception and entirely alters Schiller's view. While Schiller had put forth the thesis that a "sentimental" work must be either a satire, an elegy, or an idyll—these three substantives signifying here not the traditional genres known under these names but manners of writing and feeling—Schlegel goes a step further by locating the essence of the sentimental (i.e., modern) work of art in the union of the elegiac and the idyllic. The fragments cited earlier allow us to assume that, here too, Schlegel glimpsed the possibility of a union of the elegiac and the idyllic in the sense of that dialectical conception which distinguishes between form (or tendency) and content (or tone) and which mediates them through each other. This, in any case, is how Hölderlin views the matter when he asserts that a strophe can have an ideal (i.e., elegiac) basic tone (*Grundstimmung*) and a naive (i.e., idyllic) artistic character (*Kunstcharakter*). No. 234 of the *Fragments on Literature and Poetry* shows that this interpretation, which likens Schlegel's position to Hölderin's, is far from arbitrary: "The tone of the novel should be elegiac, the form idyllic."[66] Translated into Hölderlin's terminology, this sentence would read: The novel, which is ideal in appearance, is naive in its significance. Now, this is how Hölderlin defines the lyrical poem. This confrontation of novel and lyrical poem, which at first seems to refute the translation we propose, actually concords with the fact that Schlegel considers the novel, and Hölderlin, the lyric, as the modern literary work *par excellence.*

The most important consequence of this conception for the poetics of genre—both in Schlegel and in Hölderlin—can be seen in no. 599 of the

Fragments on Literature and Poetry: "The particularity of the poetical genres lies in the fact that form and content, and basic material and expression (language and meter) share the same characteristics."[67] The two conceptual pairs "form—content" and "basic material—expression" correspond here to Hölderlin's pair "basic tone—artistic character" (or "significance—appearance"). Given the common nature of the genres, their identical characteristic properties, we may say that the difference between genres derives not from a difference in these constitutive characteristics, but from a difference in the way the qualitative aspects combine to form a pair of opposites and from their divisions into form and content, basic material and expression. This, at least, is how one may read Schlegel's statement in the light of Hölderlin's poetics of genres, in which the basic tone of the lyrical poem is termed "ideal."[68]

What is the ultimate significance, for Schlegel's conception of poetical genres, of the adjectival use of the genre concepts and of the consequent relativization of the differences between genres, in other words, of their reduction to differences within a combinatorial system? It is nothing less than the complete elimination of—or at the least, the possibility of eliminating—the division of poetry into genres. However, it is impossible to determine if this is a logical consequence or the realization of an initial intention to transcend the poetics of genres. For the question of whether genres can exist at all is necessarily posed at the same time as the "critical" question concerning the conditions under which they are possible. A sentence like the following, from the year 1797, shows, insofar as it may be applied to the poetical genres, that Schlegel did not have the answer from the beginning: "It is not true that individuals are more real than the genres."[69] This apology for the genre, however, may be contrasted with other pronouncements, such as: "One can just as well say that there exist *infinitely many* as that there exists only *one* progressive *poetical genre (Dichtart)*. Therefore there really exists none; for a genre cannot be conceived without an accompanying genre."[70] And, "Of the modern genres there exists only one or infinitely many. Every poem [is] a genre unto itself. (*Jedes Gedicht eine Gattung für sich*)."[71] The postulate of the *unique* genre that takes the place of the system of genres is here restricted to modern poetry. This postulate, in which "one" is only another word for "infinitely many," leads, in the second fragment, to the thesis that every poem is a genre unto itself. But, in this context, a "poem" (*Gedicht*) means a "progressive," "modern" poem, i.e., a novel. Thus one of the *Philosophical Fragments* from the same period (1797) affirms that "Every novel is a type (*Art*) unto itself. Here the classification (*Rubrizieren*) is very illiberal."[72] According to Schlegel's theory, the novel is either a mixture of all the genres or a genre encompassing all the others. In a marginal note

Schlegel writes: "All the genres, except the three ancient classical ones. These basic elements then united in a progressive unity."[73] From this statement we may conclude that Schlegel restricted the domain of the traditional genres to antiquity and that it was on this basis that he claimed the poetics of genres has been surpassed only in the modern age, thanks to the novel. Admittedly, this interpretation is opposed by another note that characterizes the novel as a mixture of the dramatic, the epic, and the lyrical. This is not the first or the last time Schlegel contradicts—or corrects—himself. What he says of the "romantic genre," of the novel—that it is "still becoming," that "eternally it is only becoming and can never be completed"[74]—is no less true of its theory.

Chapter 6
Schleiermacher's Hermeneutics Today

For Paul Celan

Hermeneutics, the theory of the understanding and interpretation of texts, is an ancient science.[1] It is generally considered to have originated in the efforts of Atheneans of the classical period to establish the literal sense of the words in the Homeric epics, the language of which was no longer accessible to them. Hermeneutics is thus, in the first place, a discipline designed to mediate successive stages of a language, illuminating the obscurities and correcting the misapprehensions that result from the aging of fixed expressions. The hermeneuticist is an interpreter who, thanks to his linguistic knowledge, can render comprehensible what has become obscure by replacing a word that is no longer understood by another that belongs to his reader's own language. Yet, ever since the beginning of the discipline, this determination of the literal sense (sensus literalis) has been motivated by more than the mere intention of making the incomprehensible comprehensible. Its goal has been to overcome the historical distance of the canonical Atheneans—and to transport the text into the present as a way of demonstrating its undiminished validity and canonical stature.

Already at an early date the desire to establish the literal sense was accompanied by the quest for an allegorical sense. A new meaning was ascribed to each passage, a spiritual meaning *(sensus spiritualis)* that did

Written in 1970 for presentation on a radio program and first published in French under the title "L'herméneutique de Schleiermacher," trans. S. Buguet, in *Poetique* 2 (1970): 141-55. The German version appeared in *Sprache im technischen Zeitalter* 58 (1976): 95-110.

not exclude the literal meaning but stood alongside or above it. The allegorical interpretation, too, as it was applied in early Christianity and in the Middle Ages to the Old and New Testaments, served to make texts more "present" to a new audience. Perhaps the clearest example of this is the so-called *typological* interpretation, which sees in the Old Testament stories an anticipation, a promise of the events reported in the New Testament; thus Abraham's readiness to sacrifice Isaac becomes a prefiguration of God's sacrifice of Christ.

While both these methods of interpretation—the so-called *grammatical,* which aims at discovering the literal sense, and the *allegorical*—seek to overcome historical distance, they remain diametrically opposed. For in their efforts to resolve the problem of the aging of texts, of their increasing incomprehensibility, they adopt two radically different procedures. The grammatical interpretation seeks to recover and preserve the former meaning of a word by offering a new formulation in place of the old one, which has become obsolete and alien as a result of historical change, or, alternatively, by using a new expression to explain it in a gloss. The allegorical interpretation, in contrast, draws its inspiration from a sign that has become alien, to which it ascribes a new meaning stemming from the intellectual universe of the interpreter rather than from that of the text.

The history of hermeneutics from the church fathers to the Reformation is marked by the confrontation of these two methods of interpretation. Origen's theory of the threefold meaning of Scriptures, which, in its various versions penetrated all medieval theology, was challenged by the School of Antioch.[2] This school, whose positions can be traced to Aristotle's *Rhetoric,* rejected the allegorical interpretation altogether. After flourishing in Scholastic thought, the allegorical interpretation again came under attack when the Reformation sought to establish the exclusive legitimacy of the *sensus literalis,* drawing on the achievements of the humanist philologists of the later Middle Ages and the Renaissance. Luther himself placed his confidence in these writers when he announced his scriptural principle of the clarity of the Holy Scriptures, namely, the notion that they interpret themselves and no longer require for their interpretation an authority such as the Church had claimed to be.[3]

With the defeat of the allegorical interpretation at the beginning of the modern period, hermeneutics experienced a certain impoverishment. The subtlety of the theory of multiple textual meaning disappeared along with the emotion with which it had been contested. The theory of interpretation became rigidified into a collection of rules, and this level was rarely surpassed in the countless theological and philological manuals written during the seventeenth and eighteenth centuries. It was not until around 1800, at the high point of German idealist philosophy, that a change took place in hermeneutics. For Wilhelm Dilthey, writing a hundred years later, this change amounted to a refoundation of hermeneutics in the form of the analysis of understanding. He celebrated the theologian Friedrich D. E. Schleiermacher as the founder of this philosophical hermeneutics. Through Dilthey's writings, Schleiermacher became the model for the practitioner of the art in our century. But, whereas Dilthey still spoke of the analysis of understanding as the "secure starting point for the establishment of rules,"[4] his successors have tended increasingly to soar into the realm of a philosophy of understanding, neglecting to return to the earthly practice of interpretation and to its methodology. In 1927, in *Being and Time*,[5] Heidegger treated understanding as an "Existential." Later his student Hans-Georg Gadamer published the "Principles of a Philosophical Hermeneutics" under the title of *Truth and Method* (1960),[6] and in this book Gadamer vigorously rejected the notion that one could expect to find a methodology in it.[7]

Anyone interested in Schleiermacher's theory of understanding today would do well to concentrate less on the philosophical intentions that Dilthey emphasized so strongly and more on both Schleiermacher's ideas about the practice of understanding and his project of a new hermeneutics founded upon the observation of linguistic materials. This approach would demonstrate that Schleiermacher's theory can serve as a model for a new theory of interpretation. At present we do not possess a theory which would allow us to go beyond what ordinarily passes for interpretation but which is rarely more than a detailed report prepared by a well-read literary amateur. Such a new theory can only be elaborated by means of a close collaboration of literary theory and modern linguistics.

In 1829 Schleiermacher delivered two addresses before the Prussian Academy of Sciences, "On the Concept of Hermeneutics."[8] In an autobiographical introduction intended for the first address (which was discarded by Schleiermacher but included in a new edition of his hermeneutical writings edited by Heinz Kimmerle), Schleiermacher cites the reasons that led him to work for a quarter of a century on developing a theory of hermeneutics.[9] His courses on New Testament exegesis brought him to the realization that traditional theological hermeneutics was merely a collection of rules "lacking a genuine foundation, because the general principles had never been established."[10] Hence, right from the start, Schleiermacher's intention was not further to elaborate the traditional hermeneutics but rather to give it a theoretical foundation. He recognized that one of the reasons why his immediate predecessors, the authors of the manuals of hermeneutics in use around 1800, had not arrived at such a theory of hermeneutics was that their work always dealt with just a single kind of text, either the New Testament or the works of antiquity. Since these authors, whether they were concerned with theological or with philological hermeneutics, took as their point of departure the specific problems of the object they studied, they invariably produced only more rules designed to guide the interpretation of these particular writings; in other words, they never created a theory of hermeneutics that could claim general validity irrespective of the differences in the texts to be interpreted. Schleiermacher thought that the foundation of a general hermeneutics should be sought in the act of understanding, in interpretation itself.

Schleiermacher did not simply disregard the differences between the works of antiquity and the Holy Scriptures. He also enlarged the field of hermeneutics by turning every linguistic phenomenon, seen as a potential object of understanding, into an object of the theory of this understanding, and so of hermeneutics. Schleiermacher thought that hermeneutics should not be restricted either to literary works or to those written in a foreign language. Hermeneutical problems are likewise raised by nonartistic texts such as newspapers and advertisements. Spoken language and conversation are also possible objects of hermeneutical inquiry; indeed Schleiermacher devotes particular attention to them. In his first Academy Address he writes:

> Hermeneutics is not to be restricted solely to literary productions . . . ; for I very often find myself undertaking hermeneutical operations in the midst of private conversations, when, not satisfied with an ordinary degree of understanding, I seek to explore how, in my friend, the transition from one thought to another has taken place, or when I detect what opinions, judgments, and aims cause him to express himself on a given subject just as he does and not differently. Facts of this kind—which everyone can attest for himself if he gives the matter a little attention— indicate clearly enough, I should think, that the solution to the problem, which is the very one for which we are seeking a theory, in no way depends on the discourse being fixed for the eye through writing; rather, it will appear each time we perceive thoughts or series of thoughts expressed in words.[11]

By taking the act itself of understanding as his starting point, Schleiermacher does not merely enlarge the domain of hermeneutics; he alters its task as well. For it is no longer enough simply to decipher the meaning of a given passage. The hermeneuticist must also attempt to understand the genesis of the passage, and thus its connection with the rest of the text and its motivation. For Schleiermacher, hermeneutics first goes into operation not where understanding comes up against difficulties but where the "ordinary degree of understanding"[12] is no longer deemed sufficient:

Not all speech is an object of the art of interpretation to an equal degree. Some instances may possess zero value, others an absolute value; most lie between these two extremes. ... That which possesses no interest either as an act or as a significant fact about language has zero value. There is talk because language maintains itself only in the continuity of repetition. But that which only repeats what has already been said is nothing in itself; it is mere talk about the weather. Yet, this zero is not absolute nothing, but rather a minimum. For it is starting from this point that meaningful discourse develops.[13]

It was this modification of the task of hermeneutics that simultaneously brought about its emancipation from its previous status as an auxiliary science to other disciplines, namely, to theology, philology, and jurisprudence:

I admit that I hold this practice of hermeneutics, with respect to the mother tongue and to direct relations with people, to be an essential part of cultivated life, aside from all philological or theological studies. Who can frequent extremely brilliant persons without making just as great an effort to hear between the words as we make to read between the lines of dense and brilliant writings? Who, engaged in a meaningful conversation that can easily (and from many different sides) turn into a significant act as well, would not consider it equally worthy of close examination? And who would not want to single out the points that give it life, to grasp their inner links, and to pursue further all of the faint traces, even the most subtle?[14]

Moreover, Schleiermacher is not satisfied to set speech and writing on the same level as objects of hermeneutical study:

In particular, ... I would urgently advise the interpreter of written texts to practice assiduously the interpretation of all significant conversation. For the immediate presence of the speaker, the living expression that announces the participation of his entire intellectual being, the manner in which the thoughts take shape here out of the shared elements of existence: all this stimulates us far more than the solitary examination of an isolated text to understand a series of ideas as "a cresting moment of life" *(ein hervorbrechender Lebensmoment),* as an act linked with many others, some of which may even be of different kinds. Yet in explaining an author, this is precisely the aspect which is generally considered last, if indeed it is not entirely neglected.[15]

A passage such as this clearly reveals the motivation behind Schleiermacher's hermeneutics as well as the attraction that it was bound to exercise on Dilthey and on *Lebensphilosophie* in the final years of the nineteenth century. For, in Schleiermacher's approach, the important thing is not the interpretation of individual passages but the comprehension of the word, whether spoken or written, and its source, in the individual life of its author. Speech and writing are both conceived as "cresting moments of life"[16] and as acts; they thus cease to be mere documents and become active and current expressions of life. Schleiermacher complains that the hermeneutics of his day neglected this aspect, and the reason is not difficult to determine. As long as hermeneutics maintained a particularistic approach, namely in the form of theories of the interpretation of Holy Scriptures or of the monuments of ancient literature, problems concerning textual meaning dominated the field for the simple reason that (in the case of, say, Homer) it was very difficult to penetrate this meaning in order to grasp the author's life as a whole. One may wonder to what extent this hermeneutical aim is justified today. The answer is most readily found by considering the debates that have been going on for decades, in both German and foreign literary criticism, over the elements of *Lebensphilosophie* and *Erlebnispsychologie* inherited from Dilthey's school—debates that have engaged the energies of formalism, New Criticism, and structuralism. Curiously, Schleiermacher's decisive shift from writing back to speech, motivated by his dissatisfaction with the "solitary examination of an isolated text,"[17] is presently at the center of discussion, especially in France, although little reference has so far been made there to Schleiermacher. In this context we must mention two different approaches to literature. The first, developed by Georges Poulet, is strongly influenced by Dilthey and based on the subjective processes of perception and consciousness, while the second, a literary theory deriving from Mallarmé, centers on the notion of *écriture*, or writing. The latter tendency is represented by Roland Barthes and Gérard Genette, among others, but above all by Jacques Derrida, whose *Of Grammatology* has so far received little attention in Germany.[18]

As early as 1805, in his *Aphorisms*, Schleiermacher found his most incisive formulation for the contrast between traditional hermeneutics and the hermeneutical theory he planned to develop: "There are two contrary maxims concerning understanding. (1) I understand everything until I come up against a contradiction or nonsense. (2) I understand nothing that I do not perceive as necessary and that I cannot construct."[19] The traditional theory of interpretation becomes active in those cases in which a passage is no longer immediately comprehensible, that is, when the passage seems to contradict the context, the author's presumed intention, or accepted truth. Understanding is then the resolution of this contradition—a conception whose rationalist premise could hardly be more evident. Schleiermacher, in contrast, endorses the second maxim, according to which something is not understood until it is apprehended as necessary and can be constructed, i.e., reproduced on the basis of a concept. Both criteria require a genetic approach. The necessity of an utterance is established when it can be derived; thus, in order to understand it, one must have recourse to the person of the author, to his entire life. Schleiermacher views each particular utterance as a "cresting moment of life,"[20] as an "act."[21]

Schleiermacher discusses this same opposition between traditional hermeneutics and the one he planned to establish in a text of 1819 (henceforth referred to as the *Compendium*) in which he presents a summary of his ideas: "The more lax practice . . . starts from the notion that understanding occurs spontaneously, and it expresses its goal negatively: 'Misunderstanding must be avoided.' . . . The strict practice starts from the notion that misunderstanding occurs by itself and that understanding must be willed and sought for point by point."[22] In the early aphorism, Schleiermacher left unspecified the way in which what is to be understood can be apprehended as necessary and constructed, concluding with the laconic statement that, according to this maxim, understanding is "an infinite task."[23] In this later text he places his conception of understanding in the context of a theory of grammatical and psychological (or technical) interpretation.

Schleiermacher distinguishes two aspects of the act of understanding: speech is to be understood, first, as something carved out of language and, second, as a fact about a thinking subject:

> Every person [is], on the one hand, a locus in which a given language takes shape in a particular way, and his speech can be understood only by reference to the entire language. But he also has a constantly developing mind, and his speech exists only as a fact about that mind, in connection with all the other facts.[24] Even as a fact of the mind, speech cannot be understood if it is not understood in its linguistic context . . . ;[25] [conversely] even as modification of the language, it cannot be understood if it is not understood as a fact of the mind.[26]

Understanding is thus composed of two aspects and exists only through their "interpenetration" *(im Ineinandersein)*.[27] The first aspect, the study of speech in its relationship to the whole language, employs the grammatical interpretation; the other, the study of speech in its relationship to the mental processes of an author, employs the psychological interpretation, which Schleiermacher also calls the "technical" interpretation.

Simplifying, it could be said that in returning to Schleiermacher, *Lebensphilosophie,* in the form in which it was inaugurated by Dilthey, ignored the grammatical interpretation, retaining only the psychological, with its stress on the author's individuality. It neglected the "technical" dimension of the latter approach, which sees the author's individuality concretized in the principles of literary composition. The most influential aspect of Schleiermacher's theory around 1900 and in the following period, therefore, was the one based on empathy *(Einfühlung)* and psychological identification, and thus on the idea that the problem of temporal distance can be solved in a historicist manner. In his first Academy Address Schleiermacher writes:

There exists an entirely different kind of certainty, which is also ... more divinatory, and this arises when the interpreter enters, as best he can, into the writer's state of mind *(Verfassung).* Thus, it is not rare to see a case like that of Plato's rhapsodist, who recognizes, though very naively, that while he can elucidate Homer excellently, he often cannot come up with good insights concerning other poets and prose writers. In other words, assuming that he possesses the necessary range of knowledge, the interpreter can and should show himself to be equally excellent not just concerning everything that depends on language, but also concerning whatever depends, to however small a degree, on the historical conditions of a people and an age. In contrast, with respect to the proper conception of the writer's psychic state *(innere Hergang)* when he was outlining and composing, as well as with respect to the reflection of his personality as exhibited both in language and in the totality of his relationships: here even the most skilled interpreter will succeed best only with those writers to whom he is most closely related, that is to say, his favorite authors, into whose life he has penetrated most fully—just as in life things work out best for us with our closest friends. In the case of other writers, however, he will be satisfied with less and will not at all blush to seek advice from colleagues who are closer to these authors.[28]

Even if one does not contest the element of subjectivity in the process of understanding, one must still admit that these sentences are highly problematical. For, it is really a psychological truth that one understands *those* men and authors best to whom one is most closely related: "the favorites into whose life one has penetrated most fully?"[29] Valéry was of another opinion, as we see from these lines from *Tel Quel* under the heading "Lumières naturelles": "Hate inhabits the adversary, explores his depths, and dissects down to the finest roots his most cherished intentions. We know him better than ourselves and better than he knows himself. He forgets himself but we do not forget him."[30]

Schleiermacher distinguishes two types of understanding: that which is based on factual knowledge of language and history and which is independent of the subjectivity of the person who is attempting to understand; and that which is founded on empathy and identification. It is not astonishing that, at the turn of the century, *Lebensphilosophie* and psychology responded to the positivist overemphasis on the objective and the factual with an overemphasis on the subjective, in this case with the advocacy of "empathy." This is what makes a large portion of the criticism of that period unreadable today. Schleiermacher, however, by drawing upon his concepts of the grammatical and "technical" interpretations (the latter is a part of the "psychological" interpretation or even the whole of the latter—the terminology varies) was able to lay the foundations for a twofold understanding. This consists, on the one hand, in an understanding of the specific elements in an author's language, considered from both an individual and an historical point of view; and, on the other hand, in an understanding of literary forms and genres. He furnishes the principles for a stylistic criticism and a formal analysis that seek to grasp both the individuality and the historicity of literary phenomena. In this way his work breaks down the barriers that previously had separated hermeneutics, rhetoric, and poetics: the understanding of meaning and interpretation in the modern sense of the word mesh with one another. For Schleiermacher, "The most beautiful fruit of all aesthetic criticism [is] a heightened understanding of the inner procedures of the poet and the other artists of language of the entire process (*ganze Hergang*) of composition from the first sketch to the final execution."[31] The grammatical interpretation shows the connection between the work and the language, and the technical or psychological interpretation shows the connection between the work and the thought involved in it. A twofold conception of this sort can be convincing, however, only if the two types of interpretation do not remain external to each other, only if the way they are related is also taken into account. Consequently, in the following analysis we shall not simply outline the grammatical and psychological or technical interpretations, but also attempt to elucidate the relationships that Schleiermacher established between them.

A complete exposition of the grammatical interpretation can be found in the *Compendium* of hermeneutics that Schleiermacher wrote in 1819. It begins with two rules of the grammatical interpretation that had been basic elements of hermeneutics since its origins in antiquity. "First canon: Everything in a given [instance of] speech that requires more exact determination may be determined only on the basis of the linguistic domain common to the author and his original public."[32] "Second canon: The meaning of each word in a given passage must be determined *(bestimmt)* in the light of its coexistence *(Zusammensein)* with those that surround it."[33] These two rules serve to delimit the context, the whole in terms of which one must determine the meaning of the individual word, which, in turn, helps to determine this context. The first rule refers to the linguistic system, to the historical stage of a language, or, more precisely, to that portion of the latter suited to communication between the author and the readers whom he addresses. The second rule refers to the system constituted by the sentence itself. Expressed in the terminology of modern linguistics, the first canon concerns the level of language *(langue),* the second, that of speech *(parole).* If one considers which words can help to determine the meaning of a word on one level and which words can help on the other, a second distinction arises. In the system of the language as a whole, one is interested in those words which can take the place of the word that is to be defined: in the system constituted by the sentence, one is interested in those words with which the given word can combine to form a complete sentence.

This dichotomy yields two of the most important elements of the current conception of language: the paradigmatic relation and the syntagmatic relation. Schleiermacher speaks of two types of context, the "global context"[34] (viz., the language system) and the "immediate context"[35] (the sentence). The fundamental difference in the relationship of the individual word to these two systems, which has been elaborated by Ferdinand de Saussure, is, to be sure, never treated as a specific subject in Schleiermacher's writings, although he did take this difference into account as early as in his first *Aphorism:* "There are two types of determination: exclusion from the global context and thetic determination on the basis of the immediate context."[36] Exclusion is the method which, in the framework of the paradigmatic relation, allows one to discover, experimentally as it were, which words can replace the word to be defined without changing the meaning, and which cannot. In the process of excluding from a group of words that constitute a paradigm a portion of these words because they mean something else, the meaning of the word to be defined becomes established with ever-increasing precision. In contrast, the syntagma, i.e., the relation in which the word to be defined stands to the other words in the sentence, can help yield a positive, or "thetic" definition.[37] Schleiermacher did not distinguish the two relations, the paradigmatic and the syntagmatic, as precisely as this was later done in Saussurian linguistics, but he did think that this opposition was one of the three fundamental oppositions upon which he could base the major divisions within his theory of the grammatical interpretation.

Schleiermacher's assertion in the first canon, that a more precise definition should be sought "only on the basis of the linguistic domain common to the author and his original public,"[38] leads to the question of how to establish what this public was. The sort of reader that the author had in mind can, he states, be determined only with reference to the text itself. A general survey can furnish initial indications and thus a first delimitation of the domain common to the author and his public; but this process of delimitation must "be pursued throughout the course of the interpretation and can only be concluded at the same time as the latter."[39] Schleiermacher mentions two apparent exceptions to the first canon: archaisms and technical expressions. "*Archaisms* lie outside the author's immediate linguistic domain and therefore outside that of his readers as well. They are used to bring the past closer to the present—in writing more than in speech and in poetry more than in prose. [This is equally true of] *technical expressions*, even in the most common genres, for example, in legal or deliberative discourse, where they occur even when they are not comprehensible to the entire audience."[40] From this it follows, first, that the grammatical interpretation must always take into account the genre to which the text to be interpreted belongs—an important principle, especially in literary hermeneutics; and second, that the meaning of a passage cannot be inferred automatically from the public attributed to it (in the case, for example, of legal discourse), since it is possible that an author "does not always have his entire public in view."[41] Accordingly, this rule too, Schleiermacher adds, is a rule of art, "whose successful application depends on the right feeling."[42]

One further restriction regarding the validity or, to put it another way, the applicability of the first canon should probably be added to those indicated by Schleiermacher himself. It is not enough simply to distinguish specific audiences. The degree to which a written text is destined for a public is not constant but changes with the genre and the historical epoch. This becomes clear when one compares a poem from the eighteenth century with one from the twentieth, or a poem from the twentieth century with a play from the same period; for the play is not simply reduced to the reception that the public gives it: it draws its life also from the fiction that its characters speak to each other.

A second question to which Schleiermacher returns again and again in the various sketches of his hermeneutics concerns the supposed difference between proper *(eigentlich)* and improper *(uneigentlich)* meaning—a notion used by lexicographers to classify the multiple meanings of a given word. For example, in the *Compendium* of 1819 he writes that the opposition between proper and improper meaning:

> disappears upon closer examination. In allegories there are two
> parallel series of ideas. The word is part of its own series, and
> that is all that should be taken into account. It therefore preserves

its meaning. In metaphors this is only suggested, and often only
one characteristic of the concept is considered, for example, . . .
King of the jungle = lion. The lion does not reign, but "king"
does not then mean a monster who rips apart the others by virtue
of the law of the strongest. A particular use of this sort yields
no meaning; it is only the entire expression that can become
habitual.[43]

If one were constructing a theory of metaphor, which is among the most
important goals of literary theory, this thesis would have to be examined
in detail. In the context of Schleiermacher's hermeneutics, it is important
because it marks the frontier between the grammatical and technical interpretations and thereby helps to elucidate the relationship between the two
methods. In his first sketch of a hermeneutics, written in the years between
1810 and 1819, Schleiermacher makes the following observation:

Aspects of the technical interpretation are generally confused with
aspects of the grammatical interpretation. This is the reason for
most of the metaphors that serve as a form of epexegesis, like
coma arborum (the trees' head of hair) or *tela solis* (arrows of the
sun), in which the words used in their "figurative sense" preserve
their proper and exact *(eigentlichste)* meaning, producing their
effect only through a combination of ideas counted on by the
writer. This is precisely the source of technical allusions: plays on
words, the use of proverbs, [and] allegory—for which the grammatical interpretation is the proper explanation, whereas the
question of what the writer really meant to say lies in the domain
of the technical interpretation. In general, it may be said that in
this case the idea itself, as it is elucidated in the grammatical interpretation, belongs not to the domain of the represented but
only to the representation; it is itself a sign. Where and how this
phenomenon occurs can be discovered only through the technical
interpretation.[44]

Here Schleiermacher seems to view the relationship between the grama-
tical and technical interpretations as based on a division of labor. At the
same time, these lines help us to answer the difficult question of how the
two interpretative methods—the grammatical and psychological or technical—are related to the older Patristic and Scholastic theory of manifold
textual meaning. The mere fact that in the history of hermeneutics one
conception replaced the other does not in itself prove that the later one
is in fact somehow related to the earlier. All the same, it is necessary to
consider this question, especially since the concept of the grammatical and
historical interpretation already appears in ancient hermeneutics, in which
its task is the determination of the *sensus literalis,* the *sensus spiritualis*

being the concern of the allegorical interpretation. It is hard to believe that the new hermeneutics created by Schleiermacher and his immediate predecessors took over the concept of the grammatical-historical interpretation without adopting some definite position regarding ancient hermeneutics, even if only a critical one. Some light is shed on this question in the last lines of the above quotation, in which Schleiermacher emphasizes that even in the cases of metaphor and allegory, the meaning yielded by the grammatical interpretation is the proper one and not the improper or figurative one; on the other hand, the improper (*uneigentlich*) meaning is determined only by the technical interpretation, because this "figurative sense" is due solely to a combination of words—for example, *telum* (arrow) and *sol* (sun) and not, as might be supposed, from a doubling of the meaning of *telum,* whereby the first meaning would be "arrow" and the second "ray." We can see, therefore, that the theory of the different interpretative methods does not simply replace the theory of manifold textual meaning; it negates the latter in a determinate way, since it is linked with the anti-Scholastic tendency, already found in the Reformation, of insisting on the unity of meaning.

The same position is reflected in the postulate of the unity of the word, which Schleiermacher presents in the *Compendium* as follows:

> The essential task, even for the dictionaries, which exist expressly for the interpreter, is to find the true and *perfect unity of the word (vollkommene Einheit des Wortes).* To be sure, the particular occurrence of a word in a given passage involves an infinitely undetermined diversity, and from the unity to that diversity there exists no other transition than a determinate multiplicity in which the diversity is emcompassed, and as such it must necessarily dissolve into contradictions. However, in the particular occurrence the word is not isolated: it does not reveal itself immediately in its determinateness, but rather is revealed through its surroundings, and all we have to do is to relate the original unity of the word to these surroundings in order to find the right meaning each time. The perfect unity of the word, however, would be its explanation, and this is just as little given as the perfect explanation of objects. It is not given in the dead languages, because we have not yet examined their entire development, nor in the living languages, because their development is still continuing.[45]

It may have seemed so far as if Schleiermacher was a structuralist *avant la lettre,* but here we are reminded of the philosophical premises of his conception of language: they are those of German idealism. Nothing contradicts the methodological principles of modern linguistics more fully than the postulate that a word possesses a unity which is not given as such

but which simply represents the configuration of the word's various semantic nuances—a unity, in short, which is an "idea" in Benjamin's sense
of the word.[46] Even the way Schleiermacher establishes this thesis goes
against the rules utilized by structuralist linguistics. The fact that the living
languages are still evolving does not mean that an investigation of them
must also take into account their potential for further development and
that consequently every question must be left without a definitive answer.
What linguistics studies is not language as it may develop in the future,
and which lies potentially in today's language, but rather the current
linguistic system, a synchronic cut that entirely excludes the temporal
dimension. Although in the sentence just quoted this dimension appears
in the guise of the future, in the notion of the original unity of the word
it appears in the guise of the past. The etymology of a word can, it is true,
explain, and thus abolish, its diversity of meaning. But the decisive thing
for a synchronic linguistics is the fact that several *signifiés* can correspond
to a single *signifiant,* rather than the possibility of eliminating this diver-
gence by means of an historical examination; for such a reduction would
in fact be purely theoretical, since the multiplicity of meaning persists in
the speaker's linguistic consciousness.

Along with the antithesis "immediate context—parallel series,"[47] which
corresponds to the opposition syntagma—paradigm, Schleiermacher discusses two others which likewise serve to establish fundamental divisions
within his theory of the grammatical interpretation. These are the "formal—material" and the "qualitative—quantitative" oppositions. The former
may also be termed the "syntactic—semantic" opposition. When the grammatical interpretation examines the formal elements, it concentrates on
the connections between the elements of a sentence. When it examines the
material elements, it is concerned with the meaning of the individual
elements considered in isolation. In this regard, Schleiermacher repeated-
ly comes up against the interdependence of the two aspects. The analysis
of the formal elements also touches on questions that pertain to the realm
of the third opposition, the "qualitative—quantitative." The interrela-
tionships found in this area are illustrated in the following example. Among
the formal elements, Schleiermacher distinguishes between those which
link complete sentences and those which link the elements of a single
sentence. In the terminology of traditional grammar, this distinction corresponds to the difference between conjunctions and prepositions. (This
does not mean, of course, that the individual elements of a sentence can
be joined only by prepositions; certain suffixes, for example, such as those
of the genitive, can perform the same function.) Among the elements
serving to link whole sentences, Schleiermacher makes a further distinction between the organic and the mechanical, or, as he himself defines

them, those which produce "inner fusion" and those which produce "external coordination."[48] Examples of organic connection would be "although" and "since"; an example of mechanical connection would be "and." Yet, as Schleiermacher also observes—and this is where the question becomes pertinent for hermeneutics—, the opposition between inner fusion and external coordination is not constant: the one often seems to become transformed into the other. A causal connection sometimes serves merely to indicate coordination, while the coordinate conjunction "and," in turn, can also produce an organic connection, for example, when it expresses a result. This is only possible, however, because, in the one case, the conjunction "has lost its specific content,"[49] while, in the other, it has become "intensified."[50]

This variability points to possibilities of language that fall within the realm of quantitative understanding. Whereas qualitative understanding deals with the difference in the meanings of words and in the connections between words or sentences, quantitative understanding is concerned with intensity. The two extremes in this respect are, on the one hand, "emphasis," or a maximum of meaning, and, on the other, "abundance" (i.e., what today is termed "redundance"), or a minimum of meaning.[51] If a conjunction like "and," which otherwise produces merely a mechanical and additive connection, yields an organic one, then the result is emphasis. And if a causal conjunction has only an additive function, then it becomes "meaningless" (*nichtssagend*) and the result is abundance. Since, however, the transformation of a mechanical into an organic conjunction is realized through its emphatic employment, the qualitative difference becomes quantitative. The hermeneutical importance of these considerations will be evident to anyone who, in interpreting an older text, has puzzled over the question of whether the conjunction "as" is to be conceived temporally (or, in Schleiermacher's terminology, "mechanically") or causally (i.e., "organically"): the temporal "as" merely indicates a mechanical union, since the temporal connection is itself external to the events; whereas the causal "as" explains one event as the cause of another.

The notion of the "psychological interpretation" and the history of Schleiermacher's influence—which was strongly marked by this notion and by the related notions of "empathy" and "lived experience" (*Erlebnis*)—might give a false idea of what Schleiermacher himself meant by these concepts, especially in his early writings. To be sure, in the technical or psychological interpretation attention is directed to the man and his individuality, while in the grammatical interpretation it is directed to the language and its individual modifications. But even later, in the second Academy Address, the expression "original psychic process of the production and linking of thoughts and images,"[52] which indicates the subject matter of the psychological interpretation, implies an objective aspect, that of language as the medium of this production and linking. This view is expressed even more clearly in the earlier sketches, as well as in the notion of the technical interpretation, whose principal concept, that of style, bears directly on the treatment of language. The element that is preserved in the transition from the technical to the psychological interpretation—a transition which, strictly speaking, is really a shift in emphasis, since, even later, Schleiermacher continues to use the notion of the technical interpretation—is the conception of speech as a fact about the thinking subject. But now this fact is related to the totality of the man in question and to his life, rather than to the totality of language, as in the grammatical interpretation. The change in emphasis, however, concerns the examination of the subjectivity of this individual character. In the technical interpretation, the accent lies on the technique, on individual style as a particular modification of language and a particular manner of composition; in the psychological interpretation, it lies on the totality of the individual's existence. The opposition between the two approaches, which, as Schleiermacher himself stresses, is only relative, receives a more precise formulation in the notes he wrote at the end of his life. There he states that the psychological aspect is "more the emergence of ideas from out of the totality of the *Lebensmoment*";[53] and the technical aspect is "more the reduction to a determinate thought or to a will toward representation (*Darstellenwollen*), out of which a series develops."[54]

In the *Compendium,* Schleiermacher identifies the task of the technical interpretation as the complete understanding of style, but he does not restrict the concept of style to the treatment of language: "Idea and language everywhere merge, and the particular manner of grasping the object spills over into the arrangement of the parts and thus into the treatment of language."[55] Schleiermacher anticipates many of the ideas elaborated more than a hundred years later in Russian formalism, in New Criticism, and in the stylistic criticism of the Zurich School. His approach, in fact, surpasses the stylistic criticism taught in the 1940s and 1950s, inasmuch as he possessed a sense of the historicity of phenomena, an awareness that modern stylistic criticism developed only very late. Moreover, Schleiermacher did not consider the historical aspect as simply one more element to be considered *alongside* the psychological or technical aspect. He is fully aware that his aim of grasping the individual character in a speech or a literary work presupposes historical interpretation—and this is true for two reasons. First, the significance of the individual aspect is not constant throughout the history of literature. On this point Schleiermacher, adopting an insight of the writers of the Storm and Stress and early romanticism, contrasts classical objectivity with the subjectivity of the romantic period. Secondly, it is completely impossible to discern the individual element in the production of a literary work without knowing the history of the genre to which it belongs:

> Before undertaking the technical interpretation, one must know the manner in which the subject matter and the language were given to the author. . . . With regard to the first point, one must also take into account the previous state of the particular genre to which the work belongs. . . . Consequently, there can be no exact apprehension of this kind without a knowledge of the related contemporary literature and of what was given to the author as an earlier stylistic model. There is no substitute for this kind of overall study when it comes to this aspect of the interpretation.[56]

In his first Academy Address, Schleiermacher distinguishes, probably in an overly speculative way, two periods: one during which the literary forms gradually developed and another during which they were dominant. He somewhat lessens the rashness of this scheme, however, by remarking that the respective characteristics of these periods "later reappear simultaneously, although only in a subordinate way."[57] The decisive point, however, is this: Schleiermacher sees that, inasmuch as the mold in which an author works is given to him in advance, it is necessary to know that mold in order to understand the poet's creative activity.

> For hand in hand with the initial sketch of a particular work there also develops within the latter the governing force constituted by the already existing form, (and this form) modifies . . . in detail not only the expression but also the invention. In the practice of interpretation, therefore, it is necessary to see how the river of thinking and poetic creation rebounded against the walls of its bed and was turned in a direction other than the one it would have taken had it been unconstrained; otherwise, one can not hope to correctly understand the inner movement (*innere Hergang*) of the composition, let alone assign to the writer himself his proper place in relation to the language and its forms.[58]

If we recall the conception still dominant at the end of the eighteenth century, according to which poetic form and genres, as well as language itself, were merely vehicles for the author's subject matter and intention, we will not underestimate the contemporary relevance of these insights. Thanks to them, Schleiermacher's theory joins the company of modern poetics, as can be seen from reading Valéry, for example.

In the course of elaborating his hermeneutical ideas, Schleiermacher changed his view of the relationship between the grammatical and technical interpretations. In the first Academy Address, after the previously quoted lines on the affinity between interpreter and author, he remarks:

One is tempted to divide the entire practice of interpretation in the following way: one school of interpreters, more concerned with language and history than with people, goes through all the writers in a given language at a rather even pace, even though one may be outstanding in a certain area and another in a different area. The other school, more concerned with observing people, sees language as a mere medium through which people express themselves; and in history it sees only the modes in which people exist, restricting itself to those writers who most readily reveal themselves to it.[59]

This picture can still serve as an apt description of the current situation in literary theory, although even a critic who endorsed this methodological pluralism would have to admit that it does not provide a sufficient answer to problems concerning the relationship of the two interpretative methods. In fact, according to Schleiermacher's original conception, this relationship is not one of reciprocity: the two methods do not divide their labor between them. Instead, Schleiermacher boldly proposes the following thesis: "In this work, the perfect solution may be said to be found when each aspect [i.e., the grammatical and the technical] is treated in such a way that the treatment of the other brings about no change in the result obtained and that once [one of the aspects] is treated, it entirely replaces the other."[60]

In order to discover the motivation behind this conception, it is necessary to call to mind the position that Schleiermacher and the hermeneutics of his age adopted in their polemic against the theory of manifold textual meaning. Since Schleiermacher based his hermeneutics on the concept of understanding rather than on that of textual meaning, he was able to distinguish several types of interpretative methods without having to presuppose a diversity of meaning in the interpreted object itself. But, here too, Schleiermacher was not content simply to postulate an ideal relationship between the two methods. On the contrary, he recognized that their adequacy is determined by historical factors as well as by the genre of the work to be interpreted. Thus he links the grammatical interpretation with classicism, on the one hand, and with the most objective literary genre, that is, the epic, on the other. Likewise, he links the psychological interpretation with originality, that is to say, with romanticism as well as with the most subjective of the genres, the epistle and the lyric.

Schleiermacher, viewing understanding as the inversion of speech,[61] defined hermeneutics as "inverted grammar" and "inverted composition."[62] If he occasionally burst the limits of the linguistics and poetics of his age, boldly anticipating certain twentieth-century views, this was due to his conception of hermeneutics as an inversion of grammar and poetics.

His grasp of this reversal took Schleiermacher beyond the rigid system of rules that dominated these two disciplines, and also beyond their hypostatization of the object to be studied; it led him to an analysis of the preconditions of the facts as well as of their dialectical interdependence. It is by adopting such an approach that one can go beyond positivism. Hermeneutics, understood in this way, is an instrument of critique.

Chapter 7
Tableau and Coup de Théâtre: On the Social Psychology of Diderot's Bourgeois Tragedy

Qu'est-ce que la vertu?
C'est, sous quelque face
qu'on la considère, un
sacrifice de soi-même.

Diderot, *Eloge de Richardson*

"The bourgeois drama is the first which developed out of a conscious class conflict. It is the first which aimed at giving expression to the ways of feeling and thinking of a class struggling for freedom and power, and at showing its relationship to the other classes. It follows, therefore, that in general, both classes must appear in the drama, the class which is struggling as well as the one against which the struggle takes place."[1] This view was advanced by Georg Lukács in 1914, in an essay entitled "On the Sociology of Modern Drama." Forty years later, Arnold Hauser wrote in his *Social History of Art and Literature* that bourgeois drama is the first which makes social conflict "its explicit subject matter and which openly places itself in the service of the class struggle."[2] These observations are contradicted in an unsettling manner by the works which introduced the new genre in England, France, and Germany in the eighteenth century: Lillo's *London Merchant* (1731), Lessing's *Miss Sara Sampson* (1755), and Diderot's *Le Fils naturel* (1757) and *Le Père de famille* (1758). None of these plays depicts the conflict between the middle class and the nobility. Lessing's and Diderot's heroes, Sir William Sampson and M. d'Orbesson, belong to the aristocracy, not the bourgeoisie. To be sure, there are plays which conform much more closely to the descriptions given by Lukács

Written in 1968 and published in a French version under the title "Tableau et coup de théâtre: Pour une sociologie de la tragédie domestique et bourgeoise chez Diderot et Lessing," trans. Chantal Creusot, in *Poétique* 9 (1972): 1-14. The original German version appeared in *Lektueren und Lektionen* (Frankfurt am Main, 1973), pp. 13-43.

and Hauser, for example, Lessing's *Emilia Galotti* and Lenz's *Hofmeister;* however, as both of these were written in the 1770s, they can hardly reflect the conditions under which the genre first emerged. And an older bourgeois tragedy, like Martini's *Rhynsolt und Sapphira* (1755), which does borrow its material from an actual historical conflict between middle class and nobility, had no influence. What then is bourgeois about early bourgeois drama, the models for which were created by Lillo and Diderot? To what extent were the conditions under which it arose determined by the social and political situation of the rising bourgeoisie? These are the questions that will be addressed in the following remarks concerning Diderot's theory and practice of *tragédie domestique et bourgeoise.*[3] The discussion will also shed some light on Lillo's drama.

Diderot's theory of bourgeois drama rejects the convention, observed since late antiquity, that tragic heroes must literally be heroes, or princes, or kings (*heroes duces reges,* in the words of Diomedes). The impetus for this break with tradition can be inferred from a passage in the *Entretiens sur le Fils naturel* in which Diderot comments on a scene he admires in Racine's *Iphigénie* (V. iv): "If the mother of Iphigenia behaved for one moment as the Queen of Argos and wife of the Greek commanding general, she would seem to me the least worthy of creatures. True dignity, that which strikes me, which astounds me, is the picture (*tableau*) of maternal love in all its truth (*vérité*)."[4] For Diderot, tragedy owes its dignity and sublime character not to the fact that its heroes are kings and queens, but to the truthful depiction of the feelings which motivate them. *Tableau* and *vérité* are key words in Diderot's aesthetics to which we shall return. First we should consider that which shows Clytemnestra to be a mother instead of a queen and that which, more generally, underlines the criterion of *vérité* and determines the form that the *tableau* assumes: her love for her daughter—in short, her feelings. Later in the *Entretiens,* in a conversation between the author and his alter ego Dorval, who is also the son and main character of the *Le Fils naturel,* a second example is given, this time drawn not from tragic poetry but from the fictive reality of the *Entretiens.* Dorval tells the story of a peasant woman who sends her husband to her family in a neighboring village, where he is killed by one of her brothers. The next day Dorval goes to the house in which the deed was committed, and this is what he reports, repeating the same word used in the passage on Clytemnestra:

There I saw a picture (*tableau*) and heard a speech that I have never forgotten. The dead man lay stretched out on a bed. His naked legs hung down from the bed. His wife lay on the ground, her hair disheveled. She held on to her husband's feet; and bursting into tears and making a gesture which brought tears to the eyes of everyone present she said: "Alas! When I sent you here, I did not think that these feet would bring you to your death." Do you think that a woman of another rank could have been more moving (*pathétique*)? No. The same circumstances (*situation*) would have inspired her to make the same speech. Her soul would have been governed entirely by the moment. Thus what the artist must find is what anyone would say in a similar case; what no one would hear without immediately recognizing it in himself.

Deep concerns (*intérêts*), great passions. These are the source of all great speeches, of all true speeches.[5]

Clytemnestra and the nameless peasant woman serve as models for the heroes of Diderot's new drama. Clytemnestra receives this role because she forgets that she is a queen and gives utterance only to the mother in her, only to her private suffering, which as such is universal. The peasant woman receives it because her suffering helps her to a truthfulness of expression that could not be surpassed even by much more exalted figures. The choice in both cases is motivated by the notion of a universal human nature, a notion which constituted a decisive element in the revolutionary bourgeois ideology of the eighteenth century. (It appears for example in the theory of natural law.) At the same time, however, Diderot, like Rousseau, worshiped at the shrine of untamed nature. Accordingly, the two ideal heroes of bourgeois drama cited by Diderot, the mother and the wife, belong not to the middle class, not to the city, but to nature—whether it be that of the archaic period of Greek mythology or that of contemporary rural life.

This contradictory view of nature left its mark on the relationship between Diderot's dramatic theory and his actual dramatic practice. While *vérité* is guaranteed in the former by great passions, the source of "true speech," in the latter it is assured by the realistic representation of the author's own social surroundings. The archaic state of nature is the perspective in which Diderot's anticlassical dramaturgy places even the heroes of classical tragedy, for example, Philoctetes writhing in pain and Clytemnestra hysterical with fear for her daughter. This landscape stands in bold contrast to the *salon,* the setting in which Diderot's heroes, the *Fils naturel* and the *Père de famille,* move. Yet they are depicted according to the same principles which inform Diderot's understanding of the scenes from Racine and Sophocles, above all the principle of the *tableau.* Before the curtain falls on *Le Père de famille,* on a scene which could not be more conventional—the reconciliation of each character with all the others and the prospect of a double wedding—the paterfamilias gives this final speech (the *tableau* character of the scene having been meanwhile insured by the stage directions: "He brings together his four children and says . . ."): "A beautiful woman and an honest man are the two most moving creatures in nature. Offer this spectacle to the world twice on the same day."[6] The reconciliation of the lovers at the end is a traditional comic ending which had become virtually a convention. But it receives a new meaning here, in that it is employed in the service of sentimentality. The characters, moved to tears, observe one another and themselves and offer themselves to the gaze of the spectators. It is as though time sought to stand still in this scene, as in a picture. Walter Benjamin once alluded to the affinity between emotion and the *tableau,* when he wrote that sentimentality "is the flagging wing of feeling, which settles down just anywhere because it can go on no further."[7]

The action of *Le Père de famille* concludes with a *tableau* in which the characters, finally reconciled, present themselves to a sentimental public stirred to admiration. It also begins with a *tableau,* that of a family, all of whose members are assembled one night except for the son. Yet the conventionality of the final scene may be contrasted with the novelty of the first five scenes of the introductory *tableau,* which are dominated by the father's anxiety about his son. What is depicted—in pantomime, dialogue, and monologue—is an emotional state. No action occurs, nor does the exposition serve to prepare for any. The first five scenes attempt, like a psychograph, to portray the emotions troubling the soul of the *Pére de famille,* while at the same time painting a portrait of his family. Whereas the conclusion of the play is an apotheosis of a family which has regenerated itself and is once more living in harmony, the opening shows an injured family in a state of disorder and disintegration. The reason for all this is the son's absence (if one disregards both the mother's death, which occurred long before the events recounted, and the disturbing presence of the brother-in-law). The theme was quite new as a subject for a play. To be sure, both the tragedies and the comedies of the sixteenth and seventeenth centuries include scenes in which the father inquires about his son's absence. But in the tragedy the king asks about the prince, not because he needs his company, not because the family is not *whole* without him, but because he suspects that the prince is aiming at his crown and has joined in league with his enemies. And in the comedy, where the father is a bourgeois, the stylistic conventions of the genre prevent the audience from sympathizing with him: his inquiries about his son show that he is well cast in the role of the tyrannical pedant and fully merits the ridicule he receives. Similarly, they show that the son, too, is well suited to the role of the *jeune premier,* who seeks out amorous adventures instead of staying at home.

With Diderot, however, all of this changes. Just as the eighteenth century's sentimental interpretation of Molière is sympathetic to the comic figures, in whom it discovers a hidden tragic dimension (one thinks of Rousseau's reading of *Misanthrope,* a reading which might be said to go against the grain), the sentimental drama of the period abolishes the distance at which the burgher had previously been held by the effect of the comic element. The family is no longer seen from the outside and viewed according to the standards of the *homme de qualité;* it now makes up the entire reality of the drama. This triumph of bourgeois norms, which led to the replacement of Molière's type of comedy with serious comedy, reached its high point in those instances, as in *Le Père de famille,* where the "bourgeois" family head is actually an aristocrat. If Molière's *Bourgeois gentilhomme* makes himself ridiculous, Diderot's "Gentilhomme bourgeois" is all the more certain of eliciting tears from the audience inasmuch as in him it sees its own middle-class character (literally) ennobled.

The introductory *tableau* of Diderot's *Le Père de famille* bears witness to a social transformation. This consists less in the rise of a new social stratum than in a change in the organization of society. The life led by the lower ranks of the nobility whom Diderot brings to the stage is a bourgeois life. It illustrates the principle which best characterizes the sociohistorical basis of *tragédie domestique* or "domestic drama"—that of the patriarchal nuclear family. The latter, which "arose out of transformations in family structure developing over centuries in conjunction with the capitalist revolution, consolidated its position as the dominant type among the middle classes" during this period, as Jürgen Habermas reminds us in *Strukturwandel der Öffentlichkeit.*[8] Habermas also describes the opposite pole, the urban nobility, which continues to keep open house and to shun the inwardness of bourgeois family life:

> The family succession, which at the same time is the succession
> of inherited privileges, is sufficiently guaranteed by the name
> alone. The marriage partners need not even share a common
> household: often enough they live in their own *hôtels* and at times
> meet each other more frequently in the extrafamilial sphere of the
> *salon* than within the family circle. The institution of the
> *maîtresse* is symptomatic of the fact that the fluctuating and yet
> highly conventionalized relationships of "social life" seldom allow
> a private sphere in the middle-class sense. Intimacy, when it does
> exist, is merely coquettish and not at all like the enduring intimacy of the new family life. The latter contrasts, in turn, with older
> forms of extended-family community, which were still maintained
> by "the people" far beyond the eighteenth century, especially in

the countryside. These forms are also pre-bourgeois in the sense that they do not observe the distinction between "public" and "private."[9]

Drawing on Trevelyan's study of the cultural and social history of England, Habermas illustrates the increasingly private character of life through its architectural consequences for the houses of the English landed gentry. "The high hall, covered with ceiling beams . . . fell out of fashion. The dining room and the living room were now built only one story high, while the various purposes that the old hall had to serve were shared among a number of rooms of ordinary size."[10] This expansion of the realm of privacy could not be more evident than it is in *Le Père de famille*. The family in question is, to be sure, a noble family, and the play is set in Paris, in the *salle de compagnie,* a *salon* decorated with tapestries, mirrors, and paintings. But the first scenes and the single issue which dominates them, the son's absence and the father's anxiety about him, document, right from the start, the "enduring intimacy" evoked by Habermas in which this family is accustomed to live. Otherwise, the son's absence could hardly have become the theme of the play. This subject, moreover, places Diderot's work at the beginning of a tradition which has had a decisive influence on the history of modern drama: the tradition of the family drama, in which what for Diderot was the highest good, the only place where a man could be happy, degenerated into a hell; think of Hebbel's *Maria Magdalena,* Strindberg's *Father,* Chekhov's *Three Sisters,* and Albee's *Who's Afraid of Virginia Woolf?*

In Diderot's dramatic theory the counterpart of the *tableau* is the *coup de théâtre,* the "dramatic" turn of events. It is defined in the *Entretiens* as "an unforeseen event (*incident imprévu*) which finds expression in the action and which suddenly alters the circumstances of the characters."[11] Scorning the *coup de théâtre,* Diderot and Dorval advocate the *tableau,* the scenic picture, defined as "a disposition of the characters on stage which is so natural and so authentic (*vraie*) that it would please me if it were faithfully rendered on canvas by a painter."[12] A greater degree of truth is attributed to the *tableau* than to the *incident imprévu,* which is termed a *coup de théâtre* precisely because it is perceived as untrue, as merely theatrical, that is to say, created exclusively in response to the needs of the theater. But it must be borne in mind that the *tableau* is accorded this status not because it participates in the truth as such, in some suprahistorical realm, but because the unforeseen really was proscribed in the middle-class society of the eighteenth century. The rational conduct of life, which Max Weber analyzed as the fundamental trait of capitalism in his epoch-making essay on the *Protestant Ethic and the*

Spirit of Capitalism, aimed at the elimination of chance. *Fortuna* was the lodestar of that traditionalism which, according to Weber, capitalism supplanted. "As a rule [it was not] rash and unscrupulous economic adventurers such as are encountered in all periods of economic history, nor simply 'big financiers,' who effected this change, which, despite its seeming unimportance, was a decisive element in the penetration of economic life by this new spirit. Rather, [it was] men with strict middle-class views and 'principles,' who having grown up in the hard school of life were at once calculating and daring, but above all, *realistic* and *steady,* shrewd and fully devoted to their affairs."[13]

This type of social behavior—notable for its careful weighing of decisions, aversion to speculation, and a conception of work as a constant occupation—no doubt contributed to the proscription of the *coup de théâtre.* But probably even more important in this regard was the social setting of early capitalism, the family and the *intérieur.* The *coups de théâtre* belong to the world of the court and mirror the fickleness of princely moods and the inconstancy of alliances in a situation where everyone is hunting for power, favor, and happiness: *homo homini lupus.* A sudden reversal of fortune first becomes a *coup de théâtre* for a public which knows it only from the theater, that is to say, the middle-class public. The life of this audience is essentially life within the family. The feudal extended families, the houses and clans, do not confront court intrigues and power struggles as inviolable units, but rather—whether in history or in fiction—appear among both of the opposing parties. In contrast, the bourgeois nuclear family of the eighteenth century (unlike its successor in the nineteenth and twentieth centuries) is united in the certainty of how well disposed each of its members is towards the others, even at the price of his own happiness: *homo homini agnus.*

This cult of the family overshadows even the idea of the situation (*les conditions*), a basic concept of Diderot's dramatic theory which establishes the theory's topicality for Marxist aesthetics. In a central passage in the *Entretiens* Dorval expresses his opinion that it is not the characters but *les conditions* that should be shown on the stage.

> Up to the present, character has been the main concern in the
> theater, and the situation merely secondary; today it is necessary
> that the situation become the main concern and character second-
> ary. . . . It is the situation, its duties, its advantages, and its incon-
> veniences, which should be the basis of the work. . . . If the
> character is only slightly exaggerated, a spectator could say to
> himself, that is not I. But he cannot hide from himself the fact
> that the situation [*état*] being depicted before him is his own; he
> cannot fail to recognize his duties. He must necessarily apply
> what he hears to himself.[14]

What Diderot primarily has in mind when he calls for the drama to represent *les conditions* becomes clear in the subsequent dialogue. Furthermore, we are given an indication, in the questions that the author asks Dorval, that what ultimately interests him is not *les conditions* as a whole— not, for example, the full gamut of professions and their social context— but rather the particular condition which makes a family bourgeois. Dorval asserts that it is essential to show the duties, advantages, inconveniences, and dangers which are bound up with *les conditions*. So far, they have never served as the basis of a play's intrigue or of its moral, even though a paterfamilias has appeared in almost every drama. The author then immediately asks him: "Thus, you would like to see represented the man of letters, the philosopher, the merchant, the judge, the lawyer, the statesman (*le politique*), the citizen, the magistrate, the financier, the great nobleman, the governor (*intendant*)?"[15] And Dorval, the figure in the *Entretiens* who develops Diderot's new dramaturgy, replies: "Add to that all the family relations: father, husband, sister, brothers. The father of a family! What a subject, in a century like ours, when it seems that no one has the least idea of what a father of a family is!"[16] It is worth observing here that Dorval's interlocutor mentions various professions (merchant, judge, statesman, etc.) whose literary depiction would have illustrated in all its diversity the middle-class society which was developing in the seventeenth and eighteenth centuries, a task first accomplished by the novelists of the nineteenth century, Balzac, Dickens, and Zola. Dorval-Diderot does not amend this program explicitly but adds to the above-mentioned professions the family relationships (*les relations*), and this addition amounts to a change. Considering that neither of Diderot's own bourgeois dramas displays even the least attempt to characterize a profession, something Lillo had done for that of the merchant, it may be said that Diderot was less interested in the various social strata and occupations than in the family, or to be more specific, than in the conditions governing the lives of the members of the patriarchal nuclear family, which was establishing itself in his own time and even penetrating the ranks of the lower nobility. Diderot's *Le Père de famille* is a bourgeois drama, despite the aristocratic status of its main characters, because the form of social organization they exemplify and which the play is meant to glorify is of bourgeois origin.

The motivation for this sentimental realism regarding the family is most clearly evident in Diderot's *Eloge de Richardson* (1760), where he writes: "O Richardson, O Richardson, singular man, I will always read you! ... You will stay on the same shelf as Moses, Homer, Euripides, and Sophocles."[17]

Richardson does not cover the walls with blood; he does not carry
you off to distant lands; he does not expose you to the danger of
being devoured by savages; he does not shut himself up in secret
retreats of debauchery; he never loses himself in a fairy world.
His setting is the world we live in; the content of his story is true;
his characters are as real as they could possibly be; their personal-
ities are taken from the midst of society; his plots are in accord
with the customs of all civilized nations; the passions he depicts
are like those I myself feel; they are stirred by the same things,
and they have the same force I know them to possess; the disap-
pointments and sorrows of his characters are of the same kind as
those which constantly threaten me; he shows me the general
course of the things surrounding me.[18]

To understand Diderot's celebration of this realism and of its fidelity
to nature, they must be contrasted with the style which set the tone in the
arts in eighteenth-century France, that of a rococo classicism which either
imitated antiquity or sought to escape to distant fairy-tale lands. In this
context, Richardson's approach must have appeared to him that of a
genius come to show the way to freedom. The affinity Diderot felt between
himself and Richardson, however, was equally the product of the latter's
cult of virtue.

Richardson sows the seeds of virtue in the heart, where at first
they lie dormant; they lie still there until an occasion arises which
causes them to stir and grow. Then they develop; we feel ourselves driven toward virtue with such impetuosity that we do not
recognize ourselves. At the sight of injustice we experience a re-
vulsion that we cannot explain to ourselves. It is because we have
been with Richardson; it is because we have talked with a good
man at a time when the soul, unconcerned for a moment about
its own interests, was open to the truth.[19]

A more exact description could not be given of the effect Diderot hoped
to achieve with his two bourgeois dramas. Indeed, he did not disdain to
state this aim explicitly in the drama itself. In *Le Fils naturel* (IV, iii) it
is asserted that "there is no example more captivating than that of virtue,
not even the example of vice."[20] The play is subtitled, "Les épreuves de
la vertu," and Diderot's intent here is just as earnest as the Marquis de
Sade's was derisive when, a few decades later, he gave his novel *Justine*
the immeasurably more famous subtitle, "Les infortunes de la vertu." No
greater opposition could be imagined than that between Sade's fascination
with man's animalistic nature and Diderot's belief in his natural goodness.
To the question, whether human nature is good, Diderot replies, in his
essay *De la poésie dramatique:* "Yes, my friend, and very good. . . . It is

the miserable social conventions which corrupt man; it is these which must be condemned and not human nature. Indeed, what can move us as much as the story of a generous action?"[21] And he expresses the wish that all the imitative arts might work in concert with the laws in order to teach us to love virtue and hate vice.

This cult of virtue is one of the reasons which led Diderot to favor the *genre sérieux*. The latter is situated midway between the traditional, amusing comedy, which takes the ridiculous and vice as its objects, and tragedy, which depicts public catastrophes and the misfortunes of the great. In Diderot's systematic exposition of the drama, the genre is constituted by two new forms: the serious comedy, whose subject matter is virtue and duty, and the bourgeois tragedy, in which domestic misfortunes (*nos malheurs domestiques*) are portrayed. If Diderot prefers serious comedy to traditional comedy *à la* Molière, it is for the sake of virtue. "Honesty," he writes in the same treatise on the drama, "moves us in a more intimate and gentle way than that which excites our contempt and laughter."[22] Likewise, "men's duties are as rich a quarry for the dramatic poet as their ridiculous actions and their vices."[23] And in the utopian theater that Dorval sketches in the second *Entretien*—he speaks of the founding of a small state of happy people on the island of Lampedousa, "far from the mainland, in the middle of the waves"[24]—the citizens, on holidays, go to see tragedies which teach them to fear their passions and comedies which instruct them in their duties and instill in them a desire to fulfill these. Comedies which revolve around laughter and derision are not presented on the island of Lampedousa. Wickedness is no longer, as in traditional comedy, a convention that the author must respect if he wishes to elicit laughter from the audience by making his characters ridiculous. Instead, wickedness is treated as a theme; it is the sign of a hostile world storing up sorrows for the virtuous hero. In his essay *De la poésie dramatique* Diderot states that in comedy men must assume the role that the gods play in tragedy: human wickedness serves the same function in comedy as fate in tragedy.

The notion of virtue plays such a decisive role in Diderot's conception of the bourgeois drama (which also includes the serious comedy) that it is worthwhile to consider its social implications. The previously cited statement that men's duties are as rich a quarry for the dramatist as their vices and foolish traits is followed by the assertion that decent and serious plays would be successful everywhere, "but even more certainly in a corrupted nation (*peuple corrompu*) than elsewhere."[25] Since this remark appears in the context of the programmatic development of his theory of the *genre sérieux*, is may be assumed that by *peuple corrompu* Diderot means the French of his day. The reason for his attitude and, above all, the connection he sees between political-social reality and the necessity of a new genre dedicated to the cult of virtue can be surmised from the subsequent discussion in the essay. "It is by going to the theater that they will escape from the company of the wicked people surrounding them; it is there that they will find those with whom they would like to live; it is there that they will see the human race as it is, and that they will become reconciled with it."[26]

The display and encouragement of virtue in the theater thus enable a person to flee from his real surroundings, which are peopled by scoundrels. The world of beautiful—or, more accurately, of virtuous—appearance is not, however, merely one in which men would like to live. It is also, and this is Diderot's essential point, the true world, for it shows how man truly is, namely good. The spectator, fleeing from wicked reality into the theater, is thus able to reconcile himself with the world, since on the stage that reality is volatized into a mere appearance, with aesthetic appearance being asserted as the true reality. Diderot's theater seeks to promote such a reconciliation, and we shall see how it does this.

To explain why Diderot calls the French of his day a corrupt nation would require us to range far beyond the subject of the present essay. Accordingly, we shall simply take as our point of departure the remark that we go to the theater in order to escape from the company of the wicked who surround us. The personal tone of this statement entitles us to refer to Diderot's biography, an expedient which, admittedly, is always problematical. It may be useful to note here the following facts. In 1743, at the age of thirty, Diderot, who was then preoccupied with marriage plans, was confined to a cloister at his father's orders. In 1746, his first independent work, the *Pensées philosophiques,* was suppressed by the *Parlement* of Paris. In 1747, the *lieutenant de la Prévôte Générale des Monnaies,* Perrault, wrote as follows to a lieutenant of police named Berryer:

> I beg to inform you that I have been told that a certain Diderot, author of a work whose title is said to be *Philosophical Letters or Amusements,* which the *Parlement* of Paris ordered to be burned two years ago, as well as another work entitled *Philosophical Letters on the Immortality of the Soul [sic].* This wretched Diderot is again about to finish a work that he has been at now for a year, in the same vein as those that I have just had the honor of reporting to you. He is a very dangerous man, who speaks of the holy martyrs of our religion with contempt and who corrupts morals.[27]

In 1749 Diderot was arrested and imprisoned at Vincennes. In 1752, shortly after the appearance of the second volume of the *Encyclopédie,* the first two volumes were suppressed by order of the *Conseil du Roi.* In 1757, the year of the publication of *Le Fils naturel,* Diderot was attacked by Palissot in the *Petites lettres sur les grands philosophes* and accused of plagiarism. In the same year, his friend Rousseau broke with Diderot, having applied to himself an observation from *Le Fils naturel:* "Only the scoundrel lives alone" ("Il n'y a que le méchant qui soit seul").[28] In 1758, the *Encyclopédie* was sharply attacked by Peter Hayer in *La Religion vengée.* D'Alembert decided to end his collaboration on the *Encyclopédie,* and Voltaire requested the return of his as yet unprinted articles.

These facts color the circumstances under which Diderot wrote *Le Père de famille* and the essay on dramatic poetry. It is in these works that we find the remarks about the "corrupted nation" and the "society of the wicked." Almost all the above-mentioned problems from this fifteen-year period of Diderot's life involve a confluence of personal enmity and official acts of repression. While Diderot was committed to the cloister at his father's bidding, it was not without the intervention of the authorities. His later arrest and the suppression of the first two volumes of the *Encyclopédie* are likewise inconceivable without the initiatives of certain individuals in the form of attacks and denunciations. These actions, in turn, gave rise to personal attacks and led his friends d'Alembert and Voltaire to refuse him further collaboration. Diderot had sufficient grounds for believing in human baseness—in men's malice and cowardice—and in the interplay between these subjective traits and the objective sociopolitical conditions of the absolute monarchy of Louis XV. Nevertheless, he dedicated his bourgeois drama to the celebration of human goodness and virtue. And as the passage cited above from *De la poésie dramatique* shows, he was well aware that in this way he was not so much getting at the real state of affairs as offering a means of escaping from them. In his opinion, the spectator should encounter on the stage people with whom he would be happy to live. Now, just such a utopia had, Diderot thought, been realized, or could be realized, in the limited domain of the family. With a remarkable *ad hominem* twist in his discussion, he corroborated the reality of the world depicted in the family drama by reference to the circumstances of private life. After asserting that in the theater the spectator sees men with whom he would be happy to live, and thereby experiences what man is really like, he continues: "Decent people (*les gens de bien*) are rare; but they do exist. He who thinks otherwise accuses himself, and shows how unfortunate he is in his wife, in his family relations, in his friends, and in his acquaintances."[29]

The external conditions may vary widely, but within his four walls a man can be happy, and if he is not, he has only himself to blame. The middle-class nuclear family, unlike the feudal or peasant extended family, which recognized no separation between the private and public domains, is characterized essentially by possessing a private sphere secluded from the public area, and therefore also from the state and from politics in general. For Diderot, the possibilities offered by this new emphasis on privacy constituted a guarantee of happiness. In *Le Fils naturel* and *Le Père de famille,* stage reality is reduced to family intimacy. Moreover, while *les conditions* theoretically include the entire range of middle-class economic life as manifested in the various professions, in his actual dramatic practice Diderot confined himself to showing the relations of family members to one another. In this way he turned the *tragédie domestique et bourgeoise* into a depiction and glorification of the middle-class nuclear family, portraying it as a real utopia. Secluded within it, the citizen deprived of his rights can forget his powerlessness in the absolute monarchy and, appearances notwithstanding, reassure himself of the goodness of human nature.

This tells us nothing about Diderot's political opinions, but it does indicate something about the political and social implications of his bourgeois drama. In the articles he wrote for the *Encyclopédie* he undermined the theory of absolute monarchy, and shortly after the end of the American Revolution he celebrated the revolutionary change in these terms: "After centuries of universal oppression, may the revolution which has just taken place across the ocean, by offering to all the inhabitants of Europe an asylum from fanaticism and tyranny, instruct those who govern in the legitimate use of their powers!"[30] Yet Diderot also wrote that "the people are wicked (*méchant*), but above all they are stupid (*sot*),"[31] and that "the simple man is the stupidest and wickedest of men: to withdraw from the people and make oneself a better person, that is one and the same thing."[32] These same contradictions, which riddle Diderot's entire work and which cannot be minimized as mere idiosyncrasies, are also characteristic of his political attitude. Although it is impossible to define the latter in just a few words, one may nonetheless attempt, on the basis of the social content of Diderot's bourgeois drama and of the political implications of its theoretical foundation, to determine the function, in the France of Louis XV, of the new genre as well as of the sentimental notion of virtue upon which it is centered.

Such an investigation should, at the same time, highlight the difference between Diderot's drama and that of Lillo. The virtues that the merchant of London teaches—propriety, rectitude, punctuality, loyalty, and diligence: this canon of the ascetic Protestant virtues described by Max Weber—pertain as much to the public realm as to the private. By practicing these virtues a citizen becomes rich; by becoming rich he obtains power. In postrevolutionary England of the seventeenth and eighteenth centuries, virtue was a means of social advance. In Diderot's France, the France of the *ancien régime,* on the other hand, virtue was something private, with which the citizen could console himself as he sought refuge from the intrigues and wickedness of society within the security of his four walls, or in other words, as he fled from the world of the *coup de théâtre* into that of the *tableau.*

Excursus on Lessing

It is possible to examine this sociological interpretation of the sentimental cult of virtue in the light of Lessing's reflections on the drama. In 1760 this theoretician and playwright published German translations of *Le Fils naturel* and *Le Père de famille* as well as of the two related theoretical writings, thereby contributing to their broad success. A few months before the appearance of *Le Fils naturel,* in a letter of 29 November 1756 to Friedrich Nicolai, Lessing distinguished "three degrees of pity or compassion, tears being the middle degree" *(weinende Mitleid).*[33] The three degrees he named were those of emotion *(Rührung),* tears, and anguish *(Beklemmung).* Elaborating on this he wrote:

> Emotion is aroused when I clearly conceive neither the perfections *(Volkommenheiten)* nor the ill luck involved in the case, but rather have only an obscure notion of both; the sight of every beggar, for example, moves me in this way. He draws *tears* from me only when he makes me better acquainted with his good qualities as well as with his misfortunes, and, in fact, with both *simultaneously,* which is the real trick of eliciting tears. For it he first acquaints me with his good qualities and afterwards with his misfortunes, or first with the latter and afterwards with the former, the emotion indeed increases, but it does not reach the point of tears. Consider this example. I ask the beggar about his situation and he replies: I have been out of office for three years, and I have a wife and children; they are either sick or still too small to care for themselves; I myself rose up from a sickbed only a few days ago. — That is his misfortune! — But who are you, then? I ask further. — I am so and so, of whose skill in such and such matters you have perhaps heard; I served my office with the utmost fidelity; I could return to it any day, if I were willing to be the creature of a minister rather than an honest man, and so forth. Those are his perfections! In hearing such a story, however, no one can *weep.* If the poor wretch wishes to have my tears, he must, instead, join both parts of his story; he must say: I was dismissed from office because I was too honest, and thereby turned

the minister against me; I go hungry, and with me a sick, lovely wife; and with us our children, who otherwise are full of promise but are languishing in poverty; and we will certainly go hungry for a long time to come. Yet I would rather go hungry than be base; my wife and children, too, would rather go hungry and take their bread directly from God, that is, from the hand of a charitable man, than to know that their father and husband was corrupt, and so on. . . . For such a story I am always ready to shed tears. Misfortune and merit are here in equilibrium.[34]

It could be asked how far this story, particularly in its first variant, describing how for the sake of honesty a man gives up his post and becomes a beggar (the variant which according to Lessing is unsuited to tragedy), contained the seeds of Lessing's comedy *Minna von Barnhelm.* Here, however, we shall restrict our remarks to the political and social implications of Lessing's conception of compassion. The question at hand concerns a man who loses his office because he was too honest and thereby made himself hated by the minister. Lessing says that he is always ready to shed tears over the story of this man, whom he meets as a beggar, for here "misfortune and merit are in equilibrium."[35] He continues:

But let us increase the weight in one of the scales of the balance and watch what happens. Let us first throw something extra into the scale of goodness. The unfortunate man may go on to say: but when I and my sick wife have recovered, things shall be different. We are willing to live from the work of our hands; we are not ashamed of any kind. All the ways of earning one's bread are equally respectable for an honest man: chopping wood or sitting at the helm of state. His conscience is not concerned about how useful he is but about how useful he wants to be.—Now my tears stop, stifled by admiration. And I am scarcely still aware that this admiration arose from compassion.—Now let us perform the same experiment with the other scale. The honest beggar learns that it really is a miracle, something supernatural and rare to be fed by the charity of men, or directly by the hand of God. Everywhere he is turned away with insults; meanwhile his need grows, and with it his distress. Finally he becomes enraged; he kills his wife, his children, and himself.—Are you still crying?—Here pain stifles the tears, but not the pity, as admiration does. It is—[36]

At this point Lessing interrupts himself and concludes with the exclamation, "What a dreadful prattler I am!" Recalling the scale of compassion given earlier in the letter—emotion, tears, and anguish—one may assume that the case of the official who is dismissed because of his honesty and who, in his despair, slays his family and himself illustrates the third degree of compassion, that of anguish. Lessing seems to shrink back from this possibility. Yet it cannot be denied that the physical self-sacrifice of the helpless individual represents the logical outcome of this case, to which Lessing gives a central position in elaborating his conception of compassion. In his first example, a person sacrifices his livelihood to honesty and becomes a beggar, without then deciding to live from the work of his hands. Such a decision, we have seen, is certain to elicit admiration which, according to Lessing, is unsuited to tragedy. The theme of the helpless individual who turns himself into a physical sacrifice to the prevailing political and social conditions reappears, although treated in a different way than in Lessing, in the work that may be seen as the culmination of bourgeois tragedy in the eighteenth century: J. M. R. Lenz's *Hofmeister,* in which the tutor of the play's title castrates himself. In Lessing as in Lenz the powerless citizen directs his aggression against himself, not against those who deny him power. It does not occur to Lessing that, rather than his family and himself, the official who has become a beggar could, in his rage, have killed the minister who wished to compel him to commit a base act. This fact may reflect certain tendencies of bourgeois thinking, especially in a country whose citizens have preferred to slay revolutionaries rather than dictators.

The question now arises of whether it is permissible to infer the political and social premises of Lessing's dramaturgy from the example cited above of the honest beggar, who is presented as a kind of model for the hero of a bourgeois tragedy. For Lessing elaborates his position strictly in accord with an aesthetics of emotional effects. He does not indicate how a man ought to act, but rather how a man has to act if the spectator is to be able to shed tears of pity. Lessing refers, in passing as it were, to a social order in which he who scorns the wicked deed ordered by a minister becomes a beggar. This reference could be seen either as unintended, or else as a sign of Lessing's critique of the arbitrary power of absolute rulers—a critique of which another example can be found in *Emilia Galotti.* But such an approach would not go far enough. Instead of separating aesthetics and social criticism in Lessing's example, one should rather elucidate the political and social conditions of an aesthetics which declares *tears of pity* to be the intended effect of tragedy. It is thus necessary to read Lessing's remarks against the grain, turning his premise, "tears of pity . . . are the goal of tragedy," into a question;[37] and his question, "When does a person feel pity?" into a premise. This premise, however, is the given social order, in which a minister can solicit his subordinate to act basely and reduce him to beggary if the latter refuses in order to remain honest. In such circumstances there are other possible ways of behaving. Lessing knows this, and he goes through them. He who is chased from office can say to himself that "all ways of earning one's bread are equally respectable for an honest man: chopping wood or sitting at the helm of the state."[38] "His conscience [is] not concerned about how useful he is, but about how useful he wants to be."[39]

This possibility prefigures German idealism, which sided with the Revolution and which, instead of tearfully accepting the power of the prevailing social and political conditions, furnished the means of negating this power in the idea, thus anticipating its abolition. Out of this revolutionary consciousness grew Schiller's idealistic tragedy and German idealism's conception of tragedy. The latter, of course, recognized the role of sacrifice, but primarily in the interest of bringing about a new age. One thinks in this regard of Hegel's interpretation of the death of Socrates.[40] If Lessing rejects this possible attitude, it is only because seeing a person behaving in conformity with it would arouse an admiration for him which would stifle his tears: he would "scarcely still [be] aware that this admiration arose from compassion."[41] But if Lessing is compelled to reject this behavior exclusively out of fidelity to tragedy's purpose of calling forth tears of compassion, then it must be asked what compels him to select this purpose. In other words, this raises the question of the political and social premises of the theory of bourgeois tragedy.

The *Hamburgische Dramaturgie* should be read anew in the light of this question. With his commentaries on 104 plays, the theoretician Lessing contributed to the efforts of a group of Hamburg citizens who wished to create a national theater to counterbalance the court theaters, which favored mainly opera and ballet, and the theater of Mme. Neuber and of Gottsched in Leipzig, where French classicism was predominant, once again at the cost of a middle-class art. In many passages of the *Hamburgische Dramaturgie* Lessing elaborates his ideas on the emotional effects of tragedy, in particular on fear and pity and the relationship between them. Lessing translates *phobos* not as "terror" (*Schrecken*) but as "fear" (*Furcht*). And for him this fear is not "evoked by the misfortune awaiting another person, for this other person";[42] rather, it "arises from our similarity to the suffering person," and is "for ourselves."[43] In Lessing's well-known definition, fear is "pity brought into relation with ourselves" ("das auf uns selbst bezogene Mitleid").[44] Thus the postulate of the similarity between the characters of the drama and the spectators is integrated into the definition of the emotional effect of tragedy, and in this way it determines the nature of the tragedy itself. On the basis of his notion of pity or compassion, Lessing was able to reformulate the objection previously raised by Corneille, Lillo, and Diderot to the convention that tragic characters must come from the highest orders of society:

The names of princes and heroes can lend pomp and majesty to a play; but they can contribute nothing which makes it more moving. The misfortune of those whose circumstances are closest to our own must naturally touch us most deeply. And when we have compassion for kings, we have it for them as men, and not as kings. While their rank often makes their misfortunes more important, it does not thereby make them more interesting. Whole nations may be involved in them; our sympathy requires a single object, and a state is much too abstract a concept for our emotions.[45]

This much is certain: as long as the middle-class spectator wants to feel pity in the theater, the model hero of bourgeois tragedy will be the helpless victim of an absolute ruler's arbitrary power, his sphere of influence being limited strictly to his own family. Or, conversely, as long as the bourgeoisie does not revolt against absolutism and make a bid for power, it will live solely for its emotions, bewailing in the theater its own misery, which is inflicted upon it, as Diderot observed, as much by men as the misery of the heroes of Attic tragedy was inflicted upon them by fate. For the drama, the revolt of the middle class spells the end of sentimentality, the end of compassion and emotion as the purpose of tragedy. The state may be, as Lessing writes, much too abstract a concept for the emotions, but from this it is also possible to conclude that drama *ought not* to be concerned with emotions. This conclusion was drawn by the dramatists of the *Sturm und Drang* period, notably Lenz. They no longer directed their attention exclusively to the beggar, but also considered a social order in which an official who wishes to remain honest must become a beggar.

Chapter 8
Walter Benjamin's
"City Portraits"

For Rudolph Hirsch

1

It was perhaps no accident that Benjamin reflected upon ways of describing cities in 1929, the year that lies midway between his city portraits and his reminiscences of Berlin. For his remarks bear precisely on the difference between portraits of cities by foreigners and those by natives. Seeking to explain why the latter are so much less common than the former, Benjamin wrote: "The superficial cause [is that] the exotic, the picturesque has an effect only upon the foreigner. To portray a city, a native must have other, deeper motives—motives of one who travels into the past instead of into the distance. A native's book about his city will always be related to memoirs; the writer has not spent his childhood there in vain."[1] It is natural to look at Benjamin's city portraits in the light of this assertion. Their contours might thus become more sharply delineated and reveal whether in this observation, which appeared in a book review, Benjamin is not in essence writing about his own works. Is he not looking back critically at his descriptions of Naples (1925), Moscow (1927), and Marseilles (1929) and forward to his projected book *A Berlin Childhood around Nineteen Hundred?* In this perspective, two things become clear. While Benjamin's characterization exactly fits the book on Berlin that he intended to write at the time, his judgment regarding portraits of foreign cities hardly applies to those he had already produced. The motives un-

Written in 1962 and published in 1963 as an afterword to Walter Benjamin, *Städtebilder* (Frankfurt am Main, 1963).

derlying them scarcely differ from those that marked the book of reminiscences—in no way could the terms "superficial" and "profound" be
used to classify Benjamin's own descriptions. It appears, rather, that
in his portraits of foreign cities he wished to demonstrate the superfi-
ciality of a distinction made on the basis of the author's birthplace. It
is evident also that although his remark elucidates the city portraits, it requires elucidation in turn. This commentary is provided by his own city
portraits.

2

Anyone who describes his own city must travel into the past instead of
into the distance. One might ask why this journey is necessary at all, why
the native cannot remain in the present. *A Berlin Childhood around Nineteen Hundred* suggests in its very title that the answer is to be found in the
thesis of the kinship of such books with memoirs. At the same time, it
shows that the journey into the past, too, is a journey into the distance.
For without distance there can be no description, except that of mere
journalism. The portrait of one's own city is torn from this lower realm
by the adult's painful separation from the scenes of his childhood. The city
is still there, but that early period lies irrecoverably within it; this is a
paradox that sharpens not only our pain but also our perception. Gone,
therefore, is our familiarity with streets and houses, although they may
still surround us; we see them with a doubly alien view: with the view of
the child we no longer are, and with the view of the child to whom the city
was not yet familiar. Benjamin's Berlin book is proof of the constitutive
role of distance. In this respect, it is like Gottfried Keller's *Der grüne
Heinrich,* which was written not in Zurich but abroad; like *Buddenbrooks,*
which was written in Italy; and like the novel of Dublin, which could
be written only on the Continent because its author believed that absence is the highest degree of presence. So, too, Flaubert found himself
at the foot of an Egyptian pyramid when he conceived the name Bovary,
which was to stand as a monument to the petty narrowness of the French
provinces.

All the same, *A Berlin Childhood* differs in one crucial respect from all
other works whose mainspring is memory, and thus also from the book
to which it stands the closest and which Benjamin translated into German:
Proust's *Remembrance of Things Past (A la recherche du temps perdu).* For
Benjamin's work is devoted not so much to memory itself as to one of its
special gifts, which is captured in a sentence from his *One-Way Street:*
"Like ultraviolet rays, memory points out to everyone in the book of life
writing which, invisibly, glossed the text as prophecy." The adult's glance

does not yearn to merge with the child's glance. It is directed toward those moments when the future first announced itself to the child. In *A Berlin Childhood* Benjamin writes of "the shock with which a word startles us like a forgotten muff in our room. Just as the latter allows us to infer that some unknown woman has been there, so certain words or pauses allow us to detect the presence of that invisible stranger, the future, who left them behind with us." Everywhere in the city, in the streets and parks, the Berlin book is on the trail of such shocks, the memories of which are preserved by the child until the adult can decipher them. Thus the Tiergarten is not merely a playground but also the place where the child "first grasped, never to forget it, what only later came [to him] as a word: love." Unlike Proust, Benjamin does not flee the future. On the contrary, he deliberately seeks it out in the emotional turmoil of certain childhood experiences, where it went, as it were, into hibernation, whereas upon entering the present it passes into its grave. His "lost time" is not the past but the future. His backward glance is on the shattered utopia that can kindle "the spark of hope" only "in the past."[2] Benjamin, who in the years approaching the Third Reich could neither close his eyes to reality nor give up the promise of a time worthy of humanity, welded a paradoxical bond of hope and despair. It is only in this light that we can understand his plan for a "Prehistory of the Moderns"; and the same may be said of his anthology of letters *German Men,* on the origins of the German bourgeoisie, which—no less paradoxically—appeared as Noah's ark to the socialist driven out of Germany.[3]

3

The remark quoted at the beginning of this essay was made at the expense of foreign cities. How little Benjamin's city portraits display the qualitative difference he notes can be seen from the very first sentence of his early text on the Russian metropolis: "Quicker than Moscow itself one learns to see Berlin from Moscow." This new perspective on his own city is the most tangible of Benjamin's gains from his stay in Russia. Things foreign do not lure the visitor into self-forgetfulness; he does not become intoxicated by the picturesque and exotic but rather sees his own life, sees himself with an estranged vision. The effect of a journey into the distance is no different from that of a journey into the past, which is likewise a journey into the distance. Still, it is only because Benjamin goes still further that he can write on foreign cities. While he explores them, the same forces are at work that will later lead him to embark on the journey into his own childhood. From Benjamin's first impressions of Moscow, we learn that to the newcomer the city is a labyrinth; and the Berlin book begins with the sentence: "Not to find one's way about in a city is no great thing. But to get lost in a city, as one gets lost in the woods, requires practice." A foreign city fulfills this strange wish more easily than does one's own. But why this wish? Benjamin once described the labyrinth as the home of the tarrier and said it is the "right path for one who, in any event, always arrives early enough at his destination."[4] The labyrinth is thus in space what memory—which seeks hints of the future in the past— is in time. For the path whose milestones are the shocks of which he speaks ought confidently to choose hope as its destination; it will never reach it and so will never be proved false.

In *One-Way Street* Benjamin writes of one's first glimpse of a village or city in the countryside; this is "so incomparable and so irrecoverable" because "in it distance resonates in the closest bond with nearness. Habit has not yet done its work." The glance that the adult casts on his childhood is determined not least by the wish to escape from the ordinary. The journey, however, is not into something entirely different; it is into that time when the habitual was not yet habitual, into the experiences of the for-the-first-time. "Once we have begun to find our way about a place, that earliest image can never reappear." This earliest image, which is a promise, comes to the adult not only from early childhood but also from distant cities.

There is yet another factor that links the description of these cities with the Berlin book. The foreign surroundings do not just replace the distance of childhood for the adult; they turn him into a child again. Many passages in Benjamin's writings evince this feeling. Of San Gimignano, we read that the town "does not look as if one could ever succeed in approaching it. But once one does, one is drawn into its lap and is unable to concentrate on oneself because of the humming of crickets and the shouting of children." Here the children's real screaming illustrates the process intended by the metaphor, but it simultaneously interrupts this process as well. The conclusion of the section on Moscow's transport system, in contrast, is more straightforward. There he describes the low sledges that afford no downwards view but only "a tender and rapid skimming along stones and by people and horses," and he remarks that on them "one feels like a child gliding through the house on a stool." That this is more than a chance association is shown by an observation at the beginning of the description of Moscow: "The childhood stage starts right upon arrival. On the thick glazed ice of these streets walking must be learned anew." The intensity of the melancholy happiness accompanying these sentences, however, is not yet explicitly expressed. It is first revealed in the page of *A Berlin Childhood* that later provided a commentary on the passage. There the adult writes of the child's set of reading boxes:

The longing that it awakens in me proves how much a part of my childhood it was. What I am really seeking in it is the latter itself: my entire childhood, as it lay in the grasp with which the hand slid the letters along the ledge on which they were lined up. The hand can still dream of this grasp, but can never awake and execute the gesture. In like manner, many an individual may dream of how he learned to walk. But that is of no help to him. He can walk now, but never again learn to walk.

The repetition of the "for-the-first-time," the return to the earliest image: both of these experiences seemed to be lost forever, but they still exist in the shelter of foreign lands.

4

Benjamin's descriptions of foreign cities thus derive from impulses that are no less personal than those underlying *A Berlin Childhood.* This does not mean, however, that he was insensitive to foreign reality. Indeed, a foreign city can fulfill its secret task of turning the visitor into a child only if it appears as exotic and as picturesque as the child's own city once appeared to him. When abroad, Benjamin surrenders with astonishment and curiosity to all the impressions streaming in upon him, like a child standing wide-eyed in a labyrinth he cannot fully compass. The images he offers the reader could hardly be richer, more colorful, or more precise. And yet, *what* he experiences seems just as relevant to his "Search for Lost Time" as the way in which he experiences it. Unlike Proust's search, Benjamin's is borne along by historical and sociological impulses. He is seeking a way out of sclerotic late bourgeois society, enslaved to the principle of individualism, back to the lost origins of society itself. The protest that the young Hegel and Hölderlin raised against "positivity" in the name of life becomes audible again in Benjamin. This accounts for his participation in the German Youth Movement, as his essay on "Student Life" attests.[5]

From this point of view, the links between Benjamin's portraits of such different cities as Naples and Moscow become evident. In the South—in Marseilles, Naples, and San Gimignano—he encountered a collective life which had not yet become alienated from its origins (and which was the very opposite of the isolation he coldly describes at the beginning of the section on "The North Sea"). In the Soviet Union of 1929, on the other hand, he was able to observe a society in the process of formation. All the same, archaic and revolutionary seemed more closely related than the usual distinction between conservative and progressive would have it. And here he was not thinking solely of that idea of primitive communism which the Russia of the 1930s, already becoming a police state, betrayed with a positivity that mocked dialectical theory. The old in Naples and the new in Moscow are linked by more than just the fact that "To exist is a collective matter,"[6] as the following lines on Naples make clear:

> The architecture is as porous as [the] stone. Structures and activities merge in courtyards, arcades, and staircases. Enough room is left free everywhere to allow unforeseen constellations to form. The definitive, the sharply etched, is avoided. No situation seems to be conceived to stay forever just as it is; no shape asserts its "thus and no different." This is how architecture, that most concise and persuasive component of a community's rhythm, comes into being here.

This picture stands in bold contrast to the meticulousness characteristic of the North. Benjamin notes, for example, that the typical house in Bergen "still has strict boundaries." At the same time, the Naples portrait finds its analogy in the movement into which everything in Moscow has been plunged. Benjamin describes in detail the programmed "Remonte," which likewise did not tolerate anything definitive and which, as it were, stretched life out "on the laboratory table." "In this dominant passion there lies as much naive will to do good as boundless curiosity and playfulness. Little is more decisive in Russia today. The country is mobilized day and night. . . . " Private life, which had scarcely been allowed to develop in the South, has been "abolished" by bolshevism. There is a strange similarity in Benjamin's descriptions of the apartment houses in Moscow and in Naples. Once again, the children form the noisy background. They fill the streets and courtyards in countless hordes, as if they did not belong to individual families. The adult whose lonely youth was spent in a villa, as a "prisoner" of Berlin's old West End,[7] seems to cast a longing glance at the community these children enjoy. And it is not only the children who are childish here. The Russians, Benjamin says, are constantly playing, no matter what the situation. "If a scene for a film is being shot on the street, passersby forget where they are going and why, tag along for hours, and then arrive in a state of bewilderment at their offices." It is only the last word of the sentence that reminds the reader that it is adults, not children, who are being described. And since even the adults are like children, it becomes necessary to call upon Lenin's authority for that astonishing maxim, "time is money."

Benjamin returned from his trip "with at best mixed feelings," as Friedrich Podszus reports in his biographical sketch. Reading Benjamin's description of early Soviet Russia, we can sense his suspicion that this dynamism would turn into stasis and the freedom into terror. In particular, the display of images of Lenin seems to have intensified Benjamin's suspicion, and the last section of his essay is devoted to the cult that was growing up around them. "In corners and niches consecrated to Lenin, they appear as busts; in the larger clubs, as bronze statues or reliefs; in offices, as life-size half-length portraits; in kitchens, laundry rooms, and storerooms as small photographs." An even clearer indication of Benjamin's premonition of the threat to the living inherent in the new positivity of the dead image is his observation that babies are called "Oktjabr" ("October") "from the moment they are able to point to Lenin's picture." No less revealing is the metaphor in the final sentence describing the market on the Sucharewkaja: "Since the selling of icons is considered part of the stationery and picture business, [the] stalls with icons tend to be located near paper goods stands, so that everywhere they are flanked by pictures of Lenin, like a prisoner between two policemen."[8]

5

It is metaphor that makes Benjamin's city portraits what they are. Not only is it the source of their magic and, in a very precise sense, their status as poetic writing. The very purpose of these texts, to convey the experience of alienation and of being a foreigner, is first accomplished through the medium of language, which here is a language of images. The quest for lost time and for what takes its place is no less bound to language than the attempt to take possession of what one has already found. Name and image are the two poles of this field of force. In the labyrinth of the foreign city "every single step . . . is taken on named ground. And where one of these names happens to fall, fantasy constructs an entire quarter in next to no time. This will long defy subsequent reality, obstinately implanting itself therein, like brittle glass walls."[9] While one is waiting for reality, it is preceded by its name, which functions as its surrogate. The name, however, creates its own reality. The competition between the two always ends, to be sure, with the victory of objective reality, but this is very often a Pyrrhic victory: its name is disillusion. Many pages of Proust's novel are devoted to this same theme, which already appears in the romantic writers and which is revived by Benjamin.

The counterpart of this theme is the process by which reality becomes an image. "Finding words for what lies before one's eyes—how hard that can be! But when they do come they strike against reality with little hammers until they have knocked the image out of it, as out of a copper plate."[10] Thus begins Benjamin's description of San Gimignano, which, not without reason, is dedicated to the memory of the author of the *Lord Chandos Letter* (von Hofmannsthal) and written in the year of his death.

The potential field in which reality oscillates between name and image requires a separation; it requires the distance of time or of space. For the ordinary has long since absorbed its name and dispelled expectation; it will never again be transformed into an image. But whoever voyages into his past finds that reality and name constantly break apart again. It may be that the name has outlived the reality and now takes its place in memory as its phantom; it may be that in those "for-the-first-time" experiences the name was there before the reality was experienced; or that the experience was there before it received a name, so that it remained there without being understood, like the prophetic writing that invisibly glosses the text in the book of one's life. Whether he described the Berlin of his childhood or some foreign city, the consciousness of this separation rarely ever left Benjamin. It is difficult to say, though, if this was more a source of joy or of pain to him. In any case, it is only against this background that we can understand the following episode from his voyage on "The North Sea":

> In the evening, heart heavy as lead, full of anxiety, on the deck. For a long time I follow the play of the gulls. ... The sun has long since gone down, and in the East it is very dark. The ship travels southwards. Some brightness is left in the West. What now happened to the birds—or to myself?—that occurred by virtue of the spot that I, so domineeringly, so lonely, selected for myself in my melancholy in the middle of the quarterdeck. All of a sudden there were two flights of gulls, one to the East, one to the West, left and right, so entirely different that the name gull fell away from them.[11]

Melancholy sees only the dark side of everything. The tension between name and reality, which is the origin of poetry, is only experienced painfully, as the distance separating man from things. The experience that Benjamin reports, without reflecting upon it, breaks through this pain. The chiaroscuro of the sky tears reality asunder and abolishes the identity that made naming possible in the first place. The gulls' name falls away from them; they are now only themselves, but as such they are perhaps closer to man than if he possessed them by virtue of knowing their name.

6

These remarks do not yet adequately convey the meaning of this experience, which also brings to light the inverse of that which gives rise to metaphor in Proust as well as in Benjamin. Here the name falls away from the gulls because the sky divides them into groups, and the difference becomes greater than that which unites them, while in metaphor, two different things cease to be identical to themselves because they are superimposed through an analogy discovered by the writer. As Proust himself came to realize, metaphor aided him in his search for lost time. Like the experience with the madeleine, metaphor should lift man beyond temporality through the bond it creates between a moment in the present and a moment in the past. In Benjamin also, simile can assist memory when it seeks tokens of the future in the past. In such instances, the two members of the simile are related as a text that one actually experiences is related to its prophetic commentary, which is first deciphered by memory. We may take as an example the "Nibbling Child" of *One-Way Street,* who becomes the first-person narrator of *A Berlin Childhood;* "his hand," we read, slipped through "the crack of the barely opened cupboard like a lover through the night." Yet, in Benjamin metaphor is no more restricted to a single function than it is in Proust; on the contrary, it serves as a rule for the descriptive process itself. Benjamin seems to have shared Proust's view that the enumeration of objects in a description can never lead to truth and that truth first appears at the moment when the author takes two different objects and reveals their essence by linking them in a metaphor based on a common property.[12]

The only thing that seems foreign to Benjamin's intentions here is the mention of "essence"; for his frequent use of metaphor and simile in portraying foreign cities derives from other grounds. The language of images makes it possible to understand unfamiliar things without their ceasing to be unfamiliar. Simile brings distant things near while at the same time freezing them in an image protected from the ravaging force of habit. Metaphor helps Benjamin to paint his city portraits as miniatures, much like his preferred form, the fragment. Moreover, in their linking of nearness and distance, in their withdrawn existence, such miniatures resemble those favorite objects of Benjamin's: glass globes in which snow falls on a landscape. His figurative language evinces supreme artistic understanding. Benjamin was a master in the creation of twofold definitions by the use of images: "What is sentimentality if not the flagging wing of feeling, which settles down anywhere at all because it can go on no further, and what, then, its opposite, if not this tireless movement, which so wisely holds itself back [and] settles down on no experience or memory, but rather remains hovering, grazing one after the other."[13]

Benjamin is often dissatisfied with simple metaphors, and so he creates entire compositions with them, as in his description of Notre Dame de la Garde in Marseilles or in his evocation of the conflict between that city and its surrounding landscape. As each new image carries the comparison further, the danger grows that the bridge might not reach the other bank, and yet the link between the two banks becomes stronger with each new span. Sometimes, too, the image does not leave the language unaffected. Thus, Benjamin writes of Bergen; "Just as the inhabitants of remote mountain villages intermarry to the point of sickliness and death, so the staircases and corners of the houses have become intertwined."[14] The new images are what make the comparison evident, although they themselves become possible only as a result of the comparison. Sometimes Benjamin resorts to the metaphoric conditional tense, which in its suggestion of experiment betrays the whole playful awareness and fragility of the metaphor. For example: "If this sea is the Campagna, then Bergen lies in the Sabine Hills." Despite such artistry, Benjamin never uses figurative language without real commitment. Indeed, it is largely responsible for an effect aptly characterized by T. W. Adorno: "What Benjamin said and wrote sounds as if it derived from a secret. But its power comes from its obviousness."[15]

Neither the secret nor the obviousness would be possible if it were true, as Hugo Friedrich asserts, that "the fundamental vocation of metaphor lies not in recognizing existing similarities but rather in inventing nonexistent ones."[16] Metaphor's achievement lies beyond this alternative. It is not concerned, of course, with what is at hand, but neither is it interested in inventing similarities; it seeks, rather, to find them. Metaphor originates in the belief that the world is built up of correspondences that can and should be recognized. In his description of Weimar, Benjamin writes that "In the Goethe-Schiller Archives the staircases, drawing rooms, display cases and reading rooms are white. . . . The manuscripts are bedded down like patients in hospitals. And yet, the longer one exposes oneself to this harsh light, the more one believes that he discerns a reason, unconscious of itself, underlying such institutions."[17] The metaphorist's glance proves to be that of the theologian's. Benjamin is a student of the baroque emblematists, whom he treats in his work on *The Origins of Tragic Drama.* And what is true of them is equally true of himself: that which seems to be artistry and was once learned from books is nothing less than the exegesis of the Creation.

7

The city portraits are products of the years between 1925 and 1930; *A Berlin Childhood* was written after 1930. Anyone familiar with Benjamin's biography and works will grasp the significance of these dates. From the period before 1925, we may mention an essay he wrote at the age of twenty-two on Hölderlin, a work that would have marked a new epoch in the study of that poet had it become known at the time. (The essay was first published in 1955.) Then came the great study on "Goethe's *Elective Affinities*' " (1924) along with the major work on German baroque drama (1923-25), with which Benjamin vainly sought to qualify as a university lecturer at Frankfurt. It was only after Benjamin was obliged to give up the prospect of an academic career (his mind having been judged to be insufficiently academic) that he became a man of letters and a journalist. To earn a living, he began to write the articles for newspapers and journals that today contribute as much to his reputation as does his scholarly work. It is among these that we find the city portraits. Nothing earlier in his life had hinted at this activity, as becomes clear, for example, in reading a letter written in his student days in Bern (22 October 1917), in which he told Gershom Scholem of his plans for the future.[18] It would thus appear that it was the university, whose representatives rejected him, which was responsible for Benjamin's becoming the kind of writer it suspected him of being.

The fact that Benjamin wrote no more city portraits in the period after 1933 can likewise be explained by the date in question. At that time a story was circulating in the emigrant community about a Jew who planned to emigrate to Uruguay; when his friends in Paris seemed astonished that he wanted to go so far away, he retorted: "Far from where?" With the loss of one's homeland the notion of distance also disappears. If everything is foreign, then that tension between distance and nearness from which the city portraits draw their life cannot exist. The emigrant's travels are not the kind one looks back upon; his map has no focal point around which foreign lands assume a fixed configuration. After he had finished his book of reminiscences about Berlin, Benjamin did, it is true, devote the last ten years of his life to a work on Paris, the city in which he had long felt at home. This work, however, has nothing in common with the earlier city portraits. Benjamin had frequently written about Paris even while he was still living in Germany, but he had never tried to capture the city's traits in a miniature ("too near ," he remarked in a note reporting a dream about Paris).[19] The path he entered on in Paris in search of Paris was thus the same one that—in the remark quoted at the start of this essay—he urged upon whoever undertakes to write about his native city; a journey into the past. The projected book, a montage of historical texts presented as if the city were writing its own memoirs, was to be called *Paris: Capital of the Nineteenth Century.*

Chapter 9
Hope in the Past:
On Walter Benjamin

Walter Benjamin begins his reminiscences, *A Berlin Childhood around 1900*, with the following passage:

> Not to find one's way about in a city is of little interest. But to lose one's way in a city, as one loses one's way in a forest, requires practice. For this the street names must speak to one like the snapping of dry twigs, and the narrow streets of the city center must reflect the time of day as clearly as a mountain valley. I learned this art late in life: it fulfilled the dreams whose first traces were the labyrinths on the blotters on my exercise-books. No, not the first, for even before these there had been another which outlasted them. The way into this labyrinth, which did not lack its Ariadne, led over the Bendler Bridge, whose gentle arch was my first hillside. Not far from its foot lay the goal: Friedrich Wilhelm and Queen Luise. They towered up from their round pedestals among the flower beds as if spellbound by magic curves that a watercourse had inscribed before them in the sand. More than to the monarchs themselves, however, I headed for their pedestals, because what was happening upon them, though not clear to me, was nearer in space. That there was something special about this labyrinth I have since recognized in the wide, banal forecourt, which in no way revealed that here, only a few steps from the avenue for the droshkies and carriages, sleeps the strang-

Written in 1961 and published as "Hoffnung im Vergangenen: Über Walter Benjamin" in the *Neue Zuercher Zeitung* of 8 Oct. 1961.

est area of the park. I already had an inkling of this very early. Here or not far from here must have been the bed of that Ariadne in whose proximity I first grasped, never to forget it, what only later came to me as a word: love.[1]

A Berlin Childhood was written in the early 1930s. Benjamin published portions of it in newspapers, but the work did not appear as a whole until 1950, ten years after his death. One of the most beautiful examples of prose writing of our age, this book remained for a long time virtually unknown. Occupying less than seventy pages in the two-volume edition of Benjamin's *Schriften,* it is a series of miniature portraits conjuring up individual streets, people, objects, and interior scenes. These vignettes have titles like "Victory Column," "Halle Gate," "Loggias," "Departure and Return," and "Kaiserpanorama." Without doubt, he who undertakes to write about such things is, like Proust, whose translator Benjamin was, in search of time past, of "lost time." It is thus understandable that around the time he was writing *A Berlin Childhood* Benjamin could say to a friend that "he did not wish to read a word more of Proust than what he needed to translate at the moment, because otherwise he risked straying into an addictive dependency which would hinder his own production."[2] This remark suggests that there is more involved here than just the influence of Proust's novel on Benjamin; it hints at an elective affinity between the two authors. It is difficult otherwise to see how the reading of this foreign work could possibly have usurped the place of Benjamin's own. His statement thus has a significance beyond the history of the influence of *A la recherche du temps perdu.* Let us make the statement our starting point in attempting to convey something of the distinctive nature of Benjamin's work.

We should not, however, overlook the history of Proust's reception in Germany, which is closely linked with the names of the poet Rilke, the scholar Ernst Robert Curtius, and Walter Benjamin, a philosopher who was a poet and a scholar as well. These men were not simply among the first in Germany to come under Proust's influence; they also worked actively to extend it. Barely having finished reading the first volume of *A la recherche* in 1913, Rilke tried to persuade his publisher to acquire the German language rights for it, though without success.[3] Then, in 1925, Ernst Robert Curtius devoted a lengthy essay to Proust, and by his severe criticism of the first volume of the German edition, which had appeared in the meantime, he succeeded in having the work of translation placed in more competent hands.[4] The succeeding volumes were translated by Franz Hessel and Walter Benjamin.[5] In 1929, Benjamin also published the important study "Zum Bilde Prousts."[6] Shortly thereafter, however, translation and study of Proust were brought to a violent halt: manuscripts of the still unpublished portions of the translation were lost, and the understanding of Proust's work was buried along with them. In its place came this judgment, as delivered by Kurt Wais:

> A real explosion of the stable, firmly-rooted form of the novel ... was undertaken by two non-full Frenchmen, the half-Jew Marcel Proust and André Gide, who was brought up in the gloomiest Calvinism. ... In Proust's hands, personalities ... crumble into inconsistent individual traits. ... He who himself has not been moved cannot move others. The hundred figures remain phantoms, whose blood he silently sucks in his neurotic monologue *A la recherche du temps perdu* (which swelled from the three volumes originally planned to thirteen): Effeminate men and masculine women around whom he flutters with the hair-splitting chatter of his endlessly piled up similes and whom he analyzes with Talmudical ultra-intelligence. Indeed, the stale air of the darkened sickroom, for fifteen years the incubator of this evil-minded, dainty hair-splitter, whose sole concern revolves around the penetration of the strata of society that are closed to him; the inquisitive microscopy of the problems of puberty and of the morass of outrageously depraved sexual perversions, which Proust has in common with many of Europe's Jewish literary men ... , all this will probably keep away from this work any present-day reader who is not a neurologist.[7]

While the question of Proust's influence leads, on the one hand, into a thicket of ideological delusion which is rooted in all too real circumstances for it to merit oblivion (Benjamin himself died in flight from the Gestapo), it also leads, on the other hand, to the very core of the *A la recherche.* In the last volume, the hero decides to write the novel that the reader holds in his hands, allowing the book, as it were, to catch up with itself and, simultaneously, causing the anxiety of the beginning to join in an unforgettable manner with the triumph of the completion. It is at this very moment that a question is raised concerning the distinctive nature of the work that has already been written and yet that is now finally about to be written for the first time. The answer lies not least in something which is meant to be an unusual, indeed a unique, effect. At this point (after the famous cathedral simile), the author states:

> But to return to my own case, I thought more modestly of my book, and it would be inaccurate even to say that I thought of those who would read it as "my" readers. For it seemed to me that they would not be "my" readers but the readers of their own selves, my book being merely a sort of magnifying glass like those

which the optician at Combray used to offer his customers—it would be my book, but with its help I would furnish them with the means of reading what lay inside themselves.

Mais pour en revenir à moi-même, je pensais plus modestement à mon livre, et ce serait même inexact que de dire en pensant à ceux qui le liraient, à mes lecteurs. Car ils ne seraient pas, selon moi, mes lecteurs, mais les propres lecteurs d'eux-mêmes, mon livre n'étant qu'une sorte de ces verres grossissants comme ceux que tendait à un acheteur l'opticien de Combray; mon livre, grace auquel je leur fournirais le moyen de lire en eux-mêmes.[8]

Without knowing these lines, Rilke had shown very early that he was a "reader of himself" as Proust had imagined such a person. To be sure, the poet, who had finished the *Aufzeichnungen des Malte Laurids Brigge* a few years earlier, was a predestined reader of Proust. Yet his own work differs fundamentally from that of *A la recherche,* for in contrast to Proust's thesis of involuntary remembering *(la mémoire involontaire),* Rilke's writing represents a conscious and assiduous effort to "carry out" or "realize" *(leisten)* his childhood once again. Later Rilke was to judge his own effort abortive because the place of his own childhood was taken by that of another, the fictional hero Malte. It is possible that Rilke first became a reader of himself while reading Proust's initial volume. This may be inferred from a passage in a letter of 1914 recounting a childhood memory of a Bohemian health spa. The letter was addressed to Magda von Hattingberg, the friend to whom, shortly before, Rilke had enthusiastically sent his copy of *Du Côté de chez Swann.*[9]

Rilke here recalls Proust most vividly in the faithful way he reproduces the image of his memory. Nothing seems retouched, the faulty passages retain their imperfections, the lacunae are not skillfully filled. Thus the first name of the girl in question is not given. Nor are her facial features recorded, just something "thin, blond" floating through the memory. Even her gestures in the scene described have vanished from Rilke's memory; only the sound of laughter still rings in his ears. But this he must not pursue, for who can say that it is *her* laughter? Thus, even in the places where it is empty, the picture shows the particular name of its painter, who is not Rilke, but memory itself. And it shows, as well, memory's predilection for the aural, transmitting the family name on account of its charm and allowing the first name to slip away, preserving the laughter but not the person.

Proustian, too, in this picture, whose sketchiness would have been unthinkable in *Malte,* is its setting, the park, the promenade. Their significance in Proust's novel is well known. The park of Tansonville with its red hawthorne, where the young Marcel first glimpses Gilberte, and the gardens of the Champs-Elysées, in which he finds her once more: these, together with the boardwalk at Balbec, Albertine's kingdom, are the most important settings in *The Remembrance of Things Past*. (Rilke's memory was possibly awakened, precisely in Proust's sense, by his reading of the first scene at Tansonville.) Thus the beginning of the last volume, *Le Temps retrouvé,* recounts the occasion on which Marcel encounters once again the park of Tansonville and then, immediately before the hero of the novel solves the riddle of memory and time, that on which he once more encounters the gardens of the Champs-Elysées.

It is no accident that the book Benjamin wrote as a reader of himself, *A Berlin Childhood,* also begins with the description of a park, that of the Tiergarten zoo. However great the difference may seem between this collection of short prose pieces and Proust's three-thousand-page novel when viewed from the outside, Benjamin's book illustrates the fascination he expressed in the statement to his friend cited above. A sentence in his book points to the central experience of Proust's work: that almost everything childhood was can be withheld from a person for years, suddenly to be offered him anew as if by chance. "Like a mother who holds the new-born infant to her breast without waking it, life proceeds for a long time with the still tender memory of childhood" (p. 152). Also reminiscent of Proust is the description of the mother who, on evenings when guests are in the house, comes in to see her child only fleetingly to say good night; so, too, is that of the boy attentively listening to the noises which penetrate into his room from the courtyard below and thus from a foreign world. The studied elevation of the newly invented telephone to the level of a mythical object is anticipated in Proust as well. And the relationship to and influence of the earlier work can be demonstrated even in the use of metaphor. But little is gained by this approach, and it would not be easy to refute the objection that such similarities lie in the authors' common raw material: childhood, the fin de siècle epoch, and the attempt to bring them both into the present.

Yet, do Proust and Benjamin really share the same theme? Does their search for "lost time" arise from the same motive? Or is the common element merely an appearance that should be pointed out because it could obscure the fact that the intentions of the two works are not only not related but are in fact totally opposed? If the latter is the case, then Benjamin's statement that he feared falling into an "addictive dependency" on Proust which would impede his own work would perhaps take on a deeper significance, namely, that in his fascination with a work only apparently similar to his own, he risked becoming alienated from his innermost intention. Only a more precise comparison can provide an answer to this question.

The meaning of Proust's search for time past is explicitly stated at the end of his novel. The moment when its autobiographical hero, Marcel, recognizes this meaning is the high point of the work; for the point is simultaneously that toward which the book has been aiming and that from which it issues. This knowledge has two sources, one happy and one painful, both of which become evident very early in the book. The inexplicable feeling of happiness seizes the hero one evening when his mother offers him a madeleine dunked in tea, the taste of which brings back the whole world of his childhood, because as a child he had often eaten this pastry. The other feeling, the consternation, "the frightfully painful premonition," takes hold with his father's pronouncement that he "does not stand outside of time, but is subject to its laws." In the latter incident Marcel recognizes the connection between his two feelings of happiness and terror. That which underlies the feeling of happiness in the one case liberates him from the terror of the other:

> This cause I began to divine as I compared these diverse happy impressions, diverse yet with this in common, that I experienced them at the present moment and at the same time in the context of a distant moment, so that the past was made to encroach upon the present and I was made to doubt whether I was in the one or the other. The truth surely was that the being within me which had enjoyed these impressions had enjoyed them because they had in them something that was common to a day long past and to the present, because in some way they were extra-temporal, and this being made its appearance only when, through one of these identifications of the present with the past, it was likely to find itself in the one and only medium in which it could exist and enjoy the essence of things, that is to say: outside time.

> Cette cause, je la devinais en comparant ces diverses impressions bienheureuses et qui avaient entre elles ceci de commun que je les éprouvais à la fois dans le moment actuel et dans un moment éloigné, jusqu'à faire empiéter le passé sur le présent, à me faire hésiter à savoir dans lequel des deux je me trouvais; au vrai, l'être qui alors goûtait en moi cette impression la goûtait en ce qu'elle avait d'extra-temporel, un être qui n'apparaissait que quand, par une de ces identités entre le présent et le passé, il pouvait se trouver dans le seul milieu ou il pût vivre, jouir de l'essence des choses, c'est-à-dire en dehors du temps.[10]

Proust undertakes his search for "lost time," the past, so that through its rediscovery and in the coincidence of time past and present, he can escape from the sway of time itself. For Proust, the goal of the search for time past is the disappearance of time as such.

For Benjamin it is different. The intention behind the evocation of *A Berlin Childhood* can be readily perceived from a characteristic shared by many of the places, people, and events he selects as subjects of the individual vignettes. Recall, for example, the description of the zoological gardens, of the labyrinth in front of the pedestals of the royal statues. "Here or not far from here must have been the bed of that Ariadne in whose proximity I first grasped, never to forget it, what only later came to me as a word: love."

Another prose piece, called "The Larder," begins: "My hand slipped through the crack of the barely opened cupboard like a lover through the night. Once at home in the dark, it felt around for sugar or almonds, for sultanas or preserves. And as the lover, before he kisses her, embraces his girl, my sense of touch had a rendezvous with them before my mouth tasted their sweetness" (p. 44).

The section on the "Tiergarten" is recalled by another, with the title "Two Brass Bands," in which the author writes: "Never was music more inhuman and shameless than that played by the military band which set the pace for the people streaming in the 'zoo,' pushing between the refreshment stands along 'Gossip Row.' . . . That was the atmosphere in which for the time the boy's glance sought to catch the attention of a girl passing by, as he talked all the more eagerly to his friend" (p. 103).

What links these texts appears explicitly in another section entitled "Sexual Awakening." Yet this awakening is not confined to sex. The expressions "for the first time" and "the first traces" and the anticipation which finds completion in metaphor (for example, that of the child's hand which slips through the crack in the cupboard door "like a lover through the night") concern not only love, but all levels of a person and of his existence.

In the section entitled "Fever," Benjamin writes: "I was often sick. This is perhaps the origin of what others call patience in me, but which in truth does not resemble any virtue: the propensity for seeing everything I care about approach me from far away, as the hours approached my sickbed" (p. 94).

While here the child's illness is called back to mind because it prefigures a character trait of the adult, in another chapter, entitled "Winter Morning," the subject is a more external trait noticeable later in his life: "The fairy who grants a wish exists for everyone. It's just that only a few can remember the wish they made, and, accordingly, only a few recognize its fulfillment later in their own life" (p. 36). This passage is followed by the description of a winter morning, including the boy's painful effort to get up and the walk to school. "Once I arrived there, however, and sat down in my seat, suddenly all the tiredness which at first seemed to have vanished came back tenfold. And with it came that wish: to sleep my fill. I surely made it a thousand times, and later it was indeed fulfilled. Yet it was not until much later that I realized this was so—when I became aware that the hope I cherished of a position and an assured livelihood had always been in vain" (p. 38).

In the section called "The Reading Boxes," Benjamin writes:

> For everyone there are some things which form more enduring habits than all others. Through them the capacities are developed which help to determine the course of one's life. And since in my case these were reading and writing, of all the objects which surrounded me during my early years, nothing awakens greater longing than the reading boxes. [After describing this game, in which alphabet cards, chosen from boxes, are arranged to form words, he continues:] The longing that it awakens in me proves how much a part of my childhood it was. What I am really seeking in it is the latter itself: my entire childhood, as it lay in the grasp with which the hand slid the letters along the ledge where they were lined up. The hand can still dream of this grasp but can never awake and really execute the gesture. In like manner, many an individual may dream of how he learned to walk. But that is of no help to him. He can walk now, but never again learn to walk. [pp. 88-90]

The zoo, the larder, the reading boxes: in these Benjamin detected omens and early traces of his later life. Yet his recollective glance encountered other things, too, in which it was not his own profile but rather his historical and social environment which first became recognizable. This environment in turn acted upon Benjamin himself and became an object of his conscious reflection. Under the ambiguous title "Society" he describes the evenings on which his parents gave receptions. At first the boy still hears the guests ringing the doorbell and entering the house.

> Then came the moment when the company, which had barely begun to gather, seemed to die away. In fact, it had only withdrawn to the farther rooms, where, amidst the bubbling and sediment of the many footsteps and conversations, it disappeared, like some monster cast ashore by the ocean seeking refuge in the wet sand of the shore. The abyss from which it had been ejected was that of my class [that is to say, the upper bourgeoisie], and it was on such evenings that I first made its acquaintance. There was something queer about it. I felt that what filled the rooms was something ungraspable, slithery, ready at any instant to strangle those around whom it played; it was blind to time and place, blind to everything in its hunt for nourishment, blind in its ac-

tions. The shiny dress shirt that my father wore on that evening now appeared before me like a breastplate, and in the glance with which, an hour before, he surveyed the still empty chairs, I now discovered the man-at-arms. [pp. 81-82]

Once again metaphor is accorded a special role: the comparison brings together the present and the future, the premonition of the child and the knowledge of the grown man.

Those men whom the boy could *not* have met at his parents' receptions are also mentioned in the book.

In my childhood I was a prisoner of the old and the new quarters of western Berlin. . . . For the rich children of my age, the poor existed only as beggars. And it was a great advance in my understanding when poverty dawned on me for the first time in the ignominy of poorly paid work. That was in a short composition, perhaps the first I wrote entirely for myself. [p. 133]

We have quoted abundantly and now need only comment briefly. For the sections from *A Berlin Childhood* themselves answer the question about the difference between Proust's and Benjamin's search for time past. Proust sets off in quest of the past in order to escape from time altogether. This endeavor is made possible by the coincidence of the past with the present, a coincidence brought about by analogous experiences. Its real goal is escape from the future, filled with dangers and threats, of which the ultimate one is death. In contrast, the future is precisely what Benjamin seeks in the past. Almost every place that his memory wishes to rediscover bears "the features of what is to come," as he puts it at one point in *A Berlin Childhood* (p. 60). And it is no accident that his memory encounters a manifestation of childhood "in the office of the seer who foretells the future" (p. 57). Proust listens attentively for the echo of the past; Benjamin listens for the first notes of a future which has meanwhile become the past. Unlike Proust, Benjamin does not want to free himself from temporality; he does not wish to see things in their ahistorical essence. He strives instead for historical experience and knowledge. Nevertheless, he is sent back into the past, a past, however, which is open, not completed, and which promises the future. Benjamin's tense is not the perfect, but the future perfect in the fullness of its paradox: being future and past at the same time.

Was Benjamin aware of this difference which makes his *A Berlin Childhood* an exact counterpart of Proust's "Parisian Childhood"? In what is perhaps the most important page in his book, he seems deliberately to call attention to it. There he writes:

Déjà vu has often been described. Is the expression really a felici-
tous one? Should we not speak, instead, of incidents that come
upon us like an echo, of which it seems that the sound which
gave rise to it originated at some time in the darkness of a life
which has already passed by. This would accord, moreover, with
the fact that the shock with which a moment comes into our consciousness as having already been lived through most often strikes
us in the form of a sound. It is a word, a rustle, or a knock, which
is granted the power of calling us unexpectedly into the cool sep-
ulcher of what-has-been, from whose vaulted ceiling the present
seems to resound only as an echo. It is strange that the mirror
image of this translation in time has not yet been investigated: the
shock with which a word startles us, like a forgotten muff in our
room. Just as the latter allows us to infer that some unknown
woman has been there, so certain words or pauses allow us to
infer the presence of that invisible stranger, the future, who left
them behind with us. [pp. 48-49]

Is Benjamin speaking here of both Proust and himself? The mere fact
that he describes the phenomenon of *déjà vu,* even though it plays no role
in *A Berlin Childhood,* does not tell us much. For, first of all, he is con-
strained to use contrast in order to characterize a phenomenon which has
no name. And, in general, metaphors based on twofold definitions, to
which he owes the most masterly passages in his prose, are among Benjamin's favorite stylistic devices. In such passages his intellectual force and
imaginative power prove to be the same faculty. In any case, nothing can
obscure the fact that the translation effected by the *déjà vu* is just as much
the basis of Proust's work as its mirror image is the basis of *A Berlin
Childhood.* To conjure up the moments that are marked by this shock, so
very different from the other, is the task of Benjamin's remembering. He
states this most clearly in the book entitled *One-Way Street (Einbahn-
strasse).* "Like ultra-violet rays, memory points out to everyone in the
book of life writing which, invisibly, glossed the text as prophecy."[11]

This difference between the experience of time in Proust and in Benjamin is also responsible for the formal difference in their respective works,
that gulf which separates the three-thousand-page novel from the collection of brief prose pieces. The poet of the *déjà vu* is on the track of those
moments in which the experience of childhood shines forth anew; he
must, accordingly, recount an entire life. Benjamin, on the contrary, can
disregard later events and devote himself to the invocation of those moments of childhood in which a token of the future lies hidden. It is not
fortuitous that among his favorite objects were those glass globes containing such scenes as a snowy landscape which is brought back to life whenever the globe is shaken.[12] For the allegorist Benjamin, these globes were,

like reliquaries, very likely sheltering from events outside a representation not of the past but of the future. The experiences of *A Berlin Childhood* and the miniatures in which they are captured resemble such globes.

We must inquire, however, not only about the relationship between Proust's and Benjamin's intentions but also about the meaning of Benjamin's quest for time gone by, for lost time, which is, in sum, a quest for the lost future. This leads beyond *A Berlin Childhood* to Benjamin's philosophical-historical works, where the theme reappears in an objective context, accompanied by Benjamin's own explanations. In contrast, the biographical background of *A Berlin Childhood* could be fully grasped only if Benjamin's letters were available.* His friend T. W. Adorno, in the epilogue he wrote for the book, describes this background from personal knowledge. "A deathly air permeates the scenes poised to awaken in Benjamin's depiction. Upon them falls the gaze of the condemned man."

A knowledge of ruin obstructed Benjamin's view into the future and allowed him to see future events only in those instances where they had already moved into the past. This ruin is the ruin of his age. *A Berlin Childhood* belongs, as the epilogue observes, in the orbit of the prehistory of the modern world on which Benjamin worked during the last fifteen years of his life and which is called *Paris, die Hauptstadt des 19. Jahrhunderts.* The link to this sociohistorical investigation is formed by certain of the reminiscences, such as the one of the "Kaiserpanorama," which invoke the predecessors and, in some instances, initial forms of what has become present-day technology. This was the subject that Benjamin planned to examine, on the broadest possible basis, in *Paris: Capital of the Nineteenth Century,* of which there exist only preliminary studies and fragments. However, the conclusion of *One-Way Street,* which appeared in 1928, gives us some indication of how Benjamin viewed the technological age.

> [The] great wooing of the cosmos was carried out for the first time on a planetary scale, specifically, under the sign of technology. Since, however, the ruling class' lust for profit sought to have its way with technology, technology has betrayed mankind and turned the bridal chamber into a sea of blood. Control of nature, so the imperialists teach, is the meaning of all technology. Who, however, would wish to trust a martinet who declared that the control of children by adults is the meaning of education? Is not education, above all, the indispensable ordering of the relationship between the generations, or, if one wishes to speak of control, the control of the generational relationship rather than of the

*Since this essay was written, a large number of Benjamin's letters have been published. See *Briefe,* eds. T. W. Adorno and G. Scholem, 2 vols. (Frankfurt, 1966).—Trans.

children: Similarly, technology is not control of nature [but] control of the relationship between nature and mankind.[13]

Benjamin's conception of technology is utopian rather than critical. What he criticizes is the betrayal of utopia that was committed in realizing the idea of technology. Accordingly, he directs his attention not to the possibilities latent in technology—which today are largely destructive— but to the time when technology first represented a possibility, when its true idea still lay on the horizon of the future, an idea that Benjamin expressed as the control not of nature but of the relationship between nature and mankind. Thus his understanding of utopia is anchored in the past. This was the precondition for his projected prehistory of the modern age. The task is paradoxical, like the joining of hope and despair to which it gives voice. The way to the origin is, to be sure, a way backwards, but backwards into a future, which, although it has gone by in the meantime and its idea has been perverted, still holds more promise than the current image of the future.

This paradoxical trajectory confirms in an unexpected manner Friedrich Schlegel's definition of the historian as a prophet facing backwards. It also distinguishes Benjamin from the philosopher who, along with Ernst Bloch, stands closest to him: Theodor W. Adorno. For Adorno's writings show the eschatological impulse at work no less paradoxically in a critique of the present age, in the analysis of "damaged life" *("beschädigte Leben").* At the conclusion of *Minima Moralia* Adorno writes:

> In the face of despair, the only way philosophy can still be
> justified is as an attempt to consider all things as they look from
> the standpoint of salvation. Knowledge has no light other than
> that which shines down on the world from salvation: everything
> else spends itself in reconstruction and remains a merely technical
> matter. Perspectives must be established in which the world
> comes apart, alienates itself, and reveals its cracks and fissures, as
> it will be one day when it lies poor and disfigured in the Messian-
> ic light.[14]

Let us return, however, to the sentences quoted at the beginning. Now we can understand Benjamin's strange wish to be able to lose himself in a city—this art which, as he observes, requires practice and which he did not learn until late. It is, we should add, an art which develops at the end of an age. In the section on "Lost Objects" in *One-Way Street,* he writes "Once we have begun to find our way around in a place, our earliest image can never reappear."[15] Since this image harbors the future, it must not be allowed to disappear. It is for its sake that the ability to get lost is something to be wished for.

This theme from *A Berlin Childhood* also appears in Benjamin's historical, philosophical, and political writings. The link between the autobiographical literary work and a scholarly work such as the one on German tragedy is not really astonishing. Hegel, in his *Aesthetics,* speaks of the "blind erudition which fails to notice the depths even when they are clearly expressed and set forth."[16] The question then arises of whether the depths are not *necessarily* overlooked whenever an author eliminates his own experience due to a falsely conceived notion of science. True objectivity is bound up with subjectivity. The basic idea of Benjamin's work on the *Origins of German Tragic Drama,* a work on allegory in the baroque period, came to him, as he sometimes recounted, while looking at a king in a puppet theater whose hat sat crookedly on his head.[17]

Considering the great difficulties that a reader of Benjamin's theoretical writings confronts, a brief look at his remaining work can offer no more than hints which may serve as signposts in a terrain in which hastily cleared shortcuts are of no use.

In the theses on the concept of history that Benjamin wrote shortly before his death, we again find the statement from *One-Way Street* that "memory points out to everyone in the book of life writing which, invisibly, glossed the text as prophecy." But this time it is embedded in a philosophy of history. "The past," writes Benjamin here, "carries with it a temporal index, according to which it is assigned to salvation."[18]

Benjamin's last effort, undertaken in the face of the victory of national socialism and the failure of German and French social democracy, was devoted to formulating a new conception of history which would break with the belief in progress, with the notion of the progress of humanity in a "homogeneous and empty time."[19] He judged that fascism's opportunity lay not least in the fact that "its opponents confronted it in the name of progress as an historical norm," and that the self-deception of social democracy arose not least from the "illusion that factory work, which is caught up in the onward march of technical advance, constitutes, in itself, a political accomplishment." "The astonishment that the things we are living through are 'still' possible in the twentieth century is *in no way* philosophical. It is not the source of any knowledge, unless it be that the conception of history from which it stems cannot be defended."[20] Benjamin's new conception of history is rooted in the dialectic of future and past, of messianic expectation and remembrance. "The origin is the goal" — this phrase from Karl Kraus serves as a motto for one of the theses on the philosophy of history.

This conception sends us back not only to the prehistory of modern times on which Benjamin was working at the same time but also to the book on the *Origins of German Tragic Drama (Ursprung des deutschen*

Trauerspiels), which he had outlined more than twenty years earlier, in 1916. Here he started out from totally different premises. What concerned him was the problematic nature of the ahistorical conceptions of literary genres usually found in discussions of poetics. He arrived at the following definition:

> Origin, although a thoroughly historical category, has nevertheless nothing in common with genesis. Origin does not at all mean the formation or becoming of what has arisen *(Entsprungene),* but rather what is arising *(Entspringendes)* out of becoming and passing away. The origin is a whirlpool in the stream of becoming and draws into its rhythm the material that is to be formed. That which is original never lets itself be known in the bare, public stock of the factual, and its rhythm can be perceived only by a double insight. It wishes to be known, on the one hand, as restoration and rehabilitation and, on the other hand, in this very rehabilitation, as uncompleted and unsettled. In every origin-phenomenon *(Ursprungsphänomen)* the shape in which an idea time and again confronts the historical world gradually determines itself until it lies complete in the totality of its history. Therefore, the origin does not remove itself altogether from the actual facts, but rather, pertains to the latter's pre- and posthistory. . . . The genuine—that stamp of a phenomenon's origins *(Ursprungssiegel)*—is an object of discovery, a discovery that is linked in the most singular way with re-cognition.[21]

Between the early work on allegory in baroque drama and the last studies on *Paris, Capital of the Nineteenth Century,* the centerpiece of which was to have been the statue of Baudelaire, there exist other thematic connections which simultaneously touch on the motif of memory in Proust and in *A Berlin Childhood.* The most important category in this regard is that of experience, the atrophy of which constitutes, for Benjamin, the distinguishing mark of the moderns. In Proust's work he detects the attempt "to construct experience . . . synthetically under current social conditions," while in Baudelaire "memory *(Erinnerung)* recedes entirely in favor of remembrance *(Andenken).* There are strikingly few childhood memories in his work."[22] In remembrance, however, as Benjamin puts it in another fragment of the *Nachlass,* we find "crystallized the increasing self-alienation of man, who inventories his past like so many lifeless possessions. In the nineteenth century, allegory abandoned the outer world to settle the inner world."[23] The inventorying of the past, with which the allegory of the baroque period was turned inward, is at the same time, for Benjamin, the personal correlate of the prevailing view of history against which his *Theses on the Philosophy of History* rebelled.

The last work we shall discuss is a collection of letters for which Benjamin wrote a preface and commentaries and which was published in Switzerland in 1936 under the pseudonymn Detlef Holtz.[24] The book consists of twenty-five letters from the period 1783–1883; among the authors included are Lichtenberg, Johann Heinrich Voss, Hölderlin, the Grimm brothers, Goethe, David Friedrich Strauss, and Georg Büchner. The volume is called *Deutsche Menschen* and was to have been imported into national socialist Germany under this "camouflaged title" *(Tarntitel)*—a term that Benjamin himself used in a letter. This scheme was, of course, bound to fail, if only because of the frankness of the subtitle, which openly formulates what the letters are meant to attest: *Von Ehre ohne Ruhm. Von Grösse ohne Glanz. Von Würde ohne Sold* (Of honor without fame. Of greatness without splendor. Of dignity without pay). The book is about the German bourgeoisie, to which, however, it erects no gilded monument. In the preface Benjamin speaks with cool detachment of the years of industrial development after 1871, when the age "ended in an unsightly manner." And yet, if we recall his assertion in the book on tragedy that the origin is "what arises out of becoming and passing away," we may then say that in this volume of letters Benjamin wished to show the origin of the German bourgeoisie—an origin which still held the promise of a future for it.

A copy of the book which once belonged to Benjamin's sister was found in a Zurich antique shop. It bears the following dedication: "This ark, built on the Jewish model, for Dora—from Walter. November 1936."[25] What was supposed to be rescued by this book? What was Benjamin thinking of when he justified his refusal to emigrate overseas with the assertion that "in Europe [there are] positions to defend?"[26] The salvation project can be understood only on the basis of Benjamin's view of history, to which he gave poetic expression in *A Berlin Childhood*. One may well apply to the ark of *Deutsche Menschen* these lines from the *Theses on the Philosophy of History:* "Only *that* historian has the gift of kindling the sparks of hope in the past who is thoroughly imbued with this idea: *even the dead* will not be safe from the enemy if he wins. And this enemy has not ceased to win."[27] Benjamin did not build the ark for the dead alone; he built it for the sake of the promise that he saw in their past. For this ark was not intended to save only itself. It sailed forth in the hope that it could reach even those who viewed as a fecund inundation what was in truth the Flood.

Chapter 10
The Poetry of Constancy:
Paul Celan's Translation
of Shakespeare's Sonnet 105

Shakespeare's sonnet 105, a poem about the virtues of the author's young friend and, simultaneously, a poem about the poetic writing that extols them, ends with the couplet:

> Fair, kind, and true, have often lived alone.
> Which three till now, never kept seat in one.

Celan's translation of this sonnet concludes with the verses:

> "Schön, gut und treu" so oft getrennt, geschieden.
> In Einem will ich drei zusammenschmieden.[1]

Beauty, goodness, and fidelity are the three virtues that the poet ascribes to his friend in the preceding quatrains, and it is to their expression that he wishes to confine his writing, indeed, even its vocabulary. Whereas in these strophes Shakespeare speaks not only of his friend but also of his own love and of his own songs, the final couplet is devoted entirely to the three virtues, which are granted an independent life through the device of personification. Yet this independent life is accorded to beauty, goodness, and fidelity only so that the poet may affirm that their separation, which previously was the rule, is henceforth overcome. The "till now" of the

Written in December 1970 and published as "Poetry of Constancy—Poetik der Beständigkeit: Celans Übertragung von Shakespeares Sonett 105," in *Sprache im technischen Zeitalter* 37 (1971): 9-25.

dispersion of "fair, kind, and true" is the history of humanity until the appearance of that W. H. who is celebrated in the majority of Shakespeare's sonnets. The last two verses of Celan's translation say something different. They do not contrast the long separation of the three "virtues" with the place in which they finally have all come together. The union of "fair, kind, and true" *("Schön, gut und treu")* is due not to the appearance of the friend, but to a literary work, to the future work of the poet, who intends to "forge" the three "together" *(zusammenschmieden will)*. If Shakespeare's concluding verses are silent about the friend, this is only in order to invoke him all the more strikingly through the negation "never" and above all, through the sonnet's inconspicuous last word, "one," which is a circumlocution for him in whom "fair, kind, and true" have taken up common residence. In contrast, Celan's *in Einem* ("in one"), in which the poet "intends to forge together fair, kind, and true" *("Schön, gut und treu" zusammenschmieden will),* is not "the one *person*" (der *Eine*) extolled by the poem but "the one *thing*" (das *Eine*), most probably the *one* image that the poet sketches of him, if indeed it is not the unity of the poem, which has entirely absorbed its subject matter. To be sure, in the three quatrains of the Shakespearian sonnet the poet speaks so explicitly about his work ("my songs and praises," "my verse," "my invention"—in the third verse of each quatrain) that, despite the emphatic silence of the concluding couplet, we may interpret the "now," before which moment "fair," "kind," and "true" were separated, as being simultaneously the "now" of Shakespeare's composition of the poem. That the place where beauty, goodness, and fidelity unite could be the friend as well as the poem about him is an ingenious piece of ambiguity based on the relationship between friend and poem established by other poems in the sonnet cycle. In contrast, we may note the explicitness and pathos evident in Celan's translation, in which the poet, through the image of the "forging together," claims that what Shakespeare expresses in the form of a description—and what is linked with the act of its being described only inasmuch as it is a *described* reality—is the product solely of his own will, the result of his poetic activity alone.

This same approach, which characterizes Celan's version of the final two verses, is a decisive element of his entire translation of Shakespeare's sonnet 105:

> Let not my love be called idolatry,
> Nor my beloved as an idol show,
> Since all alike my songs and praises be
> To one, of one, still such, and ever so.
>
> Kind is my love to-day, to-morrow kind,

Still constant in a wondrous excellence,
Therefore my verse to constancy confined,
One thing expressing, leaves out difference.

Fair, kind, and true, is all my argument,
Fair, kind, and true, varying to other words,
And in this change is my invention spent,
Three themes in one, which wondrous scope affords.

Fair, kind, and true, have often lived alone,
Which three till now, never kept seat in one.[2]

Ihr sollt, den ich da lieb, nicht Abgott heissen,
nicht Götzendienst, was ich da treib und trieb.
All dieses Singen hier, all dieses Preisen:
von ihm, an ihn und immer ihm zulieb.

Gut ist mein Freund, ists heute und ists morgen,
Und keiner ist beständiger als er.
In der Beständigkeit, da bleibt mein Vers geborgen,
spricht von dem Einen, schweift mir nicht umher.

"Schön, gut und treu," das singe ich und singe.
"Schön, gut und treu"—stets anders und stets das.
Ich find, erfind—um sie in eins zu bringen,
sie einzubringen ohne Unterlass.

"Schön, gut und treu" so oft getrennt, geschieden.
In Einem will ich drei zusammenschmieden.

In the first quatrain, Celan's use of the active voice leads to the introduction of the poet's own activity into the subject matter, even though the translation, too, appears to have only the friend in view. The substantival infinitive forms of the verbs (*Singen,* "singing," and *Preisen,* "praising, extolling") replace the corresponding substantives ("my songs and praises"). Where the passive form "be called" appears in the original, in Celan's version the poet speaks of what he himself is doing (the sequence of verses 1 and 2 is reversed). And this impression is strengthened by repetition, specifically by the preservation of lexical identity (*treib/trieb,* "do/did"), coexisting with morphological difference (present tense, imperfect tense), as well as by the rhyme on *zulieb* ("for the love of ").

In the second quatrain, the poet's activity comes to the fore, since the translator, using both syntax and semantics to achieve his effect, assigns a more active function to a verse that is already personified in Shakespeare. In this way he also intensifies the personification of his own work, which increasingly takes the place of the person extolled by Shakespeare. Celan gives *Da bleibt mein Vers geborgen* ("there lies my verse sheltered") for *my verse to constancy confined;* and he gives *schweift mir nicht umher* ("does not wander round about") for *leaves out difference.*

Finally, in the third quatrain, the poet's more active role, the result of the specific accumulation of verbs referring to his own doings (*Ich find, erfind*—"I discover, invent" for "is my invention spent"; *zu bringen, einzubringen*—"to bring, to harvest") is supplemented by greater semantic specification. Thus, in place of "is all my argument," originally a standard rhetorical phrase, the translation gives *das singe ich und singe* ("that [is what] I sing and sing"), preparing the reader for the repetitions to come in verses 11 and 12.

It may seem that the main point involved here is a shift in accent from the person who is being praised to the act of praising or composing. What we are actually dealing with, however, is more than merely the "bolder display" (as Hölderlin expressed it in connection with his translations of Sophocles)[3] of a theme already present in the original, in which, however, it is entirely subordinate to the themes of the "fair friend"[4] and of the poet's love for him. The relationship of Celan's translation to the original can be appropriately described neither as a change in thematic interest or style, nor as the kind of change which, according to the tenets of traditional theories of translation, would be pertinent in judging the fidelity and success of the translation. Rather, the movement from original to translation is a change in what Walter Benjamin, in his essay on "The Task of the Translator," calls "intention toward language *(Intention auf die Sprache).*[5] Where a translation not only may but should differ from the original is in its mode of signification *(Art des Meinens).*[6] The concept of "significatio" pertains to the structure of language, to a relationship whose two members, however, should not be assigned fixed names, since such names always imply a specific relationship between the two, that is, a precise conception of the structure of signification in language. Michel Foucault calls the two elements of this relationship simply *Words and Things*—a formula that serves as the title of the book in which he interprets the historical change in this relationship as a change in the epistemological "conditions of possibility" governing the specific historical forms assumed by the various "human sciences."[7] Any less general notion would hinder the discovery of the relevant mode of signification; and this would be a serious loss, since it is always this mode that constitutes the historicity of a given linguistic constellation and thus also the goal of philological understanding.[8] Accordingly, a translation does not primarily indicate the historical state of a language (indeed, primarily it does not indicate this at all); it gives evidence, rather, of the use of language. The translation points not so much to a definite linguistic state as to a definite conception of language. Thus Benjamin saw the legitimacy, indeed the necessity, of translating as lying in the different intentions toward language and modes of signification displayed by an original text and its translation. This very difference, moreover, invalidates the premises underlying debates over the issue of fidelity versus freedom in translating.

The way in which Celan's mode of signification differs from Shakespeare's can be gathered by comparing the concluding couplet of sonnet 105 as its stands in the original and in the translation:

> Fair, kind, and true, have often lived alone.
> Which three till now, never kept seat in one.

> "Schön, gut und treu" so oft getrennt, geschieden.
> In Einem will ich drei zusammenschmieden.

The theme in both versions is the separation of the three "virtues" and their unification, the two states being contrasted in the antithetical structure of the couplet. The difference in intention toward language at work in Celan's version and in Shakespeare's text can be inferred from the way Celan expresses the dispersion, as well as the contrast between this dispersion and the ensuing union. In translating "have often lived alone" by *so oft getrennt, geschieden* ("so often separated, divided"), he enriches the discursive mode of expression with another whose poetic energy overwhelms discursiveness. What traditional stylistic criticism would consider as a varied repetition used for emphasis—*getrennt, geschieden*—serves here to express the caesurae between "Schön, gut, und treu" in other than simply a lexical manner. Modern linguistics has conceptualized that which the reader of earlier times could have perceived in analyzing the impression made on him by a phrase like *getrennt, geschieden,* if—and that is the real question—such a turn of phrase and such an intention toward language appeared at all *before* the advent of modern literature. If it is true that the understanding of language consists primarily in making distinctions, in registering "distinctive features," then the phrase *getrennt, geschieden,* is not so much an instance of varied repetition as it is, when spoken aloud *as ge-trennt, ge-schieden,* the union of the common prefix *ge* with two different, although synonymous lexemes, *trennt* and *schieden.* Understanding, which depends upon distinctions, sees intended meaning less in the literal sense of separating and dividing than in the caesura, which splits the word *geschieden* into two parts, by virtue on the one hand, of the identity of the prefix, and, on the other, of the phonological quasi-identity (the paronomasia) of *schieden* and its rhyme word *schmieden.* This separation of *ge* and *schieden* may be seen as a metadiscursive representation of the separation of *"Schön, gut und treu."*

The final rhymes of the English and German versions display a similar phenomenon. The opposition appearing in the original—"lived alone/ kept seat in one"—is, of course, reproduced in the translation, namely, in the opposition of separating and dividing, on the one hand, and forging together, on the other. Nevertheless, it is clear that in the German version the opposition is conveyed not only through lexical means but also through the difference between *schieden* ("divided") and *schmieden* ("forged"). Just as understanding, sensitive to distinctions, perceives *geschieden* coming after *getrennt* as *ge-schieden,* so, too, does it register the difference between *geschieden* and *zusammenschmieden* as the minimal consonontal variation of the rhymed syllables *schieden* and *schmieden.* The normative identity of the rhymed words, which in the German text starts from the last stressed vowel *(-ieden),* is reinforced by the *sch*-sound; yet this identity is disrupted by the variation arising from the *m*-sound in *schmieden* (inserted between the *sch*-sound and the rhymed syllable [*-ieden*] and anticipated by the separable prefix *zusammen*). Thus the metadiscursive realization of both the separation and union of the three "virtues" consists in this minimal variation, the near-identity of *schieden* and *schmieden.* In other words, the opposition is expressed by its own antithesis, paronomasia. This device, employed in the rhyme of the final couplet, enables the poem's language to go beyond the dimension of meaning and *speak* the opposition, instead of expressing it (which would represent a recourse to the literal sense); and it can do this all the more so since the only difference, except for the context (*zusammen,* "together"), between the paronomasia and total homonymy lies in the consonant.

The mode of signification which is documented here, and which stamps Celan's translation throughout, may be contrasted with the mode found in Shakespeare, which likewise exploits the possibilities offered by rhyme, although in a different fashion. In Shakespeare, the opposition is already emphasized, not, however, by near-identity but by relation, namely, between "alone" (derived from "all one") and "one." Unlike Celan's, this contrastive technique, which is confined to the lexical and etymological realm, is incapable of generating a determinate negation of discursiveness, i.e., of recourse to literal sense. More important, however, is the fact that the etymological relationship between "alone" and "one" remains external to the opposition that the poem is meant to express and in fact does express on the discursive level. Thus the relationship is an abstract point of manneristic origin. The same may be said, with even greater justification, of the following paradox: separateness is evoked by the very word ("alone") that originally reinforced the word expressing union ("one"). These remarks are not meant as criticism,[9] but simply as an indication of a particular mode of signification that may be seen as the basic premise of much of traditional rhetoric. Just as this intention toward language has changed since Mallarmé, so the very *principles* of rhetoric employed in poetry since Mallarmé differ from those of traditional rhetoric. This fact, which has been noticed by only a few authors such as Derrida[10] and Deguy,[11] becomes evident in comparing Shakespeare's sonnet 105 with Celan's translation.

From the point of view of traditional rhetoric, the sonnet's most ingenious verse is no doubt the fifth:

Kind is my love to-day, to-morrow kind.

This verse is constructed in the form of a chiasmus. The mirror symmetry directly opposes "to-day" and "to-morrow" around a central axis, thereby stressing the present-future antithesis.[12] However, inasmuch as the chiastic sentence structure results, on the lexical level, in the verse's beginning and ending with the same word, "kind," it enables the verse to stress the constancy that cannot be affected by the temporal opposition. The chiasmus in this Shakespearean verse is thus scarcely mere ornament; at the same time, however, it runs entirely counter to the specific relationship of language and "content" found in Celan's translation of this verse:

Gut ist mein Freund, ists heute und ists morgen.

The chiasmus can be rendered in German, as was shown by Stefan George, whose translation of the verse reads:

Gut ist heut meine liebe•morgen gut.[13]

If Celan gives up the chiasmus, it is only so as to allow the sentence itself to speak directly that which the chiasmus can express only abstractly and mediated by reflection: constancy. Celan's verse flows easily onward, replacing the antithetically constructed verse, which can only express constancy when it reaches its end in the retrospective glance of synthesis.[14] It is as if Celan's poem heedlessly followed the course of time, in which the friend's goodness persists as unchangingly as the one occurrence of the word *ists* follows the other, as obviously as *morgen* ("tomorrow") follows *heute* ("today"). The difference between Celan's translation and the original is not adequately grasped if one merely notes that the chiasmus is replaced by repetition, as can readily be seen from Celan's German version of the succeeding verse:

und keiner ist beständiger als er.

In Shakespeare this line reads:

Still constant in a wondrous excellence.

It appears, though, that Celan does wish to repeat the chiasmus when he follows up *Gut ist mein Freund* with *keiner ist beständiger* in the next verse. But Celan's chiasmus, distributed over two lines and affecting only parts of these two, lacks that antithesis which only becomes a sign of the intended meaning, i.e., of constancy, when it is surpassed *qua* antithesis through the repetition of the word "kind." In Celan's version, instead of concluding the first verse in a gnomic fashion ("kind is my love to-day, to-morrow kind"), the chiasmus confirms the union of the first verse with the second, in which the impression of a constant onward-flowing motion is preserved by the use of the introductory word *und* ("and") and by the repetition of the word *ist* ("is").

What distinguishes Celan's translation from the original, therefore, is not a renunciation of traditional rhetorical figures but rather a change in basic presuppositions. In other words, his version displays a different mode of signification; and this mode underlies his use of language, both generally and, more particularly, with respect to rhetorical figures, although it can only be discovered by a consideration of the "performance," that is to say, the text itself. As a result, even that type of textual analysis which inquires into these presuppositions may no more dispense with stylistic criticism than it may rely exclusively on the latter.

From this point of view, repetition appears as the most consistently employed stylistic device of Celan's translation. Naturally, the fact that in his own poetry Celan frequently repeats words and sentences lends weight to the thesis that Celan translated Shakespeare into his own language; in other words, Celan's translations are Celan poems. While both plausible and likely to find a ready welcome, not necessarily false on that account, such an approach tends to obscure the possible difference in the use of language, that is, in intention toward language, which, according to Benjamin's theory of translation, constitutes the difference between an original text and its translation.[15] Hence we should pursue the comparison of the two poems further still in order to establish the specific mode of signification that informs Celan's language in his translation of the English sonnet.

Shakespeare's own text contains a large number of repetitions, which Celan always retains, however freely he may proceed in other respects. Thus, in the two introductory verses he gives translations of the pairs of corresponding terms "love-beloved" and "idolatry-idol," although *zulieb*, which corresponds to *lieb* (v. 1), does not appear until the conclusion of the first quatrain, though it is anticipated by *trieb* as its rhyming word.

This deviation from the parallelism of the two introductory verses is made for the sake of a varied repetition in verse 2 (*was ich da treib und trieb*— "what there I do and did"), which in both its form and underlying intention toward language recalls verse 5 (*Gut ist mein Freund, ists heute und ists morgen*—"kind is my friend, [he] is it today and [he] is it tomorrow"). Celan likewise keeps the slightly modified repetition in verses 6 and 7 ("constant-constancy, *beständiger-Beständigkeit*) as well as the strict repetition of "Fair, kind and true" in verses 9, 10, and 13. One last repetition in the original is made still more emphatic in Celan's version, namely, that found in the final verse of the first quatrain:

> To one, of one, still such, and ever so.

The translation refers, however abstractly, to the *"fair friend"* a third time:

> von ihm, an ihn und immer ihm zulieb
> ("about him, to him, and always for love of him").

As in the succeeding verse, this type of repetition is qualitatively different from the type we find in Shakespeare; it also serves a different function. What Shakespeare, in the second half of the verse, expresses discursively with the words "still" and "ever" is spoken by Celan's verse *as* verse (with the exception of the word *immer*—"ever"). Unlike Shakespeare's verse 4 ("To one, of one / still such, and ever so"), Celan's is not divided into two parts, but rather proceeds in a continuous fashion, due to the lexical (*ihm-ihn-ihm*) as well as the vocalic periodicity (o-ī-a-ī-u-ī-e-i-u-ī). Here, as in verse 5, constancy is not merely the intended meaning; it characterizes the verse itself. To this extent, Celan's language does not speak *about* something but "speaks" itself. It speaks about things and about language through its very manner of speaking.

In Celan's version, therefore, repetition—the syntagmatic realization of the constancy motif—is not restricted to those passages whose explicit theme is *constancy,* but stamps the sonnet as a whole. Behind the many expressions in the original referring only indirectly to this theme, the translator discerns this same constancy and governs his language accordingly. This is evident from the way he translates *my love* in the first verse of the original:

> Let not my love be called idolatry,

where he makes the constancy implied in "my love" speak through the identity of the lexeme *treib* ("do") in verse 2

> nicht Götzendienst, was ich da treib und trieb
> ("not idolatry what I do and did").

Furthermore, Celan eliminates the discursive "all alike," which links together "songs" and "praises," and instead introduces these two words by the same phrase:

> All dieses Singen hier, all dieses Preisen
> ("All this singing here, all this praising").

Celan's intention toward language is no less clear when, in the third quatrain, after the identical first part of the two introductory verses, he repeats a word each time in the second part and also makes the sentence structure hinge on this word, as in verse 5 (*Gut ist mein Freund, ists heute und ists morgen*):

> Fair, kind, and true, is all my argument,
> Fair, kind, and true, varying to other words.

> "Schön, gut und treu," das *singe* ich und *singe*.
> "Schön, gut und treu" — *stets* anders und *stets* das.

In place of the word "argument," which itself suggests discursive, rational language, and its no less logical qualifier "all," Celan offers the stubborn repetition of his own action. By setting the words *und singe* after *das singe ich* (three words that completely disregard the content of the English phrase "is all my argument") he creates a repetition that does not simply say what is expressed in the original by the word "all;" moreover, by reducing *das singe ich* to *singe* through the omission of both subject and object, he hypostatizes, as it were, the poet's action. And this is an action that coincides with the poem instead of being its subject matter, as is the case in Shakespeare.

Even more characteristic is the rendering Celan gives of the phrase "varying to other words": *stets anders und stets das* ("always different and always that"). Varying means "diversifying by change,"[16] "restating in different words."[17] The expression, a rhetorical term, assumes that word and meaning are different and hence distinguishable. It is for this reason alone that the same thing can be designated by different words; it is for this reason alone that it is possible to vary the words without departing from the intended meaning. Celan's intention toward language, by contrast, may be viewed as the determinate negation of this theoretical linguistic premise. What was a stylistic device in traditional rhetoric, and may well have been employed by writers unaware of the conditions that make its use possible, is here recognized by Celan to be a paradox and inserted into the verse as such: *stets anders und stets das*. The continuity is conveyed not merely by the word *stets* itself, but even more by its repetition, while the difference is expressed by the fact that *anders* ("other") is followed by *das* ("that," i.e., that same thing). The paradox itself is maintained in two ways. First, the contradiction between *stets,* on the one hand, and *anders* and *das,* on the other, remains unresolved. Second, and no less important, where one expects to find an answer to the possible question of "*anders* als was?" ("different from what?") there appears a forceful *das,* which, although introduced by the same word, *stets,* is incompatible with *anders.*

Celan's translation of the next verse evinces the same rejection of the traditional conception of language, according to which different signifiers can correspond to the same signified. Indeed, we can sense a desire to abolish the distinction between signifier and signified altogether. In this verse, Shakespeare explicitly mentions that *change* (i.e., the replacement of one word by another, while the intended meaning remains the same) whose premise is precisely this traditional conception of language:

And in this change is my invention spent.

Celan refuses to concede that words may be interchangeable in this way, just as he successfully avoids using a word derived from the familiar rhetorical term *inventio* to designate the poet's activity and capacity. Designation is replaced by speaking: *Ich find, erfind.* In linguistic terms, this is one of the boldest passages in Celan's version, surpassed perhaps only by the immediately following one. For here the repetition of the verb, that is, of the word for the activity, does more than simply convey the activity's constancy (which was its sole function in the case of the expressions *Gut ist mein Freund, ists heute und ists morgen* and *das singe ich und singe*). Furthermore, to understand the phrase *Ich find, erfind,* it is not sufficient to read the expansion of "find" in the repetition (*erfind*) as a delayed translation of "invention"; nor should it be viewed as a substitute for the dimension of "change" that Celan refuses to mention explicitly or even to accept as a possible means of expressing variation. To be sure, it is also all that. At the same time, however, with the phrase *Ich find, erfind* Celan pierces the façade of linguistic performance, that is, of *parole* (speech), making it possible to glimpse the inner workings of the linguistic system, of *langue* (language). (He already did this, although in an incomparably less bold fashion, in verse 2: *was ich da treib und trieb*). What is thereby revealed are parts of the conjugation paradigm, once with respect to tense (*was ich da treib und trieb*) and once with respect to person: *ich find, erfind* (= *er find*). Admittedly, this reading is not compelling in the first case (the change of tense, accompanied by lexical constancy, has its own function, as was seen above); it becomes so only when the first case is considered together with the second (*Ich find, erfind*). Our interpretation of the second case presupposes that, in this position, the prefix *er* carries the connotation of the personal pronoun *er* ("he"). That it actually does so will perhaps be doubted. We may therefore draw attention to two points. Firstly, in the sequence *Ich find, erfind* (as in verse 13: *getrennt, geschieden*), understanding, which is concerned above all with "distinctive features" will depart from the usual pronunciation (*erfind*) to stress the prefix *er* and this is what makes it possible to defend the second meaning (i.e., of *er* as a personal pronoun). Secondly, it will be recalled that there are passages in Celan's own poems in which paradigmatic fragments of *langue* obviously mingle with *parole,* as in the introductory poem of the collection entitled *Die Niemandsrose:*

> I dig, you dig, and the worm, it digs too,
> And that singing over there says: They dig.

> Ich grabe, du gräbst, und es gräbt auch der Wurm
> und das Singende dort sagt: Sie graben.[18]

The meaning of this questioning of *parole* through the introduction of nonactualized or only partially actualized *faits bruts* of *langue*—a technique that is a constitutive element of the most recent, so-called concrete poetry—becomes evident as soon as we recognize the motivation behind Celan's specific intention toward language, which emerges ever more clearly from the examples analyzed. With this end in view, let us analyze one last instance of varied repetition. At the beginning of the third quatrain Shakespeare states that he wishes to express the theme of "Fair, kind, and true," which is to be the sole theme of his writing, exclusively by means of varying words; he then continues:

> And in this change is my invention spent,
> Three themes in one, which wondrous scope affords.

Celan translates these lines as:

> Ich find, erfind—um sie in eins zu bringen,
> sie einzubringen ohne Unterlass.

The passage *sie in eins zu bringen, / sie einzubringen* is probably the one in which Celan's method of translating lies most open to criticism, the one in which it takes the most liberties. Here, more easily than anywhere else in his German version of Shakespeare's sonnet, we can perceive the specific intention toward language underlying this translation from beginning to end. Celan, as we have seen, does not allow the poet to speak of his own inventive gifts; similarly, he forbids the poet to mention the *scope* of his poetry writing or to call it "wondrous." These words are replaced by two half-verses: *um sie in eins zu bringen* and *sie einzubringen.* Each has its specific content, which can be expressed by other words. The first, the "bringing-into-one" (which translates *Three themes in one*), should be understood as the union of *"Schön, gut und treu"* —as the poetic mimesis of that union embodied in the friend. The "Three themes" are "One thing" (v. 8). Celan, to be sure, mentions only the unity, the uniting, and not the threefold nature of the manifest reality which, in Shakespeare, is taken for granted. And his *sie* ("they") refers to the group *"Schön, gut und treu,"* which (in contrast to the practice of many critical editions) also appears each time in inverted commas in the English text printed along with Celan's version,[19] with the result that this group is presented as a quotation, that is, as a verbal entity, not as something real. Thus the grouping of the virtues, which, in Shakespeare, serves, in however fictive and fictionalized a manner, as the point of departure of the poet's activity, disappears in Celan's text in two respects: it loses both its threefold nature and its existence as something real.

The second half-verse *sie einzubringen* ("to bring them in," i.e., to harvest them) cannot be understood as a translation of a specific passage of the original. Once again, what is meant is the act of poetic composition. As metaphor, it would have to be linked with the imagery of a harvest or vintage. If one assumes that the term corresponding to the implicit "whither" of the "bringing in" or harvesting is the poem itself, then the resolution of the metaphor may be seen in the "putting in practice" [i.e., of something in a work of art = *Ins Werk Setzen*]. But such an analytic reading, dependent on "retranslation," is overwhelmed by the wave arising from the paronomasia of *sie in eins zu bringen / sie einzubringen* ("to bring them into one / to bring them in"). Unlike the case of the rhyming pair in the final couplet (*schieden / schmieden*), here the paronomasia is not confined to a portion of a word but encompasses an entire syntagma. The sequence *sie in eins zu bringen, / sie einzubringen* also differs from the other paronomasia by the fact that it does not stand in the end-rhyme position; the concordance of sounds is therefore not borne by any schema, but strikes the reader unprepared. These differences, however, constitute merely the preconditions for the really decisive difference; and it is the latter that allows us to grasp the specific character of the passage and thereby the particular motivation of Celan's intention toward language, a motivation that is manifest throughout his translation.

By rhyming *zusammenschmieden* with *geschieden*, Celan brings together two signifiers which not only are different but which have opposite signifieds ("separate" / "join"). He expresses the opposition perhaps even more forcefully through the phonological near-identity, the paronomasia, than through the semantic opposition *e contrario*. In this way he subverts the normative conception of the correspondence, in every case, of the signifieds to the signifiers, the latter of which are assumed to mirror the diversity of the former. (Polysemy is equally the scandal of semiotics, as it is the fundamental fact of poetics.) Now, in contrast to the paronomasia of the final rhyme, the paronomasia of the two syntagmata *sie in eins zu bringen* and *sie einzubringen* is determined not simply by the partial difference between the signifiers *eins* ("one") and *ein* (= *hinein,* "in"), but also through the identity of the signifieds, insofar as Saussure's distinction is at all meaningful and appropriate in the context of Celan's use of language, which seems to be the same one that has been distinctive of modern poetry since Mallarmé.[20] *Ineinsbringen* ("bringing into one," i.e., uniting) and *Einbringen* ("bringing in") do not normally mean the same thing, any more than do "joining" and "putting in practice"; yet, for Celan, to put in practice in a work of art is to unite. The paronomasia of the passage under discussion shows this, and the same is suggested by a reading of the German version of the sonnet as a whole. Here we can plainly see Celan's intention toward language and the poetics of his translation. Its program is formulated in that line which renders Shakespeare's verse

Therefore my verse to constancy confined

by

In der Beständigkeit, da bleibt mein Vers geborgen.

Constancy, the theme of Shakespeare's sonnet, becomes for Celan the medium in which his verse dwells and which impedes the flow of his verse,[21] imposing constancy upon it. Constancy becomes the constituent element of his verse, in contrast to Shakespeare's original, in which constancy is sung about and described by means of a variety of expressions. Celan's intention toward language, in his version of Shakespeare's sonnet 105, is a realization of constancy in verse.[22]

We have already seen numerous examples of recurrence of the same elements and of creation of similarities that resist the changes wrought by the lapse of time, but the catalogue is not yet complete. Constancy is also conveyed on other linguistic levels than those considered so far. For example, Celan refrains from using enjambment in this translation, whereas he does employ it in his own poetry and also in others of his translations of Shakespeare's sonnets (as does Shakespeare himself). Where this device appears in the original text:

Since all alike my songs and praises be
To one, of one, still such, and ever so.

Celan inserts a colon in order to mark the limits of the verse:

> All dieses Singen hier, all dieses Preisen:
> von ihm, an ihn und immer ihm zulieb.

In another instance he replaces a comma (or perhaps a dash)[23] by a period, and thereby turns the anaphorically linked verses 9 and 10 into two that are merely juxtaposed:

> Fair, kind, and true, is all my argument,
> Fair, kind, and true, varying to other words,

> "Schön, gut und treu", das singe ich und singe.
> "Schön, gut und treu"—stets anders und stets das.

Whereas in the original text this pair of verses ends with a comma, Celan interrupts this strophe with a period, as he already did in the first and second strophes and will do in the couplet as well. (None of Shakespeare's three quatrains consists of more than a single sentence.) It is only in those verses which follow the ones just quoted, and which form the most precarious passage of the entire translation, that one could speak of enjambment. This is with the appearance of the paronomastic sequence *um sie in eins zu bringen, / sie einzubringen,* which does not stop at the end of the verse, although, admittedly, the effect of the enjambment is essentially canceled due to internal repetition.

The syntactic constancy, that is, the regular recurrence of the verses as individual sentences, goes still further: it represents a deviation from the original, indeed a determinate negation of the latter's way of shaping language. The syntactic subordination, the hypotaxis, of the original poem disappears, and along with it, the argumentative and logical style. At the turning points of the quatrains and the couplet, Shakespeare places either causal conjunctions (or adverbs):

v. 3 *Since* all alike my songs and praises be

v. 7 *Therefore* my verse to constancy confined;

or the conjunction "and" used consecutively:

v. 11 *And* in this change is my invention spent;

or a relative pronoun:

v. 14 *Which* three till now, never kept seat in one.

Celan eliminates these connective words. His sentences are not constructed either to refer to each other or to be subordinate to one another.

Celan's translation is profoundly marked by the principle of parataxis, in the literal sense as well as in a broader sense similar to the one Adorno introduced in connection with Hölderlin's later poetry.[24] Furthermore, Celan reduces the sharpness of the division of the fourteen lines into three quatrains and a couplet, even though he does set off the quatrains typographically from each other (in accord with the Petrarchan sonnet form) as well as preserve the rhyme scheme.[25] For, in contrast to Shakespeare's procedure, Celan divides every quatrain into two in the middle, either by the sentence structure or by the punctuation. Consequently, in spite of the rhyme scheme, Celan's quatrains approximate a series of couplets, whereas his couplet is assimilated to the quatrains, through syntactic division into two equal parts. In the original we find dissimilar units (three quatrains and a couplet), and these, by virtue of the way the sentence-units are interrelated (causal connection between the halves of strophes I and II and consecutive connection in strophe III) are hypotactically structured (even if, in the strict sense, there are no subordinate clauses in II and III); as a result they in turn imply inequality. In Celan's translation, on the other hand, the verses are simply set out one after the other; each is a unit, which, if it is not autonomous, is nevertheless much less heteronomous than the corresponding verse of the original. Just as, on the semantic and phonological levels, Celan's language tends to reduce change, difference, and variety to a minimum, so, too, does it strive for syntactic constance — in this translation more than in any other.

Celan's intention toward language, as revealed by a study of his German version of Shakespeare's sonnet 105, ought not be prematurely generalized. Our investigation dealt with but one sonnet. Nevertheless, the realization of constancy in verse, which is the major finding of our analysis, is not merely a feature peculiar to this one translation. Indeed, it accords with Roman Jakobson's definition of the function of poetic language: "The poetic function projects the principle of equivalence from the axis of selection into the axis of combination. Equivalence is promoted to the constitutive device of the sequence."[26] Jakobson's definition is not a description of a poem, but a statement of the principle governing the poetic use of language in the strict sense of the term. This principle can never be fully realized on the linguistic level, if the poem is not to be tautological, in other words, if it is to say anything at all. Celan's translation of Shakespeare's sonnet 105 approaches more closely than any previous poem to the limiting value of a thoroughgoing realization of the principle of the equivalence in the syntagmatic sequence (if one leaves "concrete poetry" aside). This is so not because Celan's poem and his translation *is* a poem — is more "poetic" than other poems by him or by others (to conclude this would be to misunderstand Jakobson), but because constancy is the theme of his poem, his translation. Of course, it is also the theme of Shakespeare's sonnet, to which, however, the preceding remarks in no way apply. This point brings us back one final time to the difference between the original and the translation, in other words, to the difference between Shakespeare's and Celan's respective intentions toward language.

"Constancy" can be called the theme of Shakespeare's sonnet, insofar as it actually deals with that virtue. Shakespeare asserts and praises the constancy of his "fair friend," and he describes his own writing, whose subject matter is to be exclusively his friend's constancy and the poet's celebration of it. Constancy is, at the same time, conceived of as the means by which this virtue is to be celebrated:

> Therefore my verse to constancy confined,
> One thing expressing, leaves out difference.

But it is as a virtue of the poet's composition that "constancy" figures as the subject matter of the poem. Only in the anaphorical (and thus rhetorically consecrated) repetition of "Fair, kind, and true" does constancy enter the poem's very language.

In Celan's version we find something very different. Consistent with his overall approach, Celan leaves untranslated those passages in which Shakespeare describes his own poem, his own style, and the goal of his writing: or else he translates them so "freely" that they no longer seem to deal with these topics:

> Since *all alike* my songs and praises be

> All dieses Singen hier, all dieses Preisen:

> Therefore my verse to constancy *confined,*
> One thing expressing, *leaves out difference.*

> In der Beständigkeit, da bleibt mein Vers geborgen,
> Spricht von dem Einen, schweift mir nicht umher.

> Fair, kind, and true, *is all my argument,*
> Fair, kind, and true, *varying to other words,*
> *And in this change is my invention spent*
> *Three themes in one, which wondrous scope affords.*

> "Schön, gut und treu", das singe ich und singe.
> "Schön, gut und treu"—stets anders und stets das.
> Ich find, erfind—um sie in eins zu bringen,
> sie einzubringen ohne Unterlass.

In Celan's version the poet does not speak of his "argument," his "invention," or his "scope," but instead the verse is arranged in accordance with the exigencies of this theme and of this objective aim. Nor does the poet affirm that this verse leaves out difference; rather he speaks in a language in which differences are simply left out. Celan, writing in the wake of the later Mallarmé and[27] an attentive observer of modern linguistics, philosophy of language, and aesthetics drew the logical consequence from the symbolist conception of poetry, in which a poem is its own subject matter and both invokes and describes itself as a symbol. According to Jakobson there exists a certain kind of constancy which is projected from the paradigmatic axis (of which it is constitutive) into the syntagmatic axis and which distinguishes the poetic sequence from the prosaic in this latter axis. If we accept Jakobson's views, then we may say that in translating a poem whose subject matter is that very constancy, Celan, perhaps without knowing of Jakobson's theorem, replaced the traditional symbolist poem—which deals only with itself and which has itself as its subject matter—with a poem which does not *deal* with itself but which *is* itself! He thus produced a poem which no longer speaks about itself but whose language is *sheltered* in that very place that it assigns to its subject matter, which is none other than itself: it is sheltered "in constancy."[28]

Notes

Notes

The German texts of all the essays translated here are available in a uniform, authoritative edition: Peter Szondi, *Schriften,* ed. Jean Bollack et al., 2 vols. (Frankfurt am Main: Suhrkamp Verlag, 1978).

Foreword

1. It is this historical perspective that sets off Szondi's criticism from that of the formalist and deconstructionist schools, whose concern with "difference" is purely rhetorical. Szondi is preeminently concerned with the question of how the literary text emerges as a formal-aesthetic expression of a particular author writing in a particular cultural-historical context. The text is neither a mere linguistic interplay without an historical ground nor a "universally" meaningful document of "human experience." It is always a statement about a particular time and place, and as such is open to comprehension, but not to final definition.

2. This reflection on the barrier created by Tieck's and Szondi's texts should not be understood as simply another example of deconstructionist concern with intertextual or rhetorical "interference." (Cf. the comments on the notion "preface" in John Irwin, *American Hieroglyphics,* [Baltimore: Johns Hopkins, 1983]; Gayatri Spivak's introduction to her translation of Jacques Derrida, *Of Grammatology* [Baltimore: Johns Hopkins, 1976]; and the preface to Paul Bové, *Destructive Poetics,* [New York: Columbia University Press, 1980].) As the rest of this essay should demonstrate, an awareness of the historical boundaries of a particular literary-critical practice (in this case, writing introductions that refuse to take cognizance of the origins and uses to which the form has been put) precludes the possibility of repeating the form and thereby covering over its history, a history fraught with danger at that.

3. Cf. Derrida's discussion of "names" and "proper sense" in *Of Grammatology.*

4. T. W. Adorno, "Im Schatten junger Mädchenblüte, in *Noten zur Literatur,* vol. 11, *Gesammelte Schriften* (Frankfurt am Main: Suhrkamp, 1974), p. 670.

5. On these subjects, see Carl Schorske, *Fin-de-siècle Vienna* (New York: Knopf, 1980), and the final three chapters of Eric Auerbach, *Mimesis* (Princeton: Princeton University Press, 1953).

6. Unlike Hannah Arendt, who describes Benjamin's desire to be an independent man of letters (see her introduction to *Illuminations* [New York: Harcourt, Brace, 1969]), Szondi focuses on the moment when Benjamin still hoped to remain within the academic community. The difference in perspective highlights the fact that Szondi is reading Benjamin as a comment on the history of his own academic heritage.

7. Szondi's father, Leopold, an internationally known psychologist, had moved his family to Zurich from Budapest shortly after Szondi was born in 1929. Szondi remained in Zurich after the war and studied with Emil Staiger at the University of Zurich. He continued his education at the University of Paris, and then took his first academic position in Berlin in 1961.

8. Georg Steiner, *Language and Silence* (New York: Atheneum, 1967).

9. T. W. Adorno, *Kulturkritik und Gesellschaft,* vol. 10, *Gesammelte Schriften* (Frankfurt am Main: Suhrkamp, 1977), p. 30.

10. Such notions, though often graced with other names, are readily found in contemporary American criticism, particularly in the work of defenders of the idea of a literary canon. See, for example, Charles Altieri, "An Idea of a Literary Canon," *Critical Inquiry* 10 (1983):37-60, and M. H. Abrams, "How to do Things With Texts," *Partisan Review* 46 (1979):566-88, in which Derrida and others are viewed as threats to "civilization." In an essay of similar intent, but with far more ominous overtones, Walter Jackson Bate has suggested that the first step toward a purified and improved academic (and spiritual) world should consist not only of the censorship of theorists such as Derrida, but also the clearing away of the academic "trivialization" that he sees represented in the study of women's and minority literature. See Walter Jackson Bate, "The Crisis in English Studies," *Harvard Magazine,* Sept.–Oct. 1982; reprint in *Scholarly Publishing,* April 1983, pp. 195-212. Paul de Man responded with a critique of Bate's position in *Times Literary Supplement,* 10 Dec. 1982, pp. 1355-56. See as well Lindsay Waters's reply in *Scholarly Publishing,* July 1983, pp. 299-304.

11. In his essay on Celan's "Engführung" ("Through Narrow Straits") and in his essay on "Eden," left unfinished at the time of his death, Szondi evokes the extermination camps and the murders of Rosa Luxemburg and Karl Liebknecht, but even though his personal friendship with Celan made him privy to extratextual information about the historical references in these poems, he refused to allow this knowledge to be organized as a series of subjective judgments about them. His commentaries leave the space of the poem open to the reader rather than enclosing it in an interpretive web that would organize a "final" meaning and thereby erase the gap between the text and the reader, the gap in which history is to be discovered.

12. "City Portraits," this volume, p. 140. Cf. Martin Heidegger's discussion of the work of art as a space of struggle, a struggle that renders the name instable and incapable of holding or closing a text, in *Ursprung des Kunstwerks,* ed. H. G. Gadamer (Stuttgart: Reklam, 1960).

13. Again, it must be emphasized that these gaps are historical and not simply textual aporias, they mark the collapse of a particular socioaesthetic perspective and its historical nexus.

14. *Schriften,* vol. 2, p. 384.

15. *Minima Moralia* (Frankfurt am Main: Suhrkamp, 1951), pp. 480-81.

16. Szondi, "City Portraits," p. 140.

17. See "Hope in the Past," p. 153-59. Szondi's rejection of Adorno's and Benjamin's "utopian" perspectives, their refusal of the present, can be compared to Fredric Jameson's recovery of the idea of the utopian in *The Political Unconscious* (Ithaca, N.Y.: Cornell

University Press, 1981). Both Szondi and Jameson seem to be tracing not only the desire for a nonalienated existence in the present, but also a means of locating a space within which to demonstrate that not all possibilities for a progressive viewpoint have been foreclosed. Unlike Jameson, however, Szondi does not extend his search to a sociopolitical analysis of the critical enterprise. His method, the hermeneutic focus on textual language, precludes discussion of that extratextual, ideological ground within which Jameson locates his reading of particular texts.

18. Not included in this collection are Szondi's many essays on the drama, published in *Theorie des modernen Dramas* (Frankfurt am Main: Suhrkamp, 1956) and *Versuch über das Tragische* (Frankfurt am Main: Insel, 1961), and his work on individual authors such as Thomas Mann and Bertolt Brecht. See *Satz und Gegensatz* (Frankfurt am Main: Insel, 1964) and *Lektüren und Lektionen* (Frankfurt am Main: Suhrkamp, 1973).

19. See Philippe Lacoue-Labarthe and Jean-Luc Nancy, *L'absolue littéraire-Théorie de la littérature du romantisme allemand* (Paris: Seuil, 1978); Paul de Man, "The Rhetoric of Temporality," in *Blindness and Insight,* 2d rev. ed. (Minneapolis: University of Minnesota Press, 1983), pp. 187–228 (originally published in *Interpretation,* ed. Charles Singleton [Baltimore: Johns Hopkins University Press, 1969]), and Wallace Martin's introduction to *The Yale Critics,* ed. J. Arac, W. Godzich, and W. Martin (Minneapolis: University of Minnesota Press, 1983).

20. Cf. Thomas McFarland's effort to demystify the treatment of the romantics and their aesthetic idealism in *Romanticism and the Forms of Ruin* (Princeton: Princeton University Press, 1981).

21. Although Eric Auerbach had made a similar effort somewhat earlier, his work had not yet reentered the academic/critical mainstream. See "On the Political Theory of Pascal," in *Scenes from the Drama of European Literature* (Gloucester, Mass.: Peter Smith, 1973).

22. The original essay appeared as "Zur Erkenntnisproblematik in der Literaturwissenschaft," *Die neue Rundschau* 73 (1962): 146–54.

23. For a contemporaneous but systematically ahistorical effort at general principles, see Northrop Frye, *Anatomy of Criticism* (Princeton: Princeton University Press, 1957).

24. On this subject, see Fritz Ringer, *The Decline of the German Mandarins: The German Academic Community 1890–1933* (Cambridge, Mass.: Harvard University Press, 1969).

25. See Michel Foucault, *The Order of Things* (New York: Random House, 1970), for a deconstruction of the connection between words and things.

26. This critical movement can also be related to the rise of expressionism, an aesthetic manifestation of the theory of the formal objectification of the subjective. One might also locate I. A. Richard's criticism, particularly its expressionist impulse and its concern with empathy, in this context.

27. Eric Auerbach, Friedrich Meinecke, and Norbert Elias are only three of the many whose works and lives were affected in similar fashion, and who were "rediscovered" after the war.

28. Although Bertolt Brecht did not approach the question of empathy from the same point of view as Szondi did, his critique of the concept not only demonstrates its presence in Weimar criticism, it also shows that some of the dangers inherent in the concept had already been recognized during the Republic.

29. Manfred Frank, Rainer Nägele, and others comment on the implications of this abstinence in a discussion published in *boundary 2* 11 (1983), pp. 43–48.

30. Daniel Fallon, *The German University* (Boulder, Colo.: Associated University Presses, 1980).

31. "On Textual Understanding," p. 5.

32. See Nietzsche and Foucault on the concept of genealogy in relation to Szondi's effort

184 □ NOTES TO PP. xx-18

to make what is inherited reappear within history. Friedrich Nietzsche, *Genealogy of Morals,* trans. W. Kaufmann (New York: Vintage, 1967), and Michel Foucault, "Nietzsche, Genealogy, History," in *Language, Counter-Memory, Practice,* ed. D. Bouchard (Ithaca, N.Y.: Cornell University Press, 1977), pp. 139–64.

33. "On Textual Understanding," p. 10. Cf. Auerbach's far more subjective notion of the "starting point" (*Ansatzpunkt*) in "Philologie and Weltliteratur," in *Gesammelte Aufsätze zur romanischen Philologie* (Bern: Franke, 1967). For Auerbach, it is the critics' own position that creates the point of origin for a synthesizing critical vision.

1. On Textual Understanding

1. Here Szondi employs the favorite saying of Effi Briest's father in Theodor Fontane's novel of the same name.—Trans.

2. Friedrich Schleiermacher, *Hermeneutik,* ed. H. Kimmerle (Heidelberg, 1959), p. 20: "Das vollkommene Verstehen einer Rede oder Schrift ist eine Kunstleistung und erheischt eine Kunstlehre oder Technik, welche wir durch den Ausdruck Hermeneutik bezeichnen."

3. Proposition 4.112 in Ludwig Wittgenstein, *Schriften* (Frankfurt am Main, 1960), p. 31: "Die Philosophie ist keine Lehre, sondern eine Tätigkeit. Ein philosophisches Werk besteht wesentlich aus Erläuterungen."

4. The quotation is taken from E. Ermatinger, *Philosophie der Literaturwissenschaft* (Berlin, 1930), p. 25.

5. Eng. trans. in Friedrich Hölderlin, *Poems and Fragments,* trans. Michael Hamburger (London, 1966), p. 433 (cited hereafter as "Hamburger").—Trans.

6. Friedrich Hölderlin, *Sämtliche Werke,* Grosse Stuttgarter Ausgabe, ed. Friedrich Beissner [Stuttgart, 1946–77], vol. 3, p. 549 [cited hereafter as SW].

7. Beda Allemann, " 'Friedensfeier.' Zur Wiederentdeckung einer späten Hymne Hölderlins," *Neue Zürcher Zeitung,* 24 Dec. 1954. Similarly in Allemann, *Hölderlins Friedensfeier* (Pfullingen, 1955), p. 73. [Eng. trans. of *Bread and Wine* from Hamburger, pp. 243–53.]

8. Cf. Wilhelm Dilthey, *Die Entstehung der Hermeneutik,* in *Gesammelte Schriften* (Leipzig and Berlin, 1924), vol. 5, pp. 317ff.

9. Eng. trans. of *Patmos* from Hamburger, pp. 463–77.—Trans.

10. See Lothar Kempter, "Das Leitbild in Hölderlins Friedensfeier *Hölderlin-Jahrbuch* 9 (1955–56): 88ff.

11. Schleiermacher himself noted that it may very easily happen "that entirely false notions are associated with individual sentences of an author if the sentences, once torn from their original context, are incorporated in another context and used as examples or evidence; and this in fact occurs so frequently that one can only wonder why this fidelity on the part of the citators has not yet become proverbial." Cf. *Zweite Akademierede* (1829), in *Hermeneutik* [Heidelburg, 1959], p. 14. [This text is now available in an Eng. trans. in Schleiermacher, *Hermeneutics: The Handwritten Manuscripts,* ed. Heinz Kimmerle, trans. James Duke and Jack Forstman (Missoula, Mont., 1977), pp. 195–214.]

12. *Lyceum* fragment no. 25, in Friedrich Schlegel, *1794–1802, Seine prosaischen Jugendschriften,* ed. J. Minor (Vienna, 1882), vol. 1, p. 97: "das Postulat der Gemeinheit: Alles recht Grosse, Gute und Schöne ist unwahrscheinlich, denn es ist ausserordentlich, und zum mindesten verdächtig."

13. Ermatinger, *Philosophie,* pp. 334–35.

14. For Eng. trans. of *As on a holiday . . . ,*" see Hamburger, p. 373ff.—Trans.

15. Schleiermacher, *Hermeneutik,* p. 142: . . . wenn man die Regel stellt, ein Wort in demselben Zusammenhang nicht das eine Mal anders zu erklären als das andere, weil nämlich nicht wahrscheinlich sei, daß der Schriftsteller es das eine Mal anders werde ge-

braucht haben: so kann diese doch nur insofern gelten als auch der Satz, wo es zum andern Mal vorkommt, noch als ein Teil desselben Zusammenhanges mit Recht kann angesehen werden. Denn in einem neuen Abschnitt können unter manchen Umständen mit demselben Recht wie in einem ganz andern Werk noch andere Bedeutungen ihren Platz finden.

16. Eng. trans. Heinrich von Kleist, *Amphitryon,* trans. Charles E. Passage, in *Amphitryon: Three Plays in New Verse Translations* (Chapel Hill, 1974), pp. 230–31. Translation modified.—Trans.

17. K. Hildebrandt, *Das Werk Stefan Georges* (Hamburg, 1961), p. 359.

18. P. Valéry, "Commentaries de charmes," in *Variété* III (Paris, 1936), p. 80: "C'est une erreur contraire à la nature de la poésie, et qui lui serait même mortelle, que de prétendre qu'à tout poème correspond un sens véritable, unique, et conforme ou identique à quelque pensée de l'auteur."

19. W. Müller-Seidel, *Versehen und Erkennen: Eine Studie über H. v. Kleist* (Cologne-Graz, 1961), p. 216.

20. Quotation taken from H.-G. Gadamer, *Wahrheit und Methode* (Tübingen, 1960), p. 172.

21. T. W. Adorno, "Valérys Abweichungen," in *Noten zur Literatur,* vol. 2 (Frankfurt am Main, 1961), p. 43 (also in *Gesammelte Schriften,* vol. 11 [Frankfurt am Main, 1974], p. 159).

2. The Other Arrow: On the Genesis of the Late Hymnic Style

1. The German texts of Friedrich Hölderlin's works and letters are cited according to the *Sämtliche Werke, Grosse Stuttgarter Ausgabe,* ed. Friedrich Beissner, [Stuttgart, 1946–77], hereafter abbreviated as SW; the first number indicates the volume of this edition and the second number, the page. The English translations of the poems are taken from Hölderlin, *Poems and Fragments,* trans. Michael Hamburger (London, 1966) hereafter abbreviated as "Hamburger."—Trans.

2. See Eduard Lachmann, *Hölderlins Hymnen in freien Strophen: Eine metrische Untersuchung* (Frankfurt am Main, 1937), p. 17 and passim.

3. Eng. trans., Hamburger, p. 43.—Trans.

4. Eng. trans., Hamburger, p. 149.—Trans.

5. Letter of 4 Dec. 1801, *SW* 6: 427, l. 3.

6. *SW* 5: 41, ll. 1–3.

7. Eng. trans., Hamburger, p. 373.—Trans.

8. Cf. the prose draft: "So stehen jetzt unter günstiger Witterung die Dichter," *SW* 2: 668, l. 9.

9. Cf. Martin Heidegger, *Erläuterungen zu Hölderlins Dichtung,* 1st ed. (1951), 3d ed. (Frankfurt am Main, 1963), p. 51: "Wie ein Landmann auf seinem Gang froh ob der Behütung seiner Welt, in der Feldmark verweilt, *so stehn sie unter günstiger Witterung*—die Dichter ["As a countryman on his way, happy for the sheltering of his world, tarries in the field, *so they stand in favorable weather*—they, the poets"].

10. Eng. trans., Hamburger, p. 375.—Trans.

11. The period at the end of verse 42, which makes a new sentence out of the verses 43ff. ("Des gemeinsamen Geistes Gedanken sind, / Still endend in der Seele des Dichters", ["The thoughts of the communal spirit they are, / And quietly come to rest in the poet's soul,"]) does not exist in the manuscript (see *SW* 2: 674, l. 43). The first editor's conjecture was adopted by the subsequent editors. Yet, the fact that these verses actually belong to the preceding sentence, and therefore that the group "des gemeinsamen Geistes Gedanken" is a predicate, not a subject, can be seen both from the comma after verse 43 and from the prose

draft: " . . . das Lied, das gleich der Rebe, der Erd' entwachsen ist u. ihren Flammen u. der Sonne [des] Himmels u. den Gewittern, die in der Luft u. die / Geheimnissvoller bereitet, hinwander[n]d / Zwischen Himmel u. Erd, unter den Völkern, sind, / Gedanken sind, des göttlichen Geistes, / Still endend in der Seele des Dichters" (*SW* 2: 668–69). The first to draw attention to this point was Walter Bröcker; see "Die Auferstehung der mythischen Welt in der Dichtung Hölderlins" (1955), in his *Das was kommt, gesehen von Nietzche und Hölderlin* (Pfullingen, 1963), p. 47, n. 42.

12. *SW* 2: 110, l. 240.

13. Variant to the hymn *Der Einzige* (*The Only One*), *SW* 2: 753.

14. Third version, *SW* 4: 135, ll. 371ff.

15. Eng. trans., Hamburger, p. 375.—Trans.

16. In the manuscript, above the words *die göttlichgetroffene,* we find *Asche* and *tödli* [ch], which the editor Beissner calls "the start of a variant that was not completed" (cf. *SW* 2: 675). Hölderlin presumably contemplated this change in connection with the fragmentary concluding verses of the hymn, in which the poet becomes aware of his sacrilege. For the interpretation of these verses see p. 34 below.

17. Eng. trans., Hamburger, pp. 375, 377.—Trans.

18. *Deutsche Dichtung,* ed. and intro. Stefan George and Karl Wolfskehl, vol. 3, *Das Jahrhundert Goethes,* 2d ed. (Berlin, 1910), pp. 48–49. In this book the conclusion reads: "Und tieferschüttert, eines Gottes Leiden / Mitleidend, bleibt das ewige Herz doch fest" ["And deeply shaken, a god's sorrows / Sorrowing, the eternal heart still stands fast"]. As can be seen from the facsimile of folio 17 recto of the *Stuttgart Foliobuch,* these verses give the original wording of the MS lines that are designated in the reproduction by the letters *a* and *b*. In Beissner's edition, by contrast, the corresponding verses are given in the lines *a* (with a change in the second half of the verse: *die Leiden des Stärkeren),* *b* (with the change or conjecture: *in den hochherstür* [zen] *den* [*Stürmen*]), *and c*. In place of the single verse . . . *bleibt das ewige Herz doch fest (b),* with which the poem concludes in Hellingrath's edition [see note 18 below], Beissner puts two verses (*b* and *c*), which are not the last and in which *das Herz* appears instead of *das ewige Herz*—a change that led to his being unjustly accused of tampering with the text of Hölderlin's poetry, even though this change is simply one he made in the text of the previously accepted editions. However that may be, Beissner has given two verses in place of a single one on the basis of his observation—which can be verified against the facsimile of the manuscript—that the fragmentary conclusion of the hymn is not struck out and that the hymn is thus not complete. Whereas in the case of a completed poem later variants, which so to speak open the poem up again, rightly find their place among the variant readings in the notes, the critical edition of a poem of which no fair copy exists and which, according to the surviving manuscripts, remained unfinished, must reproduce the last recognizable stage. Hellingrath's goal, to salvage a new poem of Hölderlin's from the manuscripts, was legitimate in his time and justified his placing in an appendix whatever hampered the presentation of a completed hymn; but this can no longer be the goal of a critical edition. For this reason, and for this reason only, Beissner gives *das Herz* (*c*) and not *das ewige Herz* (*b*).

19. Hölderlin, *Sämtliche Werke,* ed. Norbert v. Hellingrath, vol. 4, *Gedichte 1800–1806* (Munich and Leipzig, 1916), pp. 151–52.

20. M. Heidegger, "Wie wenn am Feiertage . . . ," in *Erläuterungen.* See note 21 below. —E. Lachmann, "Hölderlins erste Hymne," *DVjs* 17 (1939): 221ff. E. Lachmann, Hölderlins Hymnen in freien Strophen," p. 125: "Bau und Rhythmus erweisen das Gedicht als vollendet. Es ist kein Bruchstück" ["The structure and rhythm prove the poem complete. It is no fragment"—trans. A. Warminski]. On this point see also F. Beissner, "Bemerkungen

zu Eduard Lachmanns Buch über Hölderlins Hymnen," *Dichtung und Volkstum* 38 (1937): 349: "Lachmann nennt diesen Text beharrlich die 'endgültige' Fassung. Ein Blick in die Handschrift hätte ihn überzeugen müssen, dass hier von Endgültigkeit keine Rede sein kann" ["Lachmann stubbornly calls this text the 'final' version. A look into the manuscript would have convinced him that in this case there can be no talk of finality"—trans. A. Warminski]. Beissner presents a similar view in the notes to his edition; see *SW* 2: 679. On Lachmann's essay, see also note 22 below.

21. Hölderlin, *Sämtliche Werke und Briefe*, Kritisch-historische Ausgabe von Franz Zinkernagel, vol. 1 (Leipzig, 1922), p. 320.

22. *SW* 2: 120; [Eng. trans., Hamburger, p. 377.] These verses are lacking in the text that Heidegger reproduces, which was "checked anew against the autograph drafts." Heidegger concedes, moreover, that "in many respects the poem [is] incomplete. It is impossible to determine, in particular, the form that Hölderlin might have decided to give to the conclusion." But Heidegger continues mysteriously '... all incompletion here is only the consequence of the abundance that springs forth from the inmost beginning of the poem and that requires a terse conclusion." This suppression of the "fractured concluding strophe" has been called a "crude falsification" by Walter Muschg. ("Zerschwatzte Dichtung," in *Die Zerstörung der deutschen Literatur*, 3d ed. [Bern, 1958], pp. 217-18) To be sure, when Muschg asserts that the hymn *As on a holiday...* " stands at the beginning of Hölderlin's mental derangement," he also seems to be committing the error of which he accuses Heidegger; for he makes the facts (the hymn was begun around 1800, and the first signs of the illness appeared in 1802) conform to his interpretation of the concluding strophe: "Hölderlin trembles with fear before the madness that is the punishment decreed by the gods."

23. *SW* 2: 669-70. The signs marking division into verses are Hölderlin's. [The Eng. trans. of the second and third sentences ("when of a self-inflicted ... when round about me") is taken from Hamburger, p. 8.]

24. *SW* 2: 110; [Eng. trans., Hamburger, p. 227.]

25. *SW* 2: 141; 2: 426; 2: 671; 2: 782. Cf. B. Böschenstein, *Konkordanz zu Hölderlins Gedichten nach 1800* (Göttingen, 1964), p. 60.

26. Cf. "Der Rhein": "... bedürfen / Die Himmlischen eines Dings, / So sinds Heroën und Menschen / Und Sterblich sonst. Denn weil / Die Seeligsten nichts fühlen von selbst, / Muss wohl, wenn solches zu sagen / Erlaubt ist, in der Götter Nahmen / Theilnehmend fühlen ein Andrer, / Den brauchen" sie" (*SW* 2: 145). [(... and if / The Heavenly have need of one thing, / It is of heroes and human beings / And other mortals. For since / The most blessed in themselves feel nothing / Another, if to say such a thing is / Permitted, must, I suppose, / Vicariously feel in the name of the gods, / And him they need;....) (Hamburger, p. 415).]

27. *SW* 6: 427.

28. *SW* 6: 432; [Eng. trans., Hamburger, p. 13.]

29. Cf. Beda Allemann, *Hölderlin und Heidegger* (1954); 2d ed. (Zurich, [1956]). Our interpretation of the final verses differs from Allemann's (see Allemann, p. 26).

30. E. Lachmann assumes that such a transformation occurred. In his view ("Hölderlins erste Hymne," pp. 233ff.), after the insertion of the third strophe, which is not anticipated in the prose draft (*Jetzt aber tagts!*), there seems to be no room for the ideas of the fragmentary concluding verses. "After the freely granted descent of the divine ray, and after the 'Awakening of divinely beautiful nature,' there is no longer any place for an offense against the divine will" (p. 236); as a result, Lachmann sees the offense as consisting in the circumstance that the poet approaches the "divine all too greedily, and at the wrong time." But, first of all, the hymn does not say that the poet could approach the gods "at the wrong

188 □ NOTES TO PP. 36-43

time" (*zur Unzeit*). This interpretation, which Beissner also defends ("Bemerkungen," p. 351), is contradicted by the expressions *von anderem Pfeile* and *von selbgeschlagener Wunde*. Second, the basic idea of the third strophe can already be found in the prose draft: "a new sun shines over us; the spring blooms differently than before" ("eine neue Sonne scheinet über uns, es blühet anders denn zuvor der Frühling"), *SW* 2: 668. In the metrical version these lines are replaced by the third strophe, whose metaphor of the times of day takes the place of the prose draft's metaphor of the seasons. Lachmann proposes a counterargument. He thinks that, in contrast to the third strophe, the passage of the prose draft just cited does not evoke a new "world-epoch" (*Weltaugenblick*); but this is implausible.

31. E. Lachmann, "Hölderlins erste Hymne," p. 250.

32. *SW* 2: 663–64.

33. Eng. trans., Hamburger, p. 371.—Trans.

34. The irreality of the phrase *Weh mir!... wenn* is revealed as something real by the hymn's final verses.

35. Cf. the marginal note before the verses 63–66: "Die Sphäre die höher ist, als die des Menschen diese ist der Gott" ["The sphere that is higher than that of man, this is god"]. (*SW* 2: 675).

36. See Eng. trans. Hamburger, p. 230.—Trans.

37. Eng. trans., Hamburger, p. 233.—Trans.

38. Eng. trans., Hamburger, p. 235.—Trans.

39. The verses "wir, welche die stille / Liebe bildete, wir suchen zu Göttern die Bahn" ["we, fashioned by quiet / Love, we seek the path to the gods"] are later replaced by "und wer so / Lieb, gehet, er muss, gehet zu Göttern die Bahn" ["and who so / Loved, goes, he must, goes the path to the gods"]. The second version prepares the way for the late hymnic style inasmuch as, in thematic terms, it brings its intention closer to realization (*gehen*, "go," instead of *suchen*, "seek"), while, at the same time, in formal terms, it displays doubt and menace in its "austere arrangement." As the poems *As on a holiday*...and *The Middle of Life* make clear, the genesis of this style can here be grasped in the smallest detail, in the reworking of a single sentence.

40. Karl Viëtor, "Hölderlins Liebeselegie" (1938), in his *Geist und Form* (Bern, 1952), p. 291.

41. *An die Madonna, SW* 2: 211, l. 8.

42. This remark, however, is not meant to resolve the question of when the poem *Hälfte des Lebens* (*The Middle of Life*) was completed.

3. The Notion of the Tragic in Schelling, Hölderlin, and Hegel

1. Schelling, *Briefe über Dogmatismus und Kritizismus,* Hauptwerke der Philosophie in originalgetreuen Neudrucken, vol. 3 (Leipzig, 1914), pp. 85–86 (cited hereafter as *Briefe*). Cf. E. Staiger, *Der Geist der Liebe und das Schicksal* (Frauenfeld-Leipzig, 1935), p. 41: "Man hat oft gefragt, wie die griechische Vernunft die Widersprüche ihrer Tragödie ertragen konnte. Ein Sterblicher—vom Verhängnis zum Verbrecher bestimmt, selbst gegen das Verhängnis kämpfend, und doch fürchterlich bestraft für das Verbrechen, das ein Werk des Schicksals war! Der Grund dieses Widerspruchs, das, was ihn erträglich machte, lag tiefer, als man ihn suchte, lag im Streit menschlicher Freiheit mit der Macht der objektiven Welt, in welchem der Sterbliche, wenn jene Macht eine Übermacht—(ein Fatum)—ist, notwendig unterliegen, und doch, weil er nicht ohne Kampf unterlag, für sein Unterliegen selbst bestraft werden mußte. Daß der Verbrecher, der doch nur der Übermacht des Schicksals unterlag, doch noch bestraft wurde, war Anerkennung menschlicher Freiheit, Ehre, die der Freiheit gebührte. Die griechische Tragödie ehrte menschliche Freiheit dadurch, daß sie

ihren Helden gegen die Übermacht des Schicksals kämpfen ließ: um nicht über die Schran-ken der Kunst zu springen, mußte sie ihn unterliegen, aber, um auch diese, durch die Kunst abgedrungne, Demütigung menschlicher Freiheit wieder gut zu machen, mußte sie ihn—auch für das durchs Schicksal begangne Verbrechen—büßen lassen. [. . .] Es war ein großer Gedanke, willig auch die Strafe für ein unvermeidliches Verbrechen zu tragen, um so durch den Verlust seiner Freiheit selbst eben diese Freiheit zu beweisen, und noch mit einer Erklärung des freien Willens unterzugehen."

2. Fichte, "Grundlage der gesamten Wissenschaftslehre," in *Werke,* ed. F. Medicus (Leipzig, 1911), vol. 1, p. 295.

3. *Aus Schellings Leben* (Leipzig, 1869), vol. 1, pp. 76–77: "Der eigentliche Unterschied der kritischen und dogmatischen Philosophie scheint mir darin zu liegen, dass jene vom absoluten (noch durch kein Objekt bedingten) Ich, diese vom absoluten Objekt oder Nicht-Ich ausgeht."

4. Ibid.

5. *Briefe,* p. 84: "Streben nach unveränderlicher Selbstheit, unbedingter Freiheit, uneingeschränkter Tätigkeit."

6. Ibid., p. 85: "Sie haben Recht, noch Eines bleibt übrig—zu wissen, dass es eine objektive Macht gibt, die unsrer Freiheit Vernichtung droht, und mit dieser festen und gewissen Überzeugung im Herzen—gegen sie zu kämpfen, seiner ganzen Freiheit aufzubie-ten, und so unterzugehen."

7. Ibid., p. 88: "zum System des Handelns könnte er schon deswegen nicht werden, weil ein solches System ein Titanengeschlecht voraussetzte, ohne diese Voraussetzung aber, ohne Zweifel zum grössten Verderben der Menschheit ausschlüge."

8. Throughout this essay we use the words "dialectic" and "dialectical" in a way that conforms to Hegel's usage but without accepting the implications of his system. Thus they designate the following phenomena and processes: the unity of contradictory terms, the turning of one term into its opposite, the act by which a term posits the negation of itself, and self-division.

9. Schelling, *Philosophie der Kunst,* in *Werke* (Stuttgart, 1856–61), vol. 5, sec. 1, p. 693: "Das Wesentliche der Tragödie ist [. . .] ein wirklicher Streit der Freiheit im Subjekt und der Notwendigkeit als objektiver, welcher Streit sich nicht damit endet, daß der eine oder der andere unterliegt, sondern daß beide siegend und besiegt zugleich in der vollkommenen Indifferenz erscheinen."

10. Ibid., p. 969: "Der Streit von Freiheit und Notwendigkeit [ist] wahrhaft nur da, wo diese den Willen selbst untergräbt, und die Freiheit auf ihrem eigenen Boden bekämpft wird."

11. Ibid., p. 380: "unendliche, alle Realität in sich begreifende Idealität."

12. Ibid., p. 383: "Ineinsbildung des Realen und Idealen"; "Indifferenz der Freiheit und der Notwendigkeit, in einem Realen angeschaut."

13. Ibid., p. 687: "gleichsam einen Stand der Unschuld, wo alles noch beisammen und eins ist, was später nur zerstreut existiert oder nur aus der Zerstreuung wieder zur Einheit kommt. Diese Identität entzündete sich im Fortgang der Bildung im lyrischen Gedicht zum Widerstreit, und erst die reifste Frucht der späteren Bildung war es, wodurch, auf einer höheren Stufe, die Einheit selbst mit dem Widerstreit sich versöhnte, und beide wieder in einer vollkommneren Bildung eins wurden. Diese höhere Identität ist das Drama."

14. Hölderlin, *Sämtliche Werke,* Grosse Stuttgarter Ausgabe, ed. Friedrich Beissner, [Stuttgart, 1946–77] (cited hereafter as *SW*) vol. 4, p. 275. *Sämtliche Werke,* Historisch-kritische Ausgabe, ed. L. v. Pigenot (Berlin, 1943), vol. 3, p. 274: "Die Bedeutung der Tragödien ist am leichtesten aus dem Paradoxon zu begreifen. Denn alls Ursprüngliche, weil alles Vermögen gerecht und gleich geteilt ist, erscheint zwar nicht in ursprünglicher

Stärke, sondern eigentlich in seiner Schwäche, so daβ recht eigentlich das Lebenslicht und die Erscheinung der Schwäche jedes Ganzen angehört. Im Tragischen nun ist das Zeichen an sich selbst unbedeutend wirkungslos, aber das Ursprüngliche ist gerade heraus. Eigentlich nämlich kann das Ursprüngliche nur in seiner Schwäche erscheinen, insofern aber das Zeichen an sich selbst als unbedeutend = 0 gesetzt wird, kann auch das Ursprüngliche, der verborgene Grund jeder Natur, sich darstellen. Stellt die Natur in ihrer schwächsten Gabe sich eigentlich dar, so ist das Zeichen, wenn sie sich in ihrer stärksten Gabe darstellt = 0."

Concerning line 1, *aus dem Paradoxon* is the reading proposed by Zinkernagel and Beissner (Cf. "Zum Hölderlin-Text: Neue Lesungen zu einigen theoretischen Aufsätzen," in *Dichtung Volkstum* [1938]). According to Pigenot it first read: "Die (eigentliche gestr.) Bedeutung aller Tragödien erklärt sich aus den Paradoxen, dass alles Ursprungliche, weil alles Gut gerecht und gleich geteilt ist, nicht wirklich, sondern eigentlich nur in seiner Schwäche erscheint" ["The ('authentic' crossed out) meaning of all tragedies can be explained by the paradox that everything original, because all property is distributed justly and equally, appears not in its actuality but properly only in its weakness"—trans. A. Warminski]. (Cf. *Werke*, ed. Pigenot, vol. 3, p. 589.) Concerning line 4, *recht* is the reading given by Zinkernagel and Beissner; Pigenot and Bohm give *wohl.*

15. *SW* 6, 329: "Paradoxon . . . , dass der Kunst- und Bildungstrieb mit allen seinen Modifikationen und Abarten ein eigentlicher Dienst sei, den die Menschen der Natur erweisen."

16. Ibid., p. 300.

17. Ibid., vol. 4, p. 154: "ein Sohn der gewaltigen Entgegensetzungen von Natur und Kunst in denen die Welt vor seinen Augen erschien. Ein Mensch, in dem sich jene Gegensätze so innig vereinigen, dass sie zu *Einem* in ihm werden. . . ."

18. Ibid., pp. 156–57: "weil sonst das Allgemeine im Individuum sich verlöre, und . . . das Leben einer Welt in einer Einzelheit abstürbe."

19. Ibid., p. 157.

20. Ibid.

21. "Anmerkungen zum "Ödipus," in *SW* 5, 201: "Die Darstellung des Tragischen beruht vorzüglich darauf, daβ das Ungeheure, wie der Gott und Mensch sich paart, und grenzenlos die Naturmacht und des Menschen Innerstes im Zorn Eins wird, dadurch sich begreift, daβ das grenzenlose Eineswerden durch grenzenloses Scheiden sich reiniget." [Eng. trans. in Hölderlin, *Poems and Fragments,* Michael Hamburger (London, 1966), p. 7.]

22. Ibid., p. 202: "der Gott und der Mensch, damit der Weltlauf keine Lücke hat und das Gedächtnis der Himmlischen nicht ausgehet, in der allvergessenden Form der Untreue sich mitteilt, denn göttliche Untreue ist am besten zu behalten."

23. Ibid., p. 197.

24. Hegel, "Über die wissenschaftlichen Behandlungen des Naturrechts, seine Stelle in der praktischen Philosophie, und sein Verhältnis zu den positiven Rechtswissenschaften" ["On the scientific treatment of natural right, its place in the practical philosophy, and its relation to the positive sciences of right"—trans. A Warminski], in *Werke,* Jubiläums-Ausgabe, [ed. H. G. Grochner (Stuttgart, 1927)], vol. 1, pp. 501–2. "Die Tragödie [ist] darin, daβ die sittliche Natur ihre unorganische, damit sie sich nicht mit ihr verwickele, als ein Schicksal von sich abtrennt und sich gegenüber stellt, und, durch die Anerkennung desselben in dem Kampfe, mit dem göttlichen Wesen, als der Einheit von beidem, versöhnt ist."

25. Ibid., p. 525: "alles Tun und Sein des Einzelnen als eines solchen von dem ihm entgegengesetzten Allgemeinen und der Abstraktion beaufsichtigt, gewusst und bestimmt sehen."

26. Ibid., p. 452: "[die] absolute Idee der Sittlichkeit, . . . [die den] Naturzustand [und

die] den Individuen fremde . . . Majestät und Göttlichkeit des Ganzen des Rechtzustandes [als] schlechthin identisch [enthält]."

27. Ibid., p. 527.

28. Ibid., pp. 509-10: "ist unmittelbar Sittlichkeit des Einzelnen und umgekehrt [ist] das Wesen der Sittlichkeit des Einzelnen schlechthin die reale und darum allgemeine absolute Sittlichkeit."

29. Ibid., p. 500: "Die Kraft des Opfers besteht in dem Anschauen und Objektivieren der Verwickelung mit dem Unorganischen;—durch welche Anschauung diese Verwickelung gelöst, das Unorganische abgetrennt, und, als solches erkannt, hiermit selbst in die Indifferenz aufgenommen ist: das Lebendige aber, indem es das, was es als einen Teil seiner selbst weiß, in dasselbe legt, und dem Tode opfert, dessen Recht zugleich anerkannt und zugleich sich davon gereinigt hat."

30. Ibid., p. 501: " . . . so dass ihre wilde Natur des Anschauens der ihrem unten in der Stadt errichteten Altare gegenüber auf der Burg hoch thronende Athene genösse, und hierdurch beruhigt wäre."

31. *Hegels theologische Jugendschriften*, ed. H. Nohl (Tübingen, 1907), p. 283.

32. Ibid., p. 392.

33. Ibid., p. 393, note.

34. Ibid., p. 281: "Jetzt erst tritt das verletzte Leben als eine feindsele Macht gegen den Verbrecher auf, und mißhandelt ihn, wie er mißhandelt hat; so ist die Strafe als Schicksal die gleiche Rückwirkung der Tat des Verbrechers selbst, einer Macht, die er selbst bewaffnet, eines Feindes, den er sich selbst zum Feinde machte."

35. Ibid.

36. Ibid., p. 293: " . . . die Zeit ihres Volkes war wohl eine von denen, in welcher das schöne Gemüt ohne Sünde nicht leben, aber zu dieser wie zu jeder anderen Zeit durch Liebe zum schönsten Bewußtsein zurückkehren konnte."

37. *Werke*, vol. 1, p. 441.

38. *Werke*, vol. 14, pp. 528-29: "Das eigentliche Thema der ursprünglichen Tragödie [ist] das Göttliche; aber nicht das Göttliche, wie es den Inhalt des relgiösen Bewußtseins als solchen ausmacht, sondern wie es in die Welt, in das individuelle Handeln eintritt, in dieser Wirklichkeit jedoch seinen substantiellen Charakter weder einbüßt, noch sich in das Gegenteil seiner umgewendet sieht. In dieser Form ist die geistige Substanz des Wollens and Vollbringens das Sittliche. [. . .] Durch das Prinzip der Besonderung nun, dem alles unterworfen ist, was sich in die reale Objektivität hinaustreibt, sind die sittlichen Mächte wie die handelnden Charaktere unterschieden in Rücksicht auf ihren Inhalt und ihre individuelle Erscheinung. Werden nun diese besonderen Gewalten, wie es die dramatische Poesie fordert, zur erscheinenden Tätigkeit aufgerufen und verwirklichen sie sich als bestimmter Zweck eines menschlichen Pathos, das zur Handlung übergeht, so ist ihr Einklang aufgehoben und sie treten in wechselseitiger Abgeschlossenheit gegeneinander auf. Das individuelle Handeln will dann unter bestimmten Umständen einen Zweck oder Charakter durchführen, der unter diesen Voraussetzungen, weil er in seiner für sich fertigen Bestimmtheit sich einseitig isoliert, notwendig das entgegengesetzte Pathos gegen sich aufreizt und dadurch unausweichlich Konflikte herbeileitet. Das ursprünglich Tragische besteht nun darin, daß innerhalb solcher Kollision beide Seiten des Gegensatzes für sich genommen Berechtigung haben, während sie andererseits dennoch den wahren positiven Gehalt ihres Zwecks und Charakters nur als Negation and Verletzung der anderen, gleichberechtigten Macht durchzubringen imstande sind und deshalb in ihrer Sittlichkeit und durch dieselbe ebensosehr in Schuld geraten." [The Eng. trans. of this passage is taken from G. W. F. Hegel, *Aesthetics,* trans. T. M. Knox, vol. 2 (Oxford, 1975), pp. 1195-96.]

39. Ibid., p. 567.

40. Ibid., p. 556: "... von allem Herrlichen der alten und modernen Welt [das] vortrefflichste, befriedigendste Kunstwerk."

41. This is reflected in the position that the classical (Greek) art form occupies in Hegel's *Aesthetics,* between the symbolic (including the Hebraic) and the romantic (Christian) forms. Cf. especially *Werke,* vol. 13, p. 15.

42. *Theologische Jugendschriften,* p. 260.

43. On Hegel, cf. also P. Szondi, "Versuch über das Tragische," in *Schriften,* [ed. Jean Bollack et al. (Frankfurt am Main, 1978)], vol. 1, p. 203.

4. Friedrich Schlegel and Romantic Irony, with Some Remarks on Tieck's Comedies

1. Unlike Winckelmann and the young Schlegel, Herder had already surmised the Oriental origins of Greek culture. Cf., for example, Herder, *Sämtliche Werke,* ed. B. Suphan, vol. 8, pp. 472ff. On the conception of the Orient in German romanticism, see René Gérard, *L'Orient et la pensée romantique allemande* (Paris, 1963).

2. In the context of the present sketch, we cannot attempt to situate more precisely the essay "On the Study of Greek Poetry" and its paradoxical (and thus revealing) combination of understanding and rejection of the modern age.

3. *Friedrich Schlegel, 1794–1802, Seine prosaischen Jugendschriften,* ed. J. Minor (Vienna, 1882), vol. 1, p. 97: In antiquity, understanding was "auch bei der größten Ausbildung höchstens nur der Handlanger und Dolmetscher der Neigung; der gesamte zusammengesetzte Trieb aber der unumschränkte Gesetzgeber und Führer der Bildung." In der Moderne "ist die bewegende, ausübende Macht zwar auch der Trieb; die lenkende, gesetzgebende Macht hingegen der Verstand: gleichsam ein oberstes lenkendes Prinzipium, welches die blinde Kraft leitet und führt, ihre Richtung determiniert, die Anordnung der ganzen Masse bestimmt und nach Willkür die einzelnen Teile trennt und verknüpft." Hereafter, the following abbreviations will be used: *JS* = Jugendschriften, *L* = *Lyceum* fragments, *A* = *Athenaeum* fragments, *I* = *Ideen (The Ideas).* The numbering of the fragments follows Minor's edition.

4. *JS 1,* 105: "Der isolierende Verstand fängt damit an, daβ er das Ganze der Natur trennt und vereinzelt. Unter seiner Leitung geht daher die durchgängige Richtung der Kunst auf treue Nachahmung des Einzelnen. Bei höherer intellektueller Bildung wurde also natürlich das Ziel der modernen Poesie originelle und interessante Individualität."

5. *Friedrich Schlegels Briefe an seinen Bruder August Wilhelm,* ed. O. Walzel (Berlin, 1890), pp. 94–95. "Der Gegenstand und die Wirkung dieses Stücks ist die heroische Verzweiflung d. h. eine unendliche Zerrüttung in den allerhöchsten Kräften. Der Grund seines innren Todes liegt in der Größe seines Verstandes. Wäre er weniger groβ, so würde er ein Heroe sein.—Für ihn ist es nicht der Mühe wert, ein Held zu sein; wenn er wollte, so wäre es ihm nur ein Spiel. Er übersieht eine zahllose Menge von Verhältnissen—daher seine Unentschlossenheit.—Wenn man aber so nach Wahrheit frägt, so verstummt die Natur; und solchen Trieben, und strenger Prüfung ist die Welt nichts, denn unser zerbrechliches Dasein kann nichts schaffen, das unsren göttlichen Forderungen Genüge leistete. Das Innerste seines Daseins ist ein gräβliches Nichts, Verachtung der Welt und seiner Selbst."

6. *JS 1,* 107: "Durch eine wunderbare Situation wird alle Stärke seiner edeln Natur in den Verstand zusammengedrängt, die tätige Kraft aber ganz vernichtet. Sein Gemüt trennt sich, wie auf der Folterbank nach entgegengesetzten Richtungen aus einander gerissen; es zerfällt und geht unter in Überfluβ von müβigem Verstand, der ihn selbst noch peinlicher drückt, als alle die ihm nahen. Es gibt vielleicht keine vollkommnere Darstellung der unauflöslichen Disharmonie, welche der eigentliche Gegenstand der philosophischen

Tragödie ist, als ein so grenzenloses Mißverhaltnis der denkenden und der tätigen Kraft, wie in Hamlets Charakter."

7. *L,* 69: "Es gibt auch negativen Sinn, der viel besser ist als Null, aber viel seltner. Man kann etwas innig lieben, eben weil mans nicht hat: das gibt wenigstens ein Vorgefühl ohne Nachsatz. Selbst entschiedne Unfähigkeit, die man klar weiß, oder gar mit starker Antipathie ist bei reinem Mangel ganz unmöglich, und setzt wenigstens partiale Fähigkeit und Sympathie voraus. Gleich dem Platonischen Eros ist also wohl dieser negative Sinn der Sohn des Überflusses und der Armut. Er entsteht, wenn einer bloß den Geist hat, ohne den Buchstaben; oder umgekehrt, wenn er bloß die Materialien und Förmlichkeiten hat, die trockne harte Schale des produktiven Genies ohne den Kern. Im ersten Falle gibts reine Tendenzen, Projekte, die so weit sind, wie der blaue Himmel, oder wenn's hoch kömmt, skizzierte Fantasien: im letzten zeigt sich jene harmonisch ausgebildete Kunst-Plattheit, in welcher die größten engländischen Kritiker so klassisch sind. Das Kennzeichen der ersten Gattung; des negativen Sinns vom Geiste ist, wenn einer immer wollen muß. ohne je zu können; wenn einer immer hören mag, ohne je zu vernehmen."

8. *A,* 116: "Die romantische Poesie ist eine progressive Universalpoesie. Ihre Bestimmung ist nicht bloß, alle getrennten Gattungen der Poesie wieder zu vereinigen, und die Poesie mit der Philosophie und Rhetorik in Berührung zu setzen. Sie will, und soll auch Poesie und Prosa, Genialität und Kritik, Kunstpoesie und Naturpoesie bald mischen, bald verschmelzen, die Poesie lebendig und gesellig, und das Leben und die Gesellschaft poetisch machen, den Witz poetisieren, und die Formen der Kunst mit gediegnem Bildungsstoff jeder Art anfüllen und sättigen, und durch die Schwingungen des Humors beseelen. Sie umfaßt alles, was nur poetisch ist. . . . "

9. *L,* 115: "Die ganze Geschichte der modernen Poesie ist ein fortlaufender Kommentar zu dem kurzen Text der Philosophie: Alle Kunst soll Wissenschaft, und alle Wissenschaft soll Kunst werden; Poesie und Philosophie sollen vereinigt sein."

10. *A,* 39: "Die meisten Gedanken sind nur Profile von Gedanken. Diese muss man umkehren, und mit ihren Antipoden synthesieren."

11. *L,* 23: "In jedem guten Gedicht muss alles Absicht, und alles Instinkt sein. Dadurch wird es idealisch."

12. *A,* 108: "Schön ist, was zugleich reizend und erhaben ist."

13. *A,* 409: "Um sittlich zu heissen, müssen Empfindungen nicht bloss schön, sondern auch weise, im Zusammenhange ihres Ganzen zweckmässig, im höchsten Sinne schicklich sein."

14. *I,* 130: "Nur wer einig ist mit der Welt kann einig sein mit sich selbst."

15. A, 50: "Wahre Liebe sollte ihrem Ursprunge nach, zugleich ganz willkürlich und ganz zufällig sein, und zugleich notwendig und frei scheinen; ihrem Charakter nach aber zugleich Bestimmung und Tugend sein, ein Geheimnis, und ein Wunder scheinen."

16. *A,* 53: "Es ist gleich tödlich für den Geist, ein System zu haben, und keins zu haben. Er wird sich also wohl entschliessen müssen, beides zu verbinden."

17. *A,* 344: "Philosophieren heisst die Allwissenheit gemeinschaftlich suchen."

18. *L,* 29: "Anmut ist korrektes Leben; Sinnlichkeit die sich selbst anschaut, und sich selbst bildet."

19. *A,* 238, cited in P. Szondi, *Schriften* [ed. Jean Bollack et al. (Frankfurt am Main, 1978)], vol. 2, p. 17. "Es gibt eine Poesie, deren Eins und Alles das Verhältnis des Idealen und des Realen ist, und die also nach der Analogie der philosophischen Kunstsprache Transzendentalpoesie heißen müßte. Sie beginnt als Satire mit der absoluten Verschiedenheit des Idealen und Realen, schwebt als Elegie in der Mitte, und endigt als Idylle mit der absoluten Identität beider. So wie man aber wenig Wert auf eine Transzendentalphilosophie legen würde, die nicht kritisch wäre, nicht auch das Produzierende mit dem Produkt dar-

stellte, und im System der transzendentalen Gedanken zugleich eine Charakteristik des transzendentalen Denkens enthielte: so sollte wohl auch jene Poesie die in modernen Dichtern nicht seltnen transzendentalen Materialien und Vorübungen zu einer poetischen Theorie des Dichtungsvermögens mit der künstlerischen Reflexion und schönen Selbstbespiegelung, die sich im Pindar, den lyrischen Fragmenten der Griechen, und der alten Elegie, unter den Neuern aber in Goethe findet, vereinigen, und in jeder ihrer Darstellungen sich selbst mit darstellen, und überall zugleich Poesie und Poesie der Poesie sein."

20. *A*, 116: "Sie kann sich so in das Dargestellte verlieren, daβ man glauben möchte, poetische Individuen jeder Art zu charakterisieren, sei ihr Eins und Alles; und doch gibt es noch keine Form, die so dazu gemacht wäre, den Geist des Autors vollständig auszudrücken: so daβ manche Künstler, die nur auch einen Roman schreiben wollten, von ungefähr sich selbst dargestellt haben. Nur sie kann gleich dem Epos ein Spiegel der ganzen umgebenden Welt, ein Bild des Zeitalters werden. Und doch kann auch sie am meisten zwischen dem Dargestellten und dem Darstellenden, frei von allem realen und idealen Interesse auf den Flügeln der poetischen Reflexion in der Mitte schweben, diese Reflexion immer wieder potenzieren und wie in einer endlosen Reihe von Spiegeln vervielfachen."

21. *A*, 222: "Der revolutionäre Wunsch, das Reich Gottes zu realisieren, ist der elastische Punkt der progressiven Bildung, und der Anfang der modernen Geschichte. Was in gar keiner Beziehung auf's Reich Gottes steht, ist in ihr nur Nebensache."

22. *A*, 426: "Wie wäre es möglich, die gegenwärtige Periode der Welt richtig zu verstehen und zu interpungieren, wenn man nicht wenigstens den allgemeinen Charakter der nächstfolgenden antizipieren dürfte? Nach der Analogie jenes Gedankens würde auf das chemische ein organisches Zeitalter folgen, und dann dürften die Erdbürger des nächsten Sonnenumlaufs wohl bei weitem nicht so groβ von uns denken wie wir selbst, und vieles was jetzt bloβ angestaunt wird, nur für nützliche Jugendübungen der Menschheit halten."

23. *A*, 139: "Aus dem romantischen Gesichtspunkt haben auch die Abarten der Poesie, selbst die ekzentrischen und monströsen, ihren Wert, als Materialien und Vorübungen der Universalität, wenn nur irgend etwas drin ist, wenn sie nur original sind."

24. *A*, 116: "Die romantische Poesie ist eine progressive Universalpoesie. . . . Andere Dichtarten sind fertig, und können nun vollständig zergliedert werden. Die romantische Dichtart ist noch im Werden; ja das ist ihr eigentliches Wesen, daβ sie ewig nur werden, nie vollendet sein kann. Sie kann durch keine Theorie erschöpft werden, und nur eine divinatorische Kritik dürfte es wagen, ihr Ideal charakterisieren zu wollen."

25. *A*, 24: "Viele Werke der Alten sind Fragmente geworden. Viele Werke der Neuern sind es gleich bei der Enstehung."

26. *A*, 22: "der transzendentale Bestandteil des historischen Geistes."

27. *JS 1*, 110: "Das Ubermaβ des Individuellen führt [. . .] von selbst zum Objektiven, das Interessante ist die Vorbereitung des Schönen, und das letzte Ziel der modernen Poesie kann kein andres sein als das höchste Schöne, ein Maximum von objektiver ästhetischer Vollkommenheit."

28. Ibid.: "Die Herrschaft des Interessanten ist durchaus nur eine *vorübergehende Krise des Geschmacks:* denn sie muss sich endlich selbst vernichten."

29. Ibid., pp. 21-22: "Dieser Zusammenhang gegen unsere Zerstückelung, diese reinen Massen gegen unsere unendlichen Mischungen, diese einfache Bestimmtheit gegen unsere kleinliche Verworrenheit sind Ursache, daβ die Alten Menschen im höhern Stil zu sein scheinen. Doch dürfen wir sie nicht als Günstlinge eines willkürlichen Glücks beneiden. Unsere Mängel selbst sind unsere Hoffnungen: denn sie entspringen eben aus der Herrschaft des Verstandes, dessen zwar langsame Vervollkommnung gar keine Schranken kennt. Und wenn er das Geschäft, dem Menschen eine beharrliche Grundlage zu sichern, und eine unwandelbare Richtung zu bestimmen, beendigt hat, so wird es nicht mehr zweifelhaft sein,

ob die Geschichte des Menschen wie ein Zirkel ewig in sich selbst zurückkehre, oder ins Unendliche zum Bessern fortschreite."

30. *L*, 37: "Um über einen Gegenstand gut schreiben zu können, muß man sich nicht mehr für ihn interessieren; der Gedanke, den man mit Besonnenheit ausdrücken soll muß schon gänzlich vorbei sein, einen nicht mehr eigentlich beschäftigen. So lange der Künstler erfindet und begeistert ist, befindet er sich für die Mitteilung wenigstens in einem illiberalen Zustande. Er wird dann alles sagen wollen; welches eine falsche Tendenz junger Genies, oder ein richtiges Vorurteil alter Stümper ist. Dadurch verkennt er den Wert und die Würde der Selbstbeschränkung, die doch für den Künstler wie für den Menschen das Erste und das Letzte, das Notwendigste und das Höchste ist. Das Notwendigste: denn überall, wo man sich nicht selbst beschränkt, beschränkt einen die Welt; wodurch man ein Knecht wird. Das Höchste: denn man kann sich nur in den Punkten und an den Seiten selbst beschränken, wo man unendliche Kraft hat, Selbstschöpfung und Selbstvernichtung."

31. *JS 2*, 364: "Jedes Gedicht soll eigentlich romantisch und jedes soll didaktisch sein in jenem weitern Sinne des Wortes, wo es die Tendenz nach einem tiefen unendlichen Sinn bezeichnet. Auch machen wir diese Forderung überall, ohne eben den Namen zu gebrauchen. Selbst in ganz populären Arten, wie z. B. im Schauspiel, fordern wir Ironie; wir fordern, daß die Begebenheiten, die Menschen, kurz das ganze Spiel des Lebens wirklich auch als Spiel genommen und dargestellt sei."

32. *A*, 249: "Das didaktische Gedicht sollte prophetisch sein, und hat auch Anlage, es zu werden."

33. *L*, 42: "Es gibt alte und moderne Gedichte, die durchgängig im Ganzen und überall den göttlichen Hauch der Ironie atmen. Es lebt in ihnen eine wirklich transzendentale Buffonerie. Im Innern, die Stimmung, welche alles übersieht, und sich über alles Bedingte unendlich erhebt, auch über eigne Kunst, Tugend, oder Genialität: im Äußern, in der Ausführung die mimische Manier eines gewöhnlichen guten italienischen *Buffo*."

34. *JS 2*, 169: "Es ist schön und notwendig, sich dem Eindruck eines Gedichtes ganz hinzugeben, den Künstler mit uns machen zu lassen, was er will, und etwa nur im Einzelnen das Gefühl durch Reflexion zu bestätigen und zum. Gedanken zu erheben, und wo es noch zweifeln oder streiten dürfte, zu entscheiden und zu ergänzen. Dies ist das erste und das wesentlichste. Aber nicht minder notwendig ist es, von allem Einzelnen abstrahieren zu können, das Allgemeine schwebend zu fassen, eine Masse zu überschauen, und das Ganze festzuhalten, selbst dem Verborgensten nachzuforschen und das Entlegenste zu verbinden. Wir müssen uns über unsre eigne Liebe erheben, und was wir anbeten, in Gedanken vernichten können: sonst fehlt uns, was wir auch für andre Fähigkeiten haben, der Sinn für das Unendliche und mit ihm der Sinn für die Welt."

35. *I*, 69: "Ironie ist klares Bewusstsein der ewigen Agilität, des unendlich vollen Chaos."

36. I. Strohschneider-Kohrs, in her *Die romantische Ironie in Theorie und Gestaltung* (Tübingen, 1960), pp. 59–60, rejects this interpretation as "untenable." She asserts that it does not take into account the "extremely positive meaning" implied in Schlegel's notion of chaos; but she fails to note that in the next sentence we quote fragment no. 71 of the *Ideas* (which is one of those that she herself refers to in this regard) in order to draw attention to just this positive significance of the notion, which lies in its utopian dimension.

37. *I*, 71: "Nur diejenige Verworrenheit ist ein Chaos, aus der eine Welt entspringen kann."

38. Ludwig Tieck, *Schriften* (Berlin, 1828–46), vol. 13, pp. 244ff.:

Michel   O schaun Sie, schaun Sie doch die vielen Leute!
                    Was für ein Stück gibt man denn heute?
Melantus Der Himmel weiß, ich darf es nicht entdecken,
                    Vielleicht: Irrtum an allen Ecken.

. . .

Peter	Wie einem nun die Augen helle werden!
Melantus	So gehts mit allen Dingen auf Erden.
Michel	Mich dünkt, Sie sprechen so betrübt;
	Wo fehlt's? wenn's Ihnen zu sagen beliebt.
Melantus	Ach, bester Mann, ich habe vielen Kummer,
	Wir sitzen am Ende hier im Dunst,
	Mir wird im Kopfe immer dummer,
	Und glaube dabei nicht recht an eine Kunst.
	Es kann wohl sein, daß wir vergebens harren,
	Und, lieber Freund, dann sind wir rechte Narren.
Peter	Ja wohl, das wär ein schlechter Spaß.
Michel	Mit Ihr'r Erlaubnis, erklären Sie mir das.
Melantus	Sehn Sie, wer kann uns dafür stehn,
	Daß man hier wirklich wird was sehn?
	Wir hoffen am Ende vergebens auf Lichter,
	's gibt vielleicht weder Direktor noch Dichter;
	Wird man den Vorhang aufwärts rollen?

. . .

Anthenor	Nachbarn! mit Erlaubnis, es tut mir leid,
	Allein Ihr seid alle nicht recht gescheit,
	Ich will Euch zwar Eure Hoffnung nicht rauben,
	Doch scheint mir alles nur Aberglauben.
	Denn seht! ich schwör's bei meinem Leben,
	Es hat noch nie einen Direktor gegeben,
	Wie sollte also ein Stück entstehn?
	Die Idee, geb' ich zu, ist recht schön;
	Allein wer soll sie exekutieren?
	Wir zahlen, so mein' ich, unsre Gebühren
	Und sitzen dann hier und dichten und trachten;
	Und das ist schon für ein Stück zu achten.
	Habt Ihr schon einen Direktor gekannt?
Peter	Lieber Gott, Ihr wißt's, ich komme vom Land.
Anthenor	Könnt Ihr mir einen Direktor definieren?
Peter	Ich glaube, der Mann will uns vexieren.
Anthenor	Was ist also ein Direkteur?
	Ihr denkt und ratet hin und her,
	Verwirret Euch in die Kreuz und Quer,
	Und daraus folgt denn nur am Ende—
Melantus	O schließt nur ja nicht zu behende!
Anthenor	*Daß wenn man's gründlich überlegt,*
	Sich dahinten kein Direktor rührt noch regt,
	Daß hinter dem Vorhange nichts sich rührt,
	Ein Stück wird vor dem Theater aufgeführt
	Von uns, die wir als wahre Affen
	Behaupten, alles sei nur geschaffen
	Um zu einem künftigen Zwecke zu nutzen
	Und darum verschleudern die Gegenwart.

39. Cf. P. Szondi, *Theorie des modernen Dramas,* in *Schriften,* vol. 1, p. 16ff.

40. Cf. Georg Lukács, *Die Theorie des Romans* (Berlin, 1920); new ed. (Neuwied-Berlin, 1963 and ff.). [Eng. trans. by Anna Bostock, *The Theory of the Novel* (London, 1971).]

41. Tieck, *Schriften,* vol. 10, pp. 147–48:

König	Ach! wie gesagt: wer weiß, was uns bevorsteht!
	Ein unerbittlich Schicksal lenket uns.
Hanswurst	Soll ich mal sprechen, wie's um's Herz mir ist?
König	Nie anders, wenn die Götter uns beschützen.
Hanswurst	So mein' ich denn, es ist sowohl nicht Schicksal,
	Als Eigensinn des Dichters, wie er sich
	Benannt, der so sein ganzes Stück verwandelt,
	Und keinen Menschen bei gesundem Sinne läßt.
König	Ach, Freund! was rührst Du da für eine Saite!
	Wie traurig werd' ich, wenn ich erst bedenke,
	Daß wir nun vollends gar nicht existieren.
	Der Idealist ist schon ein elend Wesen,
	Doch ist er anzunehmen stets genötigt,
	Daß sein Dasein doch etwas Wahres sei;
	Doch wir, wir sind noch weniger als Luft,
	Geburten einer fremden Phantasie,
	Die sie nach eigensinn'ger Willkür lenkt.
	Und freilich kann dann keiner von uns wissen,
	Was jener Federkiel uns noch beschert.
	O jammervoll Geschick dramat'scher Rollen!

42. Ibid., vol. 5, pp. 319–20:

Der Wirt   Wenige Gäste kehren jetzt bei mir ein, und wenn das so fort währt, so werde ich am Ende das Schild noch gar einziehen müssen.—Ja sonst waren noch gute Zeiten, da wurde kaum ein Stück gegeben, in welchem nicht ein Wirtshaus mit seinem Wirte workam. Ich weiß es noch, in wie vielen hundert Stücken bei mir in dieser Stube hier die schönste Entwickelung vorbereitet wurde. Bald war es ein verkleideter Fürst, der hier sein Geld verzehrte, bald ein Minister, oder wenigstens ein reicher Graf, die sich alle bei mir aufs Lauern legten. Ja sogar in allen Sachen, die aus dem Englischen übersetzt wurden, hatte ich meinen Taler Geld zu verdienen. Manchmal mußte man freilich auch in einen sauern Apfel beißen, und verstelltes Mitglied einer Spitzbubenbande sein, wofür man dann von den moralischen Personen rechtschaffen ausgehunzt wurde; indessen war man doch in Tätigkeit.—Aber jetzt!—Wenn auch jetzt ein fremder reicher Mann von der Reise kommt, so quartiert er sich originellerweise bei einem Verwandten ein, und gibt sich erst im fünften Akt zu erkennen; andere kriegt man nur auf der Straße zu sehn, als wenn sie in gar keinem honetten Hause wohnten;—dergleichen dient zwar, die Zuschauer in einer wunderbaren Neugier zu erhalten, aber es bringt doch unser eins um alle Nahrung.

43. Hölderlin, *Sämtliche Werke,* [Grosse Stuttgarter Ausgabe], ed. Friedrich Beissner, [Stuttgart, 1946–77], vol. 2, p. 373.

44. Tieck, *Schriften,* vol. 5, pp. 321–22:

Fremder	Guten Morgen, Herr Wirt.
Wirt	Diener, Diener von Ihnen, gnädiger Herr.—Wer in aller Welt sind Sie, daß Sie inkognito reisen und bei mir einkehren? Sie sind gewiß noch aus der alten Schule; gelt, so ein Mann vom alten Schlage, vielleicht aus dem Englishchen übersetzt?
Fremder	Ich bin weder gnädiger Herr, noch reise ich incognito.—Kann ich diesen Tag und die Nacht hier logieren?
Wirt	Mein ganzes Haus steht Ihnen zu Befehl.—Aber, im Ernst, wollen Sie hier in

	der Gegend keine Familie unvermuteterweise glücklich machen? oder plötzlich heiraten? oder eine Schwester aufsuchen?
Fremder	Nein, mein Freund.
Wirt	Sie reisen also bloß so simpel, als ein ordinärer Reisender?
Fremder	Ja.
Wirt	Da werden Sie wenig Beifall finden.
Fremder	Ich glaube, der Kerl ist rasend.

5. Friedrich Schlegel's Theory of Poetical Genres: A Reconstruction from the Posthumous Fragments

Schlegel's fragments are taken from the critical edition of his works edited by Ernst Behler, *Kritische Friedrich-Schlegel-Ausgabe*, cited hereafter as *KA*. The relevant volumes are vol. 2, *Charakteristiken und Kritiken* I (*1796-1801*), ed Hans Eichner (1967), and vol. 18, *Philosophische Lehrjahre 1796-1806*, pt. 1, ed. Ernst Behler (1963). Some fragments are taken from *Literary Notebooks 1797-1801*, ed. Hans Eichner (London, 1957), cited hereafter as *LN*. In the quotations, Schlegel's Greek abbreviations have been eliminated along with the square brackets that the editor uses to indicate their expansion. In addition, the spelling has been modernized.—Trans.

1. *KA 2*, 165: "Über keinen Gegenstand philosophieren sie seltner als über die Philosophie."

2. Cf. P. Szondi, *Hölderlin-Studien*, in *Schriften* [ed. Jean Bollack et al. (Frankfurt am Main, 1978)], vol. 1, p. 369, n. 8.

3. Cf., among other texts, *Über Solgers nachgelassene Schriften und Briefwechsel*, in *Werke*, vol. 16 (Berlin, 1834), p. 466.

4. Cf. *KA 2*, 168-69.

5. *KA 2*, 154: "Man hat schon so viele Theorien der Dichtarten. Warum hat man noch keinen Begriff von Dichtart? Vielleicht würde man sich dann mit einer einzigen Theorie der Dichtarten behelfen müssen."

6. *LN*, 186: "Alle Dichtarten sind ursprünglich—Naturpoesie—eine bestimmte, lokale, individuelle. (Es kann unendlich viele Dichtarten geben.) Das Individuelle bleibt darin, auch nach der Umbildung durch Künstler. Die Formen sind einer unendlichen Umbildung fähig. Alle griechischen und alle romantischen Formen verlieren sich ins Dunkel und sind nicht von Künstlern gemacht."

7. Cf., for example, *Friedrich Schlegel 1794-1802: Seine prosaischen Jugendschriften*, ed. J. Minor, 2d ed. (Vienna, 1906), vol. 1, p. 144. This work is cited hereafter as *JS*.

8. *JS 1*, 77ff.

9. Cf. Batteux, *Einschränkung der schönen Künste auf einen einzigen Grundsatz, Aus dem Französischen übersetzt, und mit einem Anhange einiger eignen Abhandlungen versehen* [translated from the French, and with an appendix containing seventy of his own essays], 2d ed. (Leipzig, 1759), p. 390.

10. *JS 1*, 146: "eine *ewige Naturgeschichte des Geschmacks und der Kunst*."

11. *KA 2*, 181: "Eine Klassifikation ist eine Definition, die ein System von Definitionen enthält."

12. *LN*, 19: "Nur die ganz gültigen Dichtarten können in der *reinen* Poetik deduziert werden.—Das Epos erst in der *angewandten*, so auch alles was *nur* für klassische oder nur für progressive [d. h. moderne] Poesie gilt."

13. Georg Lukács, *Die Theorie des Romans* (Berlin and Neuwied, 1974), pp. 31ff. [Eng. trans. by Anna Bostock (London, 1971).]

14. *LN,* 22: "In einer reinen Poetik wurde vielleicht *keine* Dichtart bestehen; die Poetik also *zugleich* rein und angewandt, zugleich empirisch und rational."

15. *LN,* 229, (editor's note).

16. *LN,* 29: Goethe proceeds "bei Aufsuchung des Geistes der Dichtarten *empirisch* zu Werke; nun lässt sich aber der Charakter grade dieser Dichtart [i.e. des Romans] empirisch nicht vollstänNding und richtig auffinden."

17. *LN,* 39: "Der Deduktion der Kunst muss ein empirisches oder historisches Datum vorangehn, welches die Klassifikation in Logik, Poesie, Ethik begründet."

18. *KA 18,* 197.

19. Ibid., p. 81: "jede der klassifizierten Wissenschaften—Logik, Ethik, Poetik, Politik, Historie—... progressiv behandelt, universell [und umfasse] also alle übrigen."

20. *LN,* 37: "Man soll über die Kunst philosophieren, denn man soll über alles philosophieren; nur muß man schon etwas von der Kunst wissen.—Freilich wird alles was man von der Kunst erfahren hat, erst durch Philosophie zum Wissen. Daß die Alten klassisch sind, weiß man nicht aus der Philosophie, denn Goethe weiß es auch; aber freilich weiß mans nur mit Philosophie."

21. *KA 2,* 208: "Die Philosophie über einen Gegenstand kann nur der brauchen, der den Gegenstand kennt, oder hat; nur der wird begreifen können, was sie will und meint. Erfahrungen und Sinne kann die Philosophie nicht inokulieren oder anzaubern. Sie soll es aber auch nicht wollen. Wer es schon gewußt hat, der erfährt freilich nichts Neues von ihr; doch wird es ihm erst durch sie ein Wissen und dadurch neu von Gestalt."

22. *Die Vollendung der klassischen deutschen Aesthetik durch Hegel,* reprinted in *Schriften zur Aesthetik* (Munich, 1966).

23. *KA 18,* 24: "nicht wahr, dass die Individuen mehr Realität hätten als die Gattungen."

24. *KA 2,* 221: "Alle Gattungen sind gut, sagt Voltaire, ausgenommen die langweilige Gattung. Aber welches ist denn nun die langweilige Gattung? Sie mag größer sein als alle andern und viele Wege mögen dahin führen. Der kürzeste ist wohl, wenn ein Werk nicht weiß, zu welcher Gattung es gehören will oder soll. Sollte Voltaire diesen Weg nie gegangen sein?"

25. *KA 2,* 166.

26. Ibid.: "So teilt sich zum Beispiel die Naturpoesie in die natürliche und in die künstliche, und die Volkspoesie in die Volkspoesie fur das Volk und in die Volkspoesie für Standespersonen und Gelehrte."

27. Cf. *Hölderlin-Studien,* pp. 346ff.

28. *JS 1,* 116.

29. *KA 18,* 60: "Die echte Klassifikation ist historisch, sowohl nach dem principio cognoscendi als nach dem principio existendi. Alle Einteilungen in bestimmt Viele sind historisch.—Kant immer für das nur eins oder bestimmt viel, Fichte mehr für das unendlich viele."

30. Ibid., p. 61: "Kants Moral und Fichtes Naturrecht beweisen wie dürftig alle nicht historisch-philosopischen Systeme ausfallen müssen."

31. *KA 18,* 85: "Sobald die Philosophie Wissenschaft wird, gibts Historie. Alles System ist historisch und umgekehrt."

32. *KA 2,* 252: "Soll denn die Poesie schlechthin eingeteilt sein? oder soll sie die eine und unteilbare bleiben? oder wechseln zwischen Trennung und Verbindung? Die meisten Vorstellungsarten vom poetischen Weltsystem sind noch so roh und kindisch, wie die ältern vom astronomischen vor Kopernikus. Die gewöhnlichen Einteilungen der Poesie sind nur totes Fachwerk für einen beschränkten Horizont. Was einer machen kann, oder was eben gilt, ist die ruhende Erde im Mittelpunkt. Im Universum der Poesie selbst aber ruht nichts, alles wird und verwandelt sich und bewegt sich harmonisch; und auch die Kometen haben

unabänderliche Bewegungsgesetze. Ehe sich aber der Lauf dieser Gestirne nicht berechnen, ihre Wiederkunft nicht vorherbestimmen läßt, ist das wahre Weltsystem der Poesie noch nicht entdeckt."

33. *JS 1*, 222. Cf. *Hölderlin-Studien*, p. 369, n. 8.

34. *LN*, 36: "Wie zu klassifizieren sei, können wir oft von den Alten lernen; den Grund der Klassifikation müssen wir mystisch hinzutun."

35. *LN*, 42: "*Wahre Philosophie der Kunst ist nur reine Mystik und reine Polemik.*"

36. *LN*, 175.

37. *LN*, 204.

38. Cf. Plato, *The Republic*, 394C.

39. *LN*, 95: "In allen Romanarten muss alles Subjektive objektiviert werden; es ist ein Irrtum, dass der Roman eine subjektive Dichtart wäre."

40. *JS 1*, 146: "eine *ewige Naturgeschichte des Geschmacks und der Kunst.*"

41. Ibid., "der *ganze Kreislauf der organischen Entwicklung der Kunst* abgeschlossen und vollendet."

42. *LN*, 22: "*Drei herrschende Dichtarten.* 1) *Tragödie* bei den Griechen 2) *Satire* bei den Römern 3) *Roman* bei den Modernen."

43. *KA 2*, 188: "Wie der Roman die ganze moderne Poesie, so tingiert auch die Satire, die durch alle Umgestaltungen, bei den Römern doch immer eine klassische Universalpoesie, eine Gesellschaftspoesie aus und für den Mittelpunkt des gebildeten Weltalls blieb, die ganze römische Poesie, ja die gesamte römische Literatur, und gibt darin gleichsam den Ton an."

44. *KA 2*, 178: "Der Gegenstand der Historie ist das Wirklichwerden alles dessen, was praktisch notwendig ist."

45. *LN*, 143 and 272 (editor's note): "Die Historie der modernen Poesie vielleicht in der *Ästhetik.*"

46. *LN*, 47-48: "Es gibt eine epische, lyrische, dramatische *Form* ohne den Geist der alten Dichtarten dieses Namens, aber von bestimmtem und ewigem Unterschied.—Als *Form* hat die epische offenbar den Vorzug. Sie ist subjektiv-objektiv.—Die *lyrische* ist bloss *subjektiv,* die *dramatische* bloss *objektiv.*—Auch romantisiert zu werden ist das alte Epos ganz ausschliessend geschickt. Vom Drama lässt sich nur die neue Komödie romantisieren.—Die Naturpoesie ist entweder subjektiv oder objektiv. Die gleiche Mischung ist dem Naturmenschen noch nicht möglich."

47. *LN*, 44: "Die einzige pragmatische Kunstlehre für den Künstler ist die Lehre vom Klassischen und vom Romantischen."

48. *LN*, 48.

49. Ibid.

50. Ibid.

51. Cf. P. Szondi, *Theorie des modernen Dramas*, in *Schriften*, vol. 1, pp. 11-12.

52. *LN*, 96. The manuscript does not contain the words "In the genres of the novel . . ." (i.e., *In den Romanarten . . .*), but rather (as can be seen from the text edited by Eichner, in which the editor's additions are indicated by square brackets) "In the R-genres" (*In den R-arten*). However, according to Eichner's index of abbreviations, in Schlegel a capital "R" can mean "novel" (*Roman*) as well as "romantic" (*Romantisch*)—see *LN*, 12. Since the fragment in question is built around an opposition and since the second sentence speaks without abbreviation of the "classical genres," it is possible to expand the abbreviation "R" in the first sentence as "romantic" rather than as "novel," yielding the reading "romantic genres" (*romantische Arten*, i.e., *Dichtarten;* cf. *KA 2*, lxxv, where Eichner, on the basis of *LN* no. 1096, raises this same question). In any case, changing "novel" into "romantic" does not solve the problem, but only transposes it from the realm of textual criticism to that of

historical interpretation. For in Schlegel's texts the word *romantisch* often means nothing else than *romanhaft* [i.e., in the manner of a novel] or, indeed, *Roman-* [proper to the novel]; it is therefore not a qualitative but rather a referential adjective. Accordingly, in *Athenaeum* fragment no. 116 the expression *romantische Poesie* (which is there defined as "progressive, universal poetry" and whose program is also sketched out in that fragment) does not mean the poetry of the romantic age, but rather the writing of novels, or the genre of the novel, and it is only because the latter "sets the tone" for the modern age that the expression can also be applied to poetry of the romantic age and of the modern age in general. On this point see Eichner, *KA 2*, lvii: "For Schlegel in 1798–99 *romantische Poesie* means above all the poetry of the novel (*Romanpoesie*)." See also Arthur O. Lovejoy, "The Meaning of 'Romantic' in Early German Romanticism," in *Essays in the History of Ideas* (Baltimore, 1948), p. 186, and René Wellek, "The Concept of Romanticism in Literary Criticism," in *Concepts of Criticism* (New Haven and London, 1963), p. 134.

53. Cf. *Hölderlin-Studien*, pp. 407ff. ("Exkurs über Schiller, Schlegel und Hölderlin").

54. G. Lukács, *Theorie*, p. 100.

55. *Schillers Werke*, Nationalausgabe, vol. 20/21., ed. Benno von Wiese [Weimar], vol. 20, p. 449.

56. Cf. *Hölderlin-Studien*, p. 386.

57. It should be noted, however, that Schlegel's terminology is quite variable: in different fragments several concepts appear to designate one and the same thing.

58. *LN*, 114: "Auch unter den Romanarten gibts wieder eine lyrische—epische—dramatische Gattung."

59. Cf. note 52 and *Hölderlin-Studien*, p. 407, n. 198.

60. *KA 2*, 182.

61. *KA 18*, 23: "In Shakespeares Tragödien ist die Form dramatisch der Geist und Zweck romantisch. Die Absonderung der Komödie und Tragödie ist entweder Überbleibsel oder Annäherung zur Klassik."

62. Cf. Irene Behrens, *Die Lehre von der Einteilung der Dichtkunst* (Halle, 1940), p. 187. For a different assessment see Klaus R. Scherpe, *Gattungspoetik im 18. Jahrhundert* (Stuttgart, 1968) (= *Studien zur Allgemeinen und Vergleichenden Literaturwissenschaft*, vol. 2), p. 3 and p. 262.

63. *LN*, 33: "Gibts nicht auch eine . . . epische, lyrische, dramatische, idyllische, satirische, epigrammatische Prosa?"

64. *LN*, 60: "Im *absoluten* poetischen Drama darf nichts roh episch, nichts roh lyrisch sein; sondern alles verschmolzen. Aber auch nicht roh elegisch oder roh idyllisch."

65. *LN*, 58: "*Sentimental* ist die Vereinigung des *Elegischen* und *Idyllischen*."

66. *LN*, 48: "Der Ton des Romans sollte elegisch sein, die Form idyllisch."

67. *LN*, 73: "Das Eigentümliche der Dichtungsarten ist, dass Form und Stoff und Grundstoff und Ausdruck (Sprache, Metrum) dieselben charakteristischen Eigenschaften gemein haben."

68. Cf. *Hölderlin-Studien*, p. 386.

69. *KA 18*, 24: "Es ist nicht wahr dass die Individuen mehr Realität hätten als die Gattungen."

70. *LN*, 72: "Man kann eben so gut sagen, es gibt *unendlich viele* als es gibt nur *Eine* progressive Dichtart. Also gibt es eigentlich gar keine; denn Art lässt sich ohne Mitart nicht denken."

71. *LN*, 116: "Der modernen Dichtarten sind nur Eine oder unendlich viele. Jedes Gedicht eine Gattung für sich."

72. *KA 18*, 24: "Jeder Roman ist eine Art für sich. Hier ist das Rubrizieren sehr illiberal."

73. *LN*, 25: "Alle Dichtarten, die drei alten klassischen ausgenommen. Diese Bestandteile dann zu einer progressiven Einheit verknüpft."

74. *KA 2*, 183: "[Sie ist] noch im Werden, sie [kann] ewig nur werden, nie vollendet sein."

6. Schleiermacher's Hermeneutics Today

1. In connection with the following remarks see F. Blass, *Hermeneutik und Kritik*, in *Handbuch der klassischen Altertums-Wissenschaft in systematischer Darstellung*, ed. I. von Müller (Munich, 1892), vol. 1, pp. 147ff; W. Dilthey, *Die Entstehung der Hermeneutik* (1900), in *Gesammelte Schriften* (Stuttgart-Göttingen, 1959ff.), vol. 5, pp. 317ff.; G. Ebeling, article "Hermeneutik," in *Die Religion in Geschichte und Gegenwart* (Tübingen, 1957ff.), vol. 3, cols. 242ff.

2. Cf. H. de Lubac, *Exégèse Médiévale: Les quatre sens de l'écriture* (Paris, 1959ff).

3. Cf. K. Holl, "Luthers Bedeutung für den Fortschritt der Auslegungskunst," in *Gesammelte Aufsätze zur Kirchengeschichte* (Tübingen, 1932), vol. 1, pp. 544ff.

4. W. Dilthey, *Entstehung*, p. 320.

5. M. Heidegger, *Sein und Zeit* (Halle, 1927).

6. H.-G. Gadamer, *Wahrheit und Methode: Grundzüge einer philosophischen Hermeneutik*, 2d ed. (Tübingen, 1965).

7. Ibid., pp. xiv-xv.

8. F. D. E. Schleiermacher, *Hermeneutik*, Nach den Handschriften neu herausgegeben und eingeleitet von H. Kimmerle [newly edited and introduced on the basis of the manuscripts of H. Kimmerle] (Heidelberg, 1959) (= "Abhandlungen der Heidelberger Akademie der Wissenschaften, Philosophisch-historische Klasse" [1959], 2d essay), pp. 123ff. This work is cited hereafter as "Schleiermacher"; the spelling in the quotations given here has been modernized. [After completing my translation of this essay, I discovered the recently published translations by James Duke and Jack Forstman contained in F. D. E. Schleiermacher, *Hermeneutics: The Handwritten Manuscripts*, ed. Heinz Kimmerle (Missoula, Mont. 1977), and I have made several changes in my own translations of Schleiermacher on the basis of this edition.—Trans.]

9. Schleiermacher, p. 123, n. 4.

10. Ibid.: "die rechte Begründung [fehlte], weil die allgemeinen Prinzipien nirgends aufgestellt waren."

11. Ibid., pp. 129-30: "... die Hermeneutik [ist] auch nicht lediglich auf schriftstellerische Produktionen zu beschränken [...]; denn ich ergreife mich sehr oft mitten im vertraulichen Gespräch auf hermeneutischen Operationen, wenn ich mich mit einem gewöhnlichen Grade des Verstehens nicht begnüge, sondern zu erforschen suche, wie sich wohl in dem Freunde der Übergang von einem Gedanken zum anderen gemacht habe, oder wenn ich nachspüre, mit welchen Ansichten, Urteilen und Bestrebungen es wohl zusammenhängt, daß er sich über einen besprochenen Gegenstand grade so und nicht anders ausdrückt. Dergleichen Tatsachen, die wohl jeder Achtsame von sich wird einzeugen müssen, bekunden, dächte ich, deutlich genug, daß die Auflösung der Aufgabe, für welche wir eben die Theorie suchen, keineswegs an dem für das Auge durch die Schrift fixierten Zustande der Rede hängt, sondern daß sie überall vorkommen wird, wo wir Gedanken oder Reihen von solchen durch Worte zu vernehmen haben."

12. Ibid., p. 130: "gewöhnliche Grad des Verstehens."

13. Ibid., pp. 82-83: "Nicht alles Reden ist gleich sehr ein Gegenstand der Auslegungskunst; einige haben für dieselbe einen Nullwert, andere einen absoluten, das meiste liegt zwischen diesen beiden Punkten. [...] Einen Nullwert hat, was weder Interesse hat als Tat noch Bedeutung für die Sprache. Es wird geredet, weil die Sprache sich nur in der Kontinuität der Wiederholung erhält. Was aber nur schon vorhanden Gewesenes wiederholt, ist an sich nichts. Wettergespräche. Allein dies Null ist nicht das absolute Nichts, sondern nur das Minimum. Denn es entwickelt sich an demselben das Bedeutende."

14. Ibid., p. 130: "Ich gestehe, daβ ich diese Ausübung der Hermeneutik im Gebiet der Muttersprache und im unmittelbaren Verkehr mit Menschen für einen sehr wesentlichen Teil des gebildeten Lebens halte, abgesehn von allen philologischen oder theologischen Studien. Wer könnte mit ausgezeichnet geistreichen Menschen umgehn, ohne daβ er eben so bemüht wäre, zwischen den Worten zu hören, wie wir in geistvollen und gedrängten Schriften zwischen den Zeilen lesen, wer wollte nicht ein bedeutsames Gespräch, das leicht nach vielerlei Seiten hin auch bedeutende Tat werden kann, eben so genauer Betrachtung wert halten, die lebendigen Punkte darin herausheben, ihren innern Zusammenhang ergreifen wollen, alle leisen Andeutungen weiter verfolgen?"

15. Ibid., p. 131: "Insbesondere aber möchte ich [. . .] dem Ausleger schriftlicher Werke dringend anraten, die Auslegung des bedeutsameren Gesprächs fleiβig zu üben. Denn die unmittelbare Gegenwart des Redenden, der lebendige Ausdruck, welcher die Teilnahme seines ganzen geistigen Wesens verkündigt, die Art, wie sich hier die Gedanken aus dem gemeinsamen Leben entwickeln, dies alles reizt weit mehr als die einsame Betrachtung einer ganz isolierten Schrift dazu, eine Reihe von Gedanken zugleich als einen hervorbrechenden Lebensmoment, als eine mit vielen anderen auch anderer Art zusammenhängende Tat zu verstehen, und eben diese Seite ist es, welche bei Erklärung der Schriftsteller am meisten hintangestellt, ja groβenteils ganz vernachlässigt wird."

16. Ibid.: "hervorbrechender Lebensmoment."

17. Ibid.

18. J. Derrida, *De la grammatologie* (Paris, 1967), Ger. trans. by A. J. Rheinberger and H. Zischler (Frankfurt am Main, 1974). [Perhaps the appearance of German translations of several other works of Derrida's, including a paperback edition of *De la grammatologie,* would have led Szondi to modify this statement.—Trans.]

19. Schleiermacher, p. 31: "Zwei entgegengesetzte Maximen beim Verstehen. 1) Ich verstehe alles, bis ich auf einen Widerspruch oder Nonsens stosse, 2) ich verstehe nichts, was ich nicht als notwendig einsehe und konstruieren kann."

20. Ibid., p. 131.

21. Ibid.: "Tat."

22. Ibid., p. 86: "Die laxere Praxis in der Kunst geht davon aus, daβ sich das Verstehen von selbst ergibt, und drückt das Ziel negativ aus: 'Miβverstand soll vermieden werden'. [. . .] Die strengere Praxis geht davon aus, daβ sich das Miβverstehen von selbst ergibt und daβ Verstehen auf jedem Punkt muβ gewollt und gesucht werden."

23. Ibid., p. 31.

24. Ibid., p. 81: "Jeder Mensch [ist] auf der einen Seite ein Ort, in welchem sich eine gegebene Sprache auf eine eigentümliche Weise gestaltet, und seine Rede ist nur zu verstehen aus der Totalität der Sprache. Dann aber auch ist er ein sich stetig entwickelnder Geist, und seine Rede ist nur als eine Tatsache von diesem, im Zusammenhange mit den übrigen."

25. Ibid.: "Die Rede ist auch als Tatsache des Geistes nicht verstanden, wenn sie nicht in ihrer Sprachbeziehung verstanden ist. . . . "

26. Ibid.: "auch als Modifikation der Sprache nicht verstanden, wenn sie nicht als Tatsache des Geistes verstanden ist."

27. Ibid.

28. Ibid., pp. 132-33: "Es ist eine ganz andere Art der Gewiβheit, auch [. . .] mehr divinatorisch, die daraus entsteht, daβ der Ausleger sich in die ganze Verfassung des Schriftstellers möglichst hineinversetzt; daher es sich denn auch hier nicht selten in der Tat so verhält, wie der Platonische Rhapsode, dieser jedoch sehr naiv, von sich gesteht, daβ er den Homer vortrefflich zu erklären vermöge, über einen andern aber, Dichter oder Prosaisten, ihm oft kein rechtes Licht aufgehen wolle. Nämlich in allem, was von der Sprache nicht nur sondern auch irgend von dem geschichtlichen Zustande des Volks und der Zeit abhängt,

204 NOTES TO PP. 102-6

kann und soll sich der Ausleger, wenn ihm der gehörige Umfang von Kenntnissen zu Gebote steht, überall gleich trefflich zeigen. Was hingegen von richtiger Auffassung des innern Herganges, als der Schriftsteller entwarf und komponierte, abhängt, was das Produkt seiner persönlichen Eigentümlichkeit in die Sprache und in die Gesamtheit seiner Verhältnisse ist, das wird auch dem gewandtesten Ausleger nur bei den ihm verwandtesten Schriftstellern, nur bei den Lieblingen, in die er sich am meisten hineingelebt hat, am besten gelingen, wie es uns auch im Leben nur mit den genauesten Freunden am besten vonstatten geht, bei andern Schriftstellern aber wird er sich auf diesem Gebiet weniger genügen, und sich auch gar nicht schämen, bei andern Kunstverwandten, die diesen näher stehen, sich Rats zu erholen."

29. Ibid., p. 133.

30. P. Valéry, *Oeuvres,* vol. 2, Bibliothèque de la Pléiade (Paris, 1960), pp. 684-85: "La haine habite l'adversaire, en développe les profondeurs, dissèque les plus délicates racines des desseins qu'il a dans le coeur. Nous le pénétrons mieux que nous-mêmes, et mieux qu'il ne fait soi-même. Il s'oublie et nous ne l'oublions pas."

31. Schleiermacher, p. 138: "Die schönste Frucht von aller ästhetischen Kritik ist ein erhöhtes Verständnis von dem inneren Verfahren der Dichter und anderer Künstler der Rede, von dem ganzen Hergang der Komposition, vom ersten Entwurf an bis zur letzten Ausführung."

32. Ibid., p. 90: "Erster Kanon: Alles, was noch näheren Bestimmung bedarf in einer gegebenen Rede, darf nur aus dem dem Verfasser und seinem ursprünglichen Publikum gemeinsamen Sprachgebiet bestimmt werden."

33. Ibid., p. 95: "Zweiter Kanon: Der Sinn eines jeden Wortes an einer gegebenen Stelle muss bestimmt werden nach seinem Zusammensein mit denen, die es umgeben."

34. Ibid., p. 42.

35. Ibid.

36. Ibid.: "Es gibt zwei Arten von Bestimmung, die Exklusion aus dem ganzen Zusammenhang und die thetische aus dem unmittelbaren."

37. Ibid.

38. Ibid., p. 90: "nur aus dem Verfasser und seinem ursprünglichen Publikum gemeinsamen Sprachgebiet."

39. Ibid., p. 91: "während der Auslegung fortgesetzt werden und [sei] erst mit ihr zugleich vollendet."

40. Ibid.: "*Archaismen* liegen ausser dem unmittelbaren Sprachgebiet des Verfassers, also ebenso seiner Leser. Sie kommen vor, um die Vergangenheit mit zu vergegenwärtigen, im Schreiben mehr als im Reden, in der Poesie mehr als in der Prosa.... *Technische Ausdrücke* selbst in den populärsten Gattungen, wie z. E. in gerichtlichen und beratenden Reden, letzteres auch, wenn nicht alle Zuhörer es verstehen."

41. Ibid.: "nicht immer sein ganzes Publikum im Auge hat."

42. Ibid.: "deren glückliche Anwendung auf einem richtigen Gefühle beruht."

43. Ibid., pp. 91-92: "verschwindet bei näherer Betrachtung. In Gleichnissen sind zwei parallele Gedankenreihen. Das Wort steht in der seinigen und es soll damit nur gerechnet werden. Also behält es seine Bedeutung. In Metaphern ist dies nur angedeutet und oft nur Ein Merkmal des Begriffs herausgenommen, z. E. [. . .] König der Tiere = Löwe. Der Löwe regiert nicht, aber König heißt deswegen nicht ein nach dem Recht des Stärkeren Zerreißender. Solch ein einzelner Gebrauch gibt keine Bedeutung, und habituell kann nur die ganze Phrasis werden."

44. Ibid., pp. 59-60: "Daß man, was zur technischen Interpretation gehört, mit dem verwechselt, was zur grammatischen gehört. Hieher die meisten Metaphern, die als Epexegese stehen wie coma arborum, tela solis, wo die übertragenen Worte ganz ihre eigentlichste

Bedeutung behalten und ihre Wirkung nur durch eine Ideenkombination tun, auf welche der Schriftsteller rechnet. Eben daher die technischen Anspielungen: die Wortspiele, der Gebrauch der Sprichwörter, die Allegorie, wo die grammatische Auslegung ganz eigentlich ist und die Frage, was der Schriftsteller eigentlich gemeint hat, zur technischen gehört. Das Allgemeinste ist hier, daß der Gedanke selbst so, wie er sich durch die grammatische Interpretation ergibt, nicht zum Dargestellten gehört, sondern nur zur Darstellung, selbst wieder Zeichen ist. Wo nun und wie dieses stattfinde, ist nur durch die technische Interpretation zu finden."

45. Ibid., p. 92: "Die ursprüngliche Aufgabe auch für die Wörterbücher, die aber rein für den Ausleger da sind, ist die, die wahre vollkommene Einheit des Wortes zu finden. Das einzelne Vorkommen des Wortes an einer gegebenen Stelle gehört freilich der unendlich unbestimmten Mannigfaltigkeit, und zu dieser gibt es von jener keinen anderen Übergang als eine bestimmte Vielheit, unter welcher sie befaßt ist; und eine solche wieder muß notwendig in Gegensätze aufgehen. Allein, im einzelnen Vorkommen ist das Wort nicht isoliert: es geht in seiner Bestimmtheit nicht aus sich selbst hervor, sondern aus seinen Umgebungen, und wir dürfen nur die ursprüngliche Einheit des Wortes mit diesen zusammenbringen, um jedesmal das rechte zu finden. Die vollkommene Einheit des Wortes aber wäre seine Erklärung, und die ist ebensowenig als die vollkommene Erklärung der Gegenstände vorhanden. In den toten Sprachen nicht, weil wir ihre ganze Entwicklung noch nicht durchschaut haben, in den lebenden nicht, weil sie wirklich noch fortgeht."

46. See W. Benjamin, *Ursprung des deutschen Trauerspiels*, in *Gesammelte Schriften*, vol. 1, pt. 1 (Frankfurt am Main, 1974), p. 214; Eng. trans. by John Osborne, *The Origin of German Tragic Drama* (London, 1977), p. 34.

47. Schleiermacher, p. 96.

48. Ibid.: "innere Verschmelzung," "äussere Aneinanderreihung."

49. Ibid.

50. Ibid.: "gesteigert."

51. Ibid., pp. 104ff.

52. Ibid., p. 148: "ursprünglichen psychischen Prozess der Erzeugung und Verknüpfung von Gedanken und Bildern."

53. Ibid., p. 163: "mehr die Entstehung der Gedanken aus der Gesamtheit des Lebensmoments."

54. Ibid.: "mehr Zurückführung auf ein bestimmtes Denken oder Darstellenwollen, woraus sich eine Reihe entwickelt."

55. Ibid., p. 108: "Gedanke und Sprache gehen überall ineinander über, und die eigentümliche Art, den Gegenstand aufzufassen, geht in die Anordnung und somit auch in die Sprachbehandlung über."

56. Ibid.: "Vor dem Anfang der technischen Auslegung muß gegeben sein die Art, wie dem Verfasser der Gegenstand und wie ihm die Sprache gegeben war. [. . .] Zu dem ersten ist mitzurechnen der Zustand, in welchem sich die bestimmte Gattung, der das Werk angehört, vor seiner Zeit befand. [. . .] Also kein genaues Verständnis dieser Art ohne Kenntnis der gleichzeitigen verwandten Literatur und dessen, was dem Verfasser als früheres Muster des Stils gegeben war. Ein solches zusammenhängendes Studium kann in Beziehung auf diese Seite der Auslegung durch nichts ersetzt werden."

57. Ibid., p. 135.

58. Ibid., p. 136: "Denn gleich mit dem ersten Entwurf zu einem bestimmten Werk entwickelte sich auch in ihm die leitende Gewalt der schon feststehenden Form, sie [. . .] modifiziert [. . .] im einzelnen nicht nur den Ausdruck, sondern auch [. . .] die Erfindung. Wer also in dem Geschäft der Auslegung das nicht richtig durchsieht, wie der Strom des Denkens und Dichtens hier gleichsam an die Wände seines Bettes anstieß und

zurückprallte, und dort in eine andere Richtung gelenkt ward, als die er ungebunden würde genommen haben; der kann schon den inneren Hergang der Komposition nicht richtig verstehen und noch weniger dem Schrifsteller selbst hinsichtlich seines Verhältnisses zu der Sprache und ihren Formen die richtige Stelle anweisen."

59. Ibid., p. 133: "Man könnte versucht sein zu behaupten, die ganze Praxis der Auslegung müsse sich auf diese Weise teilen, daβ die eine Klasse von Auslegern, mehr der Sprache und der Geschichte zugewendet als den Personen, durch alle Schriftsteller einer Sprache ziemlich gleichmäβig durchginge, wenngleich auch unter ihnen der eine mehr in dieser, der andere in einer andern Region hervorragt; die andere Klasse aber, mehr der Beobachtung der Personen zugewendet, die Sprache nur als das Medium, durch welches sie sich äuβern, die Geschichte nur als die Modalitäten, unter denen sie existierten, betrachtend, sich nur jeder auf diejenigen Schriftsteller beschränkte, die sich ihm am willigsten aufschlieβen."

60. Ibid., p. 81: "Die absolute Lösung der Aufgabe ist die, wenn jede Seite für sich [i.e. die grammatische und die technische] so behandelt wird, daβ die Behandlung der andern keine Änderung im Resultat hervorbringt, [wenn jede Seite für sich] behandelt, die andere völlig ersetzt."

61. See ibid., p. 80.

62. See ibid., p. 48 and p. 56.

7. *Tableau* and *Coup de Théâtre:* On the Social Psychology of Diderot's Bourgeois Tragedy

1. Georg Lukács, *Schriften zur Literatursoziologie,* ed. P. Ludz (Neuwied, 1961), p. 277.

2. Arnold Hauser, *Sozialgeschichte der Kunst und Literatur* (1953; rpt. Munich, 1967), p. 599.

3. [The expressions for the dramatic genre usually called "domestic drama" in English will be translated here as "bourgeois drama" in conformity with the corresponding French and German terms, *le drame bourgeois* and *das bürgerliche Drama,* respectively.—Trans.]

4. Denis Diderot, *Oeuvres esthétiques,* ed. P. Vernière (Paris, 1965) (hereafter cited as *Oe. e.*), p. 91: "Si la mère d'Iphigénie sé montrait un moment reine d'Argos et femme du général des Grecs, elle ne me paraîtrait que la dernière des créatures. La véritable dignité, celle qui me frappe, qui me renverse, c'est le tableau de l'amour maternel dans toute sa vérité."

5. Ibid., p. 99: "J'y vis un tableau, et j'y entendis un discours que je n'ai point oubliés. Le mort était étendu sur un lit. Ses jambes nues pendaient hors du lit. Sa femme échevelée était à terre. Elle tenait les pieds de son mari; et elle disait en fondant en larmes, et avec une action qui en arrachait à tout le monde: "Hélas! quand je t'envoyai ici, je ne pensais pas que ces pieds te menaient à la mort." Croyez-vous qu'une femme d'un autre rang aurait été plus pathétique? Non. La même situation lui eût inspiré le même discours. Son âme eût été celle du moment; et ce qu'il faut que l'artiste trouve, c'est ce que tout le monde dirait en pareil cas; ce que personne n'entendra, sans le reconnaître aussitôt en soi.

"Les grands intérêts, les grandes passions. Voilà la source des grands discours, des discours vrais."

6. Denis Diderot, *Oeuvres complètes,* ed J. Assézat, vol. 7 (Paris, 1875), p. 298 (hereafter cited as *Oe. c.*): "Il unit ses quatres enfants, et il dit: une belle femme, un homme de bien sont les deux êtres les plus touchants de la nature. Donnez deux fois, en un même jour, ce spectacle aux hommes."

7. Walter Benjamin [Detlef Holz], *Deutsche Menschen: Eine Folge von Briefen* (Lu-

cerne, 1936), p. 74. New ed., without pseudonym (Frankfurt, 1962), and in *Gesammelte Schriften* (Frankfurt, 1972), sec. 1, p. 198.

8. Jürgen Habermas, *Strukturwandel der Öffentlichkeit* (Neuwied, 1962), p. 56.

9. Ibid.

10. Trevelyan, cited in Habermas, *Strukturwandel,* pp. 56–57.

11. *Oe. e.,* 88: "un incident imprévu qui se passe en action, et qui change subitement l'état des personnages."

12. Ibid.: "une disposition de ces personnages sur la scène, si naturelle et si vraie, que, rendu fidèlement par un peintre, elle me plairait sur la toile."

13. Max Weber, *Die protestantische Ethik und der Geist des Kapitalismus,* vol. 1 of *Gesammelte Aufsätze zur Religionssoziologie* (Tübingen, 1920), pp. 53–54.

14. *Oe. e.,* 153: "Jusqu'à présent, dans la comédie, le caractère a été l'objet principal, et la condition n'a été que l'accessoire; il faut que la condition devienne aujourd'hui l'objet principal, et que le caractère ne soit que l'accessoire. C'est du caractère qu'on tirait toute l'intrigue. On cherchait en général les circonstances qui le faisaient sortir, et l'on enchaînait ces circonstances. C'est la condition, ses devoirs, ses avantages, ses embarras, qui doivent servir de base à l'ouvrage. Il me semble que cette source est plus féconde, plus étendue et plus utile que celle des caractères. Pour peu que le caractère fût chargé, un spectateur pouvait se dire à lui-même, ce n'est pas moi. Mais il ne peut se cacher que l'état qu'on joue devant lui, ne soit le sien; il ne peut méconnaître ses devoirs. Il faut absolument qu'il s'applique ce qu'il entend."

15. Ibid, p. 154: "Ainsi, vous voudriez qu'on jouât l'homme de lettres, le philosophe, le commerçant, le juge, l'avocat, le politique, le citoyen, le magistrat, le financier, le grand seigneur, l'intendant."

16. Ibid.: "Ajoutez à cela, toutes les relations: le père de famille, l'époux, la soeur, les frères. Le père de famille! Quel sujet dans un siècle tel que le nôtre, où il ne paraît pas qu'on ait la moindre idée de ce que c'est qu'un père de famille!"

17. Ibid., p. 33: "O Richardson, Richardson, homme unique à mes yeux, tu seras ma lecture dans tous les temps! . . . Tu me resteras sur le même rayon avec Moïse, Homère, Euripide et Sophocle."

18. Ibid., pp. 30–31: "Cet auteur ne fait point couler le sang le long des lambris: il ne vous transporte point dans des contrées éloignées; il ne vous expose point à être dévore par des sauvages; il ne se renferme point dans des lieux clandestins de débauche; il ne se perd jamais dans les régions de la féerie. Le monde où nous vivons est le lieu de la scène; le fond de son drame est vrai; ses personnages ont toute la réalitè possible; ses caractères sont pris du milieu de la société; ses incidents sont dans les moeurs de toutes les nations policées; les passions qu'il peint sont telles que je les éprouve en moi; ce sont les mêmes objets qui les émeuvent, elles ont l'énergie que je leur connais; les traverses et les afflictions de ses personnages sont de la nature de celles qui me menacent sans cesse; il me montre le cours général des choses qui m'environnent."

19. Ibid., p. 31: "Richardson sème dans les coeurs des germes de [vertus] qui y restent d'abord oisifs et tranquilles: ils y sont secrètement, jusqu'à ce qu'il se présente une occasion qui les remue et les fasse éclore. Alors ils se développent; on se sent porter au bien avec une impétuosité qu'on ne se connaissait pas. On éprouve, à l'aspect de l'injustice, une révolte qu'on ne saurait s'expliquer à soi-même. C'est qu'on a fréquenté Richardson; c'est qu'on a conversé avec l'homme de bien, dans des moments où l'âme désintéressée était ouverte à la vérité."

20. *Oe. c. 7,* 67–68: "Il n'y a point d'exemple qui captive plus fortement que celui de la vertu, pas même l'exemple du vice."

21. *Oe. e.,* 195–96: "Oui, mon ami, et très bonne. . . . Ce sont les misérables conventions

qui pervertissent l'homme, et non la nature humaine qu'il faut accuser. En effet, qu'est-ce qui nous affecte comme le récit d'une action généreuse?"

22. *Oe. e.,* 195 (*De la poésie dramatique*): "nous touche d'une manière plus intime et plus douce que ce qui excite notre mépris et nos ris."

23. Ibid., p. 192 (*De la poésie dramatique*): "Les devoirs des hommes sont un fonds aussi riche pour le poète dramatique, que leurs ridicules et leurs vices."

24. Ibid., p. 105 (*Entretiens sur le fils naturel*): "loin de la terre, au milieu des flots de la mer."

25. Ibid., p. 192: "mais plus surement encore chez un peuple corrompu qu'ailleurs."

26. Ibid., pp. 192–193: "C'est en allant au théâtre qu'ils se sauveront de la compagnie des méchants dont ils sont entourés; c'est là qu'ils trouveront ceux avec lesquels ils aimerai à vivre; c'est là qu'ils verront l'espèce humaine comme elle est, et qu'ils se réconcilieront avec elle."

27. Cited in Charly Guyot, *Diderot par lui-même* (Paris, 1953), p. 7.

28. *Oe. c. 7,* 66.

29. *Oe. e.,* 193: "Les gens de bien sont rares; mais il y en a. Celui qui pense autrement s'accuse lui-même, et montre combien il est malheureux dans sa femme, dans ses parents, dans ses amis, dans ses connaissances."

30. Diderot, "*Aux insurgents d'Amérique,"* in *Oeuvres politiques,* ed. P. Vernière (Paris, 1963), p. 491: "Après des siècles d'une oppression générale, puisse la révolution qui vient de s'opérer au-delà des mers, en offrant à tous les habitants de l'Europe un asile contre le fanatisme et la tyrannie, instruire ceux qui gouvernent les hommes sur le légitime usage de leur autorité!"

31. Cited in Guyot, *Diderot par lui-même,* p. 66: "Le peuple est méchant, mais il est encore plus sot."

32. Ibid.: "L'homme peuple est le plus sot et le plus méchant des hommes: se dépopulariser, ou se rendre meilleur, c'est la même chose."

33. *Lessings Briefwechsel mit Mendelssohn und Nicolai über das Trauerspiel,* ed. R. Petsch (1910; rpt. Darmstadt, 1967), p. 69—henceforth cited as *B.*: "drei Grade des Mitleids, deren mittelster das weinende Mitleid [sei]."

34. Ibid., pp. 69ff.: "Rührung ist, wenn ich weder die Vollkommenheiten, noch das Unglück des Gegenstandes deutlich denke, sondern von beiden nur einen dunkeln Begriff habe: so rührt, mich z. E. der Anblick jedes Bettlers. Tränen erweckt er nur dann in mir, wenn er mich mit seinen guten Eigenschaften sowohl, als mit seinen Unfällen bekannter macht, und zwar mit beiden zugleich, welches das wahre Kunststück ist, Tränen zu erregen. Denn macht er mich erst mit seinen guten Eigenschaften und hernach mit seinen Unfällen, oder erst mit diesen und hernach mit jenen bekannt, so wird zwar die Rührung stärker, aber zu Tränen kömmt sie nicht. Z. E. Ich frage den Bettler nach seinen Umständen, und er antwortet: ich bin seit drei Jahren amtlos, ich habe Frau und Kinder; sie sind teils krank, teils noch zu klein, sich selbst zu versorgen; ich selbst bin nur vor einigen Tagen vom Krankenbette aufgestanden.—Das ist sein Unglück!—Aber wer sind Sie denn? frage ich weiter.—Ich bin der und der, von dessen Geschicklichkeit in diesen oder jenen Verrichtungen Sie vielleicht gehört haben: ich bekleidete mein Amt mit möglichster Treue; ich könnte es alle Tage wieder antreten, wenn ich lieber die Kreatur eines Ministers, als ein ehrlicher Mann sein wollte usw. Das sind seine Vollkommenheiten! Bei einer solchen Erzählung aber kann niemand weinen. Sondern wenn der Unglückliche meine Tränen haben will, muß er beide Stücke verbinden; er muß sagen: ich bin vom Amte gesetzt, weil ich zu ehrlich war, und mich dadurch bei dem Minister verhaßt machte; ich hungere, und mit mir hungert eine kranke liebenswürdige Frau; und mit uns hungern sonst hoffnungsvolle, jetzt in der Armut vermodernde Kinder; und wir werden gewiß noch lange hungern müssen. Doch

ich will lieber hungern, als niederträchtig sein; auch meine Frau und Kinder wollen lieber hungern, und ihr Brot lieber unmittelbar von Gott, das ist, aus der Hand eines barmherzigen Mannes, nehmen, als ihren Vater und Ehemann lasterhaft wissen usw.—[. . .] Einer solchen Erzählung habe ich immer Tränen in Bereitschaft. Unglück und Verdienst sind hier im Gleichgewicht."

35. Ibid., pp. 70-71.

36. Ibid., p. 71: "Aber lassen Sie uns das Gewicht in der einen oder andern Schale vermehren, und zusehen, was nunmehr entsteht. Lassen Sie uns zuerst in die Schale der Vollkommenheit eine Zulage werfen. Der Unglückliche mag fortfahren: aber wenn ich und meine kranke Frau uns nur erst wieder erholt haben, so soll es schon anders werden. Wir wollen von der Arbeit unsrer Hände leben; wir schämen uns keiner. Alle Arten, sein Brot zu verdienen, sind einem ehrlichen Manne gleich anständig; Holz spalten oder am Ruder des Staates sitzen. Es kömmt seinem Gewissen nicht darauf an, wie viel er nützt, sondern wie viel er nützen wollte. —Nun hören meine Tränen auf; die Bewundrung erstickt sie. Und kaum, daβ ich es noch fühle, daβ die Bewundrung aus dem Mitleiden entsprungen. —Lassen Sie uns eben den Versuch mit der andern Wagschale anstellen. Der ehrliche Bettler erfährt, daβ es wirklich einerlei Wunder, einerlei übernatürliche Seltenheit ist, von der Barmherzigkeit der Menschen, oder unmittelbar aus der Hand Gottes gespeist zu werden. Er wird überall schimpflich abgewiesen; unterdessen nimmt sein Mangel zu, und mit ihm seine Verwirrung. Endlich gerät er in Wut; er ermordet seine Frau, seine Kinder und sich. —Weinen Sie noch? —Hier erstickt der Schmerz die Tränen, aber nicht das Mitleid, wie es die Bewundrung tut. Es ist—"

37. G. E. Lessing, "Des Herrn Jakob Thomson sämtliche Trauerspiele," in *Sämtliche Werke,* vol. 7, ed. Lachmann and Muncker (Stuttgart, 1891), p. 68: "Tränen des Mitleids . . . sind die Absicht des Trauerspiels."

38. *B.,* 71.

39. Ibid.

40. G. W. F. Hegel, *Vorlesungen über die Geschichte der Philosophie,* vol. 18, *Sämtliche Werke,* ed. H. Glockner (Stuttgart, 1928), pp. 119-20.

41. *B.,* 71.

42. G. E. Lessing, *Gesammelte Werke,* ed. W. Stammler, Hamburgische Dramaturgie, no. 75 (Munich, 1959), vol. 2, p. 649: "[als eine, die uns nicht] das bevorstehende Übel eines andern, für diesen andern, erweckt, [sondern die] aus anserer Ähnlichkeit mit der leidenden Person für uns selbst entspringt."

43. Ibid.

44. Ibid.

45. Ibid., no. 14, vol. 2, p. 388: "Die Namen von Fürsten und Helden können einem Stücke Pomp und Majestät geben; aber zur Rührung tragen sie nichts bei. Das Unglück derjenigen, deren Umstände den unsrigen am nächsten kommen, muβ natürlicherweise am tiefsten in unsere Seele dringen; und wenn wir mit Königen Mitleidhaben, so haben wir es mit ihnen als mit Menschen, und nicht als mit Königen. Macht ihr Stand schon öfters ihre Unfälle wichtiger, so macht er sie darum nicht interessanter. Immerhin mögen ganze Völker darein verwickelt werden; unsere Sympathie erfordert einen einzelnen Gegenstand, und ein Staat ist ein viel zu abstrakter Begriff für unsere Empfindungen."

8. Walter Benjamin's "City Portraits"

The "City Portraits" are quoted from the texts published as *Städtebilder* in volume 17 of the series *edition suhrkamp,* which also contains a selection from *A Berlin Childhood around 1900.* (Now reprinted in Benjamin, *Gesammelte Schriften,* vol. 4, pt. 1, pp. 235ff.)—Trans.

1. Walter Benjamin, "Die Wiederkehr des Flaneurs," in *Gesammelte Schriften,* vol. 3 (Frankfurt am Main, 1972), p. 194: "Der oberflächliche Anlaß, das Exotische, Pittoreske wirkt nur auf Fremde. Als Einheimischer zum Bild einer Stadt zu kommen, erfordert andere, tiefere Motive. Motive dessen, der ins Vergangene statt ins Ferne reist. Immer wird das Stadtbuch des Einheimischen Verwandtschaft mit Memoiren haben, der Schreiber hat nicht umsonst seine Kindheit am Ort verlebt."

2. Walter Benjamin, "Über den Begriff der Geschichte," in *Gesammelte Schriften,* vol. 1, pt. 2, p. 695. [See the author's essay "Hope in the Past: On Walter Benjamin," this volume.—Trans.]

3. This is how Benjamin expressed it in a dedication. See the essay cited in note 2 above.

4. "Zentralpark," in *Gesammelte Schriften,* vol. 1, pt. 2, p. 668.

5. Benjamin, *Gesammelte Schriften,* pp. 75ff.

6. Benjamin, "Denkbilder: Neapel," in *Gesammelte Schriften,* vol. 4, p. 314: "Porös wie dieses Gestein ist die Architektur. Bau und Aktion gehen in Höfen, Arkaden und Treppen ineinander über. In allem wahrt man den Spielraum, der es befähigt, Schauplatz neuer unvorhergesehener Konstellationen zu werden. Man meidet das Definitive, Geprägte. Keine Situation erscheint so, wie sie ist, für immer gedacht, keine Gestalt behauptet ihr 'so und nicht anders.' So kommt die Architektur, dieses bündigste Stück der Gemeinschaftsrhythmik, hier zustande."

7. Benjamin, "Berliner Kindheit," in *Gesammelte Schriften,* p. 287.

8. Cited in P. Szondi, *Schriften,* [ed. Jean Bollack et al. (Frankfurt am Main, 1978)], vol. 2, p. 302: "Da der Verkaufszweig der Ikonen zum Papier- und Bilderhandel rechnet, so kommen diese Buden mit Heiligenbildern neben die Stände mit Papierwaren zu stehen, so dass sie überall von Lenin-Bildern flankiert sind, wie ein Verhafteter von zwei Gendarmen."

9. Cited in ibid., p. 303: ". . . ein jeder Schritt und Tritt [wird] auf benannten Grunde getan. Und wo nun einer dieser Namen fällt, da baut sich Phantasie um diesen Laut im Handumdrehen ein ganzes Viertel auf. Das wird der späteren Wirklichkeit noch lange trotzen und spröd wie gläsernes Gemäuer darin steckenbleiben."

10. Cited in ibid.: "Worte zu dem zu finden, was man vor Augen hat—wie schwer kann das sein. Wenn sie dann aber kommen, stossen sie mit Kleinen Hämmern gegen das Wirkliche, bis sie das Bild aus ihm wie aus einer kupfernen Platte getrieben haben."

11. Cited in ibid., p. 304: "Abends, das Herz bleischwer, voller Beklemmung, auf Deck. Lange verfolge ich das Spiel der Möwen [. . .] Die Sonne ist längst untergegangen, im Osten ist es sehr dunkel. Das Schiff fährt südwärts. Einige Helle ist im Westen geblieben. Was sich nun an den Vögeln vollzog—oder an mir?—das geschah kraft des Platzes, den ich so beherrschend, so einsam in der Mitte des Achterdecks mir aus Schwermütigkeit gewählt hatte. Mit einem Male gab es zwei Möwenvölker, eines die östlichen, eines die westlichen, linke und rechte, so ganz verschieden, daß der Name Möwen von ihnen abfiel."

12. Marcel Proust, *A la Recherche du Temps perdu,* Pléiade ed., 3 vols. (Paris, n.d.), vol. 3, p. 889.

13. Walter Benjamin, *Deutsche Menschen* (Frankfurt am Main, 1962), pp. 75-76 (Now in *Gesammelte Schriften,* vol. 4, pt. 1, p. 198.)

14. Cited in Szondi, *Schriften,* vol. 2, p. 306: "Wie die Bewohner entlegener Bergdörfer einander bis auf Tod und Siechtum versippt sein können, so haben sich die Häuser vertreppt und verwinkelt."

15. T. W. Adorno, in his "Introduction" to W. Benjamin, *Schriften,* vol. 1 (Frankfurt am Main, 1955), p. x.

16. H. Friedrich, in his "Afterword" to Karl Krolow, *Ausgewählte Gedichte* (Frankfurt am Main, 1962).

17. Cited in Szondi, *Schriften,* vol. 2, p. 307: "Im Goethe-Schiller-Archiv sind Trep-

penhäuser, Säle, Schaukästen, Bibliotheken weiß [. . .] Wie Kranke in Hospitälern liegen die Handschriften hingebettet. Aber je länger man diesem barschen Lichte sich aussetzt, desto mehr glaubt man, eine ihrer selbst unbewußte Vernunft auf dem Grunde dieser Anstalten zu erkennen."

18. In Walter Benjamin, *Briefe,* vol. 1, ed. G. Scholem and T. W. Adorno (Frankfurt am Main, 1966), no. 55.

19. Cf. "Paris, die Stadt im Spiegel," *Vogue,* 30 Jan. 1929, p. 27 (cf. *Gesammelte Schriften,* vol. 4, pt. 2, pp. 356ff.); and "Pariser Tagebuch," *Die literarische Welt,* 6th year, nos. 16/17, 18, 21, 25 (17 April, 2 May, 23 May, and 20 June 1930) (cf. *Gesammelte Schriften,* vol. 4, pt. 2, pp. 567ff.).

9. Hope in the Past: On Walter Benjamin

1. Walter Benjamin, *Berliner Kindheit um Neunzehnhundert* (Frankfurt am Main, 1950), pp. 9-10. Hereafter page references to this work will appear in the text.

2. W. Adorno, "Im Schatten junger Mädchenblute," in *Dichten und Trachten,* Jahresschau des Suhrkamp-Verlages 4 (Frankfurt am Main, 1954), p. 74.

3. "Here is a very important book, Marcel Proust, Du Côté de chez Swann (chez Bernard Grasset): a book of unparalleled strangeness by a new author[:] if it is offered for translation, it must absolutely be accepted; to be sure, 500 pages in the most peculiar style and two volumes just as large still to come!" Letter of 3 Feb. 1914 in Rainer Maria Rilke's *Briefe an seinen Verleger* (Leipzig, 1934), p. 216.

4. Ernst Robert Curtius, "Marcel Proust," in *Französischer Geist im neuen Europa* (Stuttgart, [1925]) and "Die deutsche Marcel-Proust-Ausgabe," *Die literarische Welt,* 8 Jan. 1926.

5. Marcel Proust, *Im Schatten der jungen Mädchen,* trans. Walter Benjamin and Franz Hessel (Berlin, [1927]); *Die Herzogin von Guermantes,* trans. Walter Benjamin and Franz Hessel, (Munich, 1930).

6. Now in Benjamin's *Schriften,* 2 vols. (Frankfurt am Main, 1955), vol. 2, pp. 132-47.

7. Kurt Wais, "Französische und französisch-belgische Dichtung," in *Die Gegenwartsdichtung der europäischen Völker,* ed. Wais (Berlin, 1939), pp. 214-15. In the editor's preface Wais states: "Our selection and judgment also have their limits. These are the natural ones of our hereditary points of view, of which we are not ashamed."

8. Marcel Proust, *A la recherche du temps perdu,* Pléiade ed., 3 vols. (Paris, n.d.), vol. 3, p. 1033. [Eng. trans., Marcel Proust, "Time Regained," in *Remembrance of Things Past,* vol. 3, trans. C. K. Scott Moncrieff, Terence Kilmartin, and Andreas Mayor (New York, 1981), p. 1089.]

9. Rilke, letter of 12 Feb. 1914, *Briefwechsel mit Benvenuta* (Esslingen, 1954), pp. 58ff.

10. Proust, *A la recherche,* vol. 3, p. 871. [Eng. trans., Proust, *Remembrance of Things Past,* p. 904.]

11. Benjamin, *Schriften,* vol. 1, p. 575.

12. T. W. Adorno, "Charakteristik Walter Benjamins," in *Prismen* (Frankfurt am Main, 1955), p. 289.

13. Benjamin, *Schriften,* vol. 1, pp. 580-81.

14. T. W. Adorno, *Minima Moralia* (Frankfurt am Main, 1951), pp. 480-81.

15. Benjamin, *Schriften,* vol. 1, p. 552.

16. G. W. F. Hegel, *Aesthetik,* Jubiläumsausgabe (Stuttgart, 1927-40), vol. 13, p. 342.

17. A private communication to the author from Prof. Adorno.

18. Benjamin, *Schriften,* vol. 1, p. 495.

19. Ibid., p. 502.

20. Ibid., p. 498.
21. Ibid., pp. 161-62.
22. Ibid., pp. 428, 492.
23. Ibid., p. 487.
24. *Deutsche Menschen, Eine Folge von Briefen,* Auswahl und Einleitung von Detlef Holz [selection and introduction by Detlef Holz] (Lucerne, 1936); new ed., without pseudonym (Frankfurt am Main, 1962).
25. In the possession of Dr. Achim von Borries.
26. Benjamin, *Schriften,* vol. 2, p. 535 (biographical remarks by Friedrich Podszus).
27. Ibid., vol. 1, p. 497.

10. The Poetry of Constancy: Paul Celan's Translation of Shakespeare's Sonnet 105

1. William Shakespeare, *Eindundzwanzig Sonette,* trans. Paul Celan (Frankfurt am Main, 1967), p. 35. (This is book no. 898 in the series Insel-Bücherei).
2. William Shakespeare, *The Sonnets,* ed. John Dover Wilson (Cambridge, 1966), p. 55.
3. Letter of 2 April 1804 to Friedrich Wilmans.
4. Sonnet 104, v. 1.
5. Charles Baudelaire, *Tableaux Parisiens,* Ger. trans. with a preface on "The Task of the Translator" ("Die Aufgabe des Übersetzers") by Walter Benjamin (Heidelberg, 1923), pp. xiff. Rpt. in Charles Baudelaire, *Ausgewählte Gedichte,* Ger. trans. by Walter Benjamin (Frankfurt am Main, 1970), pp. 14ff. (An English translation of this preface can be found in the collection of Benjamin's essays entitled *Illuminations,* ed. Hannah Arendt, trans. Harry Zohn (New York, 1973), pp. 69ff.

In Benjamin's essay, "intention" (*Intention*) does not mean "purpose" (*Absicht*). What Benjamin means can perhaps best be understood from the following passage from Fritz Mauthner: "Throughout the Middle Ages the concept of *intentio* did not [apply] to the will, but rather to knowing, or to the energy or tension involved in knowing. The Schoolmen's Latin was bad, and in *intentio* they could still detect the original meaning, the metaphor of the taut bow and the aiming of the arrow; hence for them *intentio* was directedness of attention or of consciousness to a perceived or perceptible object. (F. Mauthner, *Wörterbuch der Philosophie: Neue Beiträge zu einer Kritik der Sprache* [Munich and Leipzig, 1910], vol. 1, pp. 584-85). In the following discussion the concept of "intention toward language is not used strictly in Benjamin's sense, insofar as it has been divorced from the theoretical background of Benjamin's views on language and contains ideas deriving from modern linguistics. For our present purposes "intention toward language" may be defined as the directedness of consciousness toward language, that is, as the linguistic conception preceding all speech; in other words, it may be seen as the mode of signification that stamps linguistic usage.
6. Ibid.
7. *Les mots et les choses* (Paris, 1966); Eng. trans. as *The Order of Things* (New York, 1973).
8. [See P. Szondi, "On Textual Understanding," in this volume.—Trans.]
9. An analysis of Shakespeare's sonnet that would do justice to it would have to proceed from its own distinctive features, but that would carry us beyond the bounds of the present essay.
10. See Jacques Derrida, "La double séance," *Tel Quel* 41 (Spring 1970) and 42 (Summer 1970); rpt. in *La dissémination* (Paris, 1972).
11. See Michel Deguy, "Vers une théorie de la figure généralisée," *Critique* 269 (October 1969).

12. Cf. Heinrich Lausberg, *Handbuch der literarischen Rhetorik* (Munich, 1960), p. 361.
13. Stefan Georg, *Werke* (Munich and Düsseldorf, 1958), vol. 2, p. 203.
14. Cf. Theodor W. Adorno, *Negative Dialektik* (Frankfurt am Main, 1966), pp. 156ff.; trans. as *Negative Dialectics,* by E. B. Ashton (New York, 1973). See also "Parataxis: Zur späten Lyrik Hölderlins," in *Noten zur Literatur* [Frankfurt, 1980], vol. 3, pp. 184ff.
15. Cf. Benjamin, "Die Aufgabe des Übersetzers."
16. Alexander Schmidt, *Shakespeare-Lexikon,* 5th ed. (Berlin, 1962), vol. 2, p. 1310.
17. Gerald Willen and Victor B. Reed, eds., *A Casebook on Shakespeare's Sonnets* (New York, 1964), p. 107.
18. Paul Celan, *Die Niemandsrose* (Frankfurt am Main, 1963), p. 9. [Eng. trans., Paul Celan, *Paul Celan: Poems,* trans. Michael Hamburger (New York, 1980), p. 131. Trans. modified.]
19. The English text printed in the Insel-Bücherei volume was not suggested by Celan, nor did he provide the publisher with it; he did, however, examine and approve it. (This information was kindly given me by Mr. Klaus Reichert.)
20. See Derrida, "La double séance," and also his "Sémiologie et grammatologie," *Information sur les sciences sociales* 7, no. 3 (1968) (Recherches Sémiotiques).
21. See note 26.
22. It would be worthwhile to examine the function of this program (or experiment) of a poetics of constancy in Celan's own poetry and in its development.
23. See note 19.
24. See the reference in note 14. In Hölderlin, to be sure, parataxis serves to isolate individual words, whereas in Celan, at least in this translation, it pertains more to the relationship of the verses and sentences. In Celan's own poetry, parataxis involving individual words plays a decisive role.
25. See note 19. The typographical separation of the quatrains was probably made in order to have the corresponding lines of the original and the translation face each other in the dual language edition.
26. Roman Jakobson, "Linguistics and Poetics," in *Style in Language,* ed. Thomas A. Sebeok (Cambridge, Mass., 1960), p. 358.—In the poetic sequence the equivalences correspond to the passage of time. It is perhaps no accident that sonnets are the subject both of Jakobson's most important interpretations of poems and of the present essay: "Le sonnet est fait pour le simultané. Quatorze vers *simultanés,* et fortement désignés comme tels par l'enchaînement et la conservation des rimes: type et structure d'un poème *stationnaire*" ["The sonnet is made for the simultaneous. Fourteen *simultaneous* verses, and vigorously designated as such by the linking and conserving of rhymes: type and structure of a *stationary* poem"—trans. A. Warminski]. (Paul Valéry, *Tel Quel,* in *Oeuvres,* Pléiade ed. [Paris, 1960], vol. 2, p. 676.—In the framework of Jakobson's definition of the "poetic function," the conjugation paradigm, which was discussed in connection with the passages *was ich da treib und treib* and *Ich find, erfind,* turns out to be a special case of what modern linguistics terms "paradigmatics."
27. The present essay is concerned with Celan's intention toward language. It should be completed by an analysis of his way of fashioning language. Such an analysis would have to devote particular attention to the expressive value and tone of turns of phrase like "*den ich da lieb,*" "*was ich da treib,*" and "*all dieses Singen.*" It would show that with these linguistic means Celan expresses not only the contemplative distance of the melancholic to himself and to the object of his love—and the "I" who speaks in Shakespeare's sonnets may rightly be termed a melancholic; he also expresses the distance between himself and the subjective dimension as such, from which Celan turns away in favor of the objectivity of the poem, which is concerned only with itself. This objectivity is established by a language

which, like the one examined here, no longer serves the function of representation. Yet, in the final verse (*In Einem will ich drei zusammenschmieden*) intense light falls on the "I" that sets itself this task, in opposition not only to the "I" standing behind the veil of melancholy, an "I" that lives *there* (*da*), but also to the programmatic objectivity of the poem.

Index

Index

217

50-53; deduction and induction, 81;
notion of the tragic, 49-55
*Hegel's Completion of Classical German
Aesthetics*, 82
Heidegger, Martin, ix, xx, 30; influence on
hermeneutics, 97
Herder, Johann Gottfried, 57-58, 77
Hermeneutical consciousness: absence of,
in German literary study, xvi, 4-6
Hermeneutics, 2, 4, 9, 18, 107; definition
of, 95, 112; grammatical vs.
psychological interpretation, 96,
101-112; history of, 95-97, 106; inquiry
into nonliterary texts and speech,
98-100; model for a new theory of
interpretation, 97; of Schleiermacher,
95-113; and Szondi's method, ix, xvi,
xxi
Historian: as prophet, 156
Historicity: of aesthetic consciousness, viii,
164-168, 170-171; of facts, 113; of
genre and genre theory, xx, 77, 83-84,
87-88; of language, xiii, 164; of literary
phenomena, 13, 103, 110
History: Benjamin's conception of
technological age, 155-159; and
German literary study, xviii, 5, 6, 13;
as realization of necessity, 88; and
romantic eschatology, xiv, 63-64, 156;
and Szondi's perspective, 181n.1 & 2
Hölderlin, Friedrich, xi-xxi passim, 137,
142, 164, 176; genesis of hymnic style,
23-42; language, xx, 6, 25-26;
metaphor, 8-16, 26-27; notion of the
tragic, 46-48; theory of tones, 91-92;
and traditional genre, xx, 41-42
Hofmannsthal, Hugo von, 139
Hofmeister, Der, 130
Homer, 95, 100
Hymn: 8-12, 16, 23-42; transformation of
structure in, 24-25, 41-42

Identity: identity and conflict, 49-51; of
real and ideal in poetry, 62; in
Schelling's aesthetic theory, 45
Idyll, 62, 92
Iliad, The, 51
Illusion: in drama, 71-73
Imagery: in Benjamin, 137, 139-142; in
Celan, 162, 173; in Hölderlin, 9-11,

27-28, 38, 40
Indifferenz, 45, 50
Induction: and deduction, in poetics of
Schlegel, 80-81, 88
Influence: concept of, ix-x; on Szondi,
xiv-xv, xix
Intention, 61; in Celan, 164-178; and
meaning, 20-21; toward language,
concept of, 164, 212n.5
Interpretation, 17-22; grammatical vs.
psychological, 96, 101-112; new theory
of, 97; objective and subjective, 7-8,
13, 15-17. *See also* Ambiguity,
Hermeneutics, Language, Meaning
"Inversion method," 68-69
Iphigénie, 116
Iphigenia in Aulis, 53
Irony: romantic, 57-63; Schlegel's
definition of, 67-68

Jakobson, Roman, 176-178
Joyce, James, 134
Judaism: and Christianity, 50-52

Kafka-Pro und Contra, 68
Kant, Immanuel, 44, 49, 50; influence on
Schlegel, 62, 63, 75, 83
Kierkegaard, Søren, 66
Kleist, Heinrich von, 13, 19, 21
Kraus, Karl, 157
Kritische Journal der Philosophie, 49
Kunstpoesie, 61, 77, 79, 82-83, 87

Lachmann, Eduard, xx, 36
Language: in Benjamin, 139; in Celan,
170-171, 174, 175, 213-214n.27; and
fascism, xii-xiii; historicity of, 164-168;
about language, 169; Mallarmé's
conception of, 22, 174
Language and Silence, xii
Langue: and *parole*, 104, 171-172
"Lebenslauf." *See* "Course of Life, The"
Lebensphilosophie, 100, 102, 103
Lectures on the Philosophy of Art, 45
Lenz, J. M. R., 116, 130, 132
Lessing, Gotthold Ephraim, 85, 116,
128-132
Lillo, George, 115, 116, 122, 127-128, 131
Linguistics: and hermeneutics, 97-98; 104,
107-108; in study of poetry, 165;

Philosophy of history, xv, xxi; of
Benjamin, 157; and Schlegel's poetics
of genre, 57-68, 82, 84-94
Philosophy of Rhetoric, The, 6
Pindar, 23, 24, 25, 62, 83
Pity and fear: effects of tragedy, 131-132
Play: in romantic art, 66-68, 75
Pliny, 87
Poetic genre. *See* Genre
Poetic language: function of, 176
Poetic process, 11, 20, 22, 36
Poetics: pure and applied, 79-82, 85
Poetry: ancient vs. modern, 77, 79, 82-83,
87, 90-91; about poetry, 26-35, 62, 169;
postmodern, xxi, 161-178; as
provisional, 64-65; romantic, 59-67
Positivism, xvi-xviii, 7, 15
Positivity, 137
Poststructuralism, ix, xxi
Poulet, Georges, 100
Prince Zerbino, 70-71
Progressive poetry, 61, 94. *See also* Poetry,
romantic
Prologue, vii-viii, 68-70
Prologue, A, vii-viii, 68-70
Prophecy: and memory, 134-135, 140,
152-154, 157
"Prose," 20
*Protestant Ethic and the Spirit of
Capitalism, The,* 120-121
Proust, Marcel, ix, xxi; and Benjamin,
134-149 passim
Provisionalness: in romantic art, 64-65,
68-70
Psychological interpretation: vs.
grammatical, 96, 101-111

Racine, Jean Baptiste, 116, 117
Reader, ix, xiv, xviii, 105; of oneself in
literature, 147-148
Reality: and language, viii, xiii, 139-142;
as provisional, 68-72; quotation and,
173
Reflection: and modern consciousness,
58-68, 90; in novel, 61-63; in romantic
drama, 71-73
Remarks on Antigone, 48
Remarks on Oedipus, 48
*Remembrance of Things Past. See A la
recherche du temps perdu*

Repetition, 11, 168-172
Research: concept of, 7-8
Rhetoric, 61, 103, 167-168
Rhetoric, 96
Rhyme, 166, 173, 176
Richardson, Samuel, 122-123
Rilke, Rainer Maria, 122-123
Role: self-consciousness of, vii-viii. *See
also* Character, Tragic Hero
Romantic drama, 46, 68-73, 85-89. *See
also* Drama
Romantic ego, viii, x, 59, 61-63, 67-68,
71-72
Romantic irony, 57-68
Romantic poetry, 60-65. *See also* Genre,
Novel, Synthesis
Romantisch, 9, 91, 94, 200-201n.52
Rousseau, Jean-Jacques, 126
Russian formalism, xvii, 110

Sacrifice: tragedy as, 47, 50
Satire, 62, 87, 92
Saussure, Ferdinand de, 104, 174
Schelling, F. W. J., xx-xxi, 75, 85; notion
of the tragic, 43-46
Schiller, Friedrich, 23, 62, 75, 92, 131; and
Schlegel's genre theory, 90, 91, 92
Schlegel, August Wilhelm von, 59
Schlegel, Friedrich von, ix, xvi, xix, xxi;
philosophy of history, 57-68; and
poetic genre, 75-94. *See also* Genre,
Negativity, Romantic Poetry,
Synthesis, Universality
Schlegel, Johann Adolf, 77-78
Schleiermacher, Friedrich, ix, x, xviii-xix,
95-113; definition of textual
understanding, 3-4, 18; and Dilthey, 97,
100; and modern poetics, 107-108, 111,
112
Science: literary criticism as, xvi, 4-5,
12-14, 19, 22, 157. *See also* Natural
sciences, Objectivity
Scriptural Hermeneutics, 96
Scriptures, 96-98, 100, 106-107
Self-consciousness: of dramatic role,
vii-viii, 69-73; and romantic poetry,
58-63; and romantic subject, 59, 61,
66-68
Self-restraint, ix, 66
Sentimental realism, 122-123

Peter Szondi was head of the Institute for General and Comparative Literature at the Free University of West Berlin and then, shortly before his death in 1971, he was appointed to a similar position at the University of Zürich.

Harvey Mendelsohn is a bookseller specializing in antiquarian books on the history of architecture. He is the principal translator of the French and German entries in the sixteen-volume *Dictionary of Scientific Biography.*

Michael Hays is associate professor of theater studies at Cornell University. He is author of *The Public and Performance: Essays in the History of French and German Theatre, 1870-1900*; he also served as editor of *The Criticism of Peter Szondi*, a special issue of *boundary 2* (1983).